The Fall of Communism and the Rise of Nationalism

Over the past quarter of a century, *Index on Censorship* has been an unflinching witness to the many and varied workings of tyranny, from the persecution of dissidents behind the Iron Curtain to Latin America's 'dirty wars' and the troubled legacy of colonialism in Africa. By the same token, the magazine has also borne eloquent testimony to the flipside of repression, to the human spirit's extraordinary capacity for survival and its unquenchable appetite for freedom. In the process, *Index* has published some of the world's finest writers, sharpest analysts and foremost thinkers all of whom, at one time or another, have been exercised by questions of rights, liberties, toleration and dissent. This series brings together some of the most important materials from 25 years of *Index* according to theme, beginning with *The Fall of Communism and the Rise of Nationalism* and *Film and Censorship.*

INDEX ON CENSORSHIP

Lancaster House
33 Islington High Street
London N1 9LH
Telephone: (0171) 278 2313
Fax: (0171) 278 1878
e-mail: indexoncenso@gn.apc.org

The Fall of Communism and the Rise of Nationalism

The **INDEX** Reader

Edited by Ruth Petrie
Introduced by Irena Maryniak

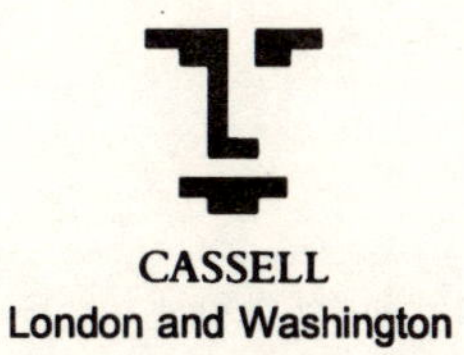

CASSELL
London and Washington

Cassell
Wellington House
125 Strand
London WC2R 0BB

PO Box 605
Herndon
Virginia 20172

First published 1997

British Library Cataloguing in Publication Data
A catalogue record for this book is available from the British Library.

ISBN 0 304 33938 5 (hardback)
0 304 33939 3 (paperback)

Typeset by BookEns Ltd, Royston, Herts.
Printed and bound in Great Britain by Biddles Ltd, Guildford and King's Lynn.

Contents

Acknowledgements vii
Contributors viii
Introduction IRENA MARYNIAK 1
Andrei Amalrik's Final Plea ANDREI AMALRIK 12
Interview with Swedish RTV ANDREI SAKHAROV 14
The Orlov Tribunal LYUDMILA ALEXEYEVA AND OTHERS 23
The Future of Soviet Dissent ROY MEDVEDEV 39
Christian Poland and Human Rights LESZEK KOLAKOWSKI 50
Goulash Archipelago MARK FRANKLAND 59
After Tito CHRIS CVIIC 66
Poland's Lesson in Freedom ADAM MICHNIK 73
Rumania: A Simple Solution IVAN KRAUS 81
USSR: Hope for Dissenters? SALLY LAIRD 85
Czechoslovakia: Stories and Totalitarianism VÁCLAV HAVEL 91
USSR: Why the Empire's Subjects are Restless BOHDAN NAHAYLO 111
A Trip to Moscow ANDREI SINYAVSKY 120
Uzbekistan: The Hostile Earth of the Friendly People SHIRIN AKINER 128
Berlin–East: The Other Side of the City LUTZ RATHENOW 136
The Rapid Demise of Sarajevo TV NENAD PEJIC 141
The Last Albanian Waiter ROBERT ELSIE 150
Former Yugoslavia: Embargo on People SVETLANA SLAPŠAK 154
Goodnight, Croatian Writers DUBRAVKA UGREŠIĆ 157
Former Yugoslavia: Close-up of Death SLAVENKA DRAKULIĆ 163
Bosnia on My Mind SALMAN RUSHDIE 167
Post-German, Post-Jewish LESZEK SZARUGA 171
Outsiders in Russia IRENA MARYNIAK 176

CONTENTS

A Season of Hell ZORAN FILIPOVIC 179
Freedom and Garbage IVAN KLÍMA 184
Small War, Big Deal JUDITH VIDAL-HALL 190
Who Goes Home? W.L. WEBB 197
1991 and All That VERA RICH 204
Surviving Communism GEOFFREY HOSKING 210
Old Griefs Revisited SERGEI KOVALEV 215
Of Blood and Votes IRENA MARYNIAK 219

Editorial Note

The essays in this collection have been reprinted from *Index on Censorship* in their original form apart from minor alterations. No attempt has been made to update political, social and artistic references.

Acknowledgements

Grateful acknowledgement is made to the individuals who allowed their articles to be reproduced for this collection. Thanks also to Faber and Faber Ltd, London and to Alfred A. Knopf, New York for permission to reproduce *Czechoslovakia: Stories and Totalitarianism*, by Václav Havel, from their publication entitled *Open Letters: Selected Prose 1965–1990*.

Contributors

Shirin Akiner is a lecturer in Central Asian Studies at the University of London.

Chris Cviic was born in Croatia and educated at the Universities of Zagreb, London and Oxford. He worked for the BBC, was the East Europe Correspondent at *The Economist* from 1969–90 and was editor of *The World Today* at The Royal Institute of International Affairs from 1984 to 1995. He is currently Associate Fellow of the Institute's European Programme and is the author of *Remaking the Balkans*.

Slavenka Drakulić is a Croatian journalist and writer. Her published works include *How We Survived Communism and Even Laughed* (Hutchinson, 1992, reprinted by Vintage, 1993), *Balkan Express* and *Marble Skin* (Hutchinson, 1993).

Robert Elsie was born in Vancouver, Canada in 1950 and is currently based in Germany. He is a specialist in Albanian affairs and author of *Anthology of Modern Albanian Poetry* (London, 1993), *History of Albanian Literature* (New York, 1995), *Studies in Modern Albanian Literature and Culture* (New York, 1996) and of the forthcoming political reader on the Kosovo crisis, *Kosovo: In the Heart of the Powder Keg* (New York, 1997).

Zoran Filipovic was born in Bosnia and has written widely about the Balkan war. His photographs have appeared in *Life* magazine, *Die Zeit*, *Le Figaro* and *The Times*. He currently lives in Zagreb.

Mark Frankland was born in London 1934 and is an author and journalist. From 1962 to 1996 he was Foreign Correspondent for the *Observer* in the USSR, Indochina, the United States and East Europe. He is the author of three books on Soviet and East European affairs.

Václav Havel, the world renowned playwright, was a prominent member of the Czech cultural underground in the 1960s, with the literary magazine *Tvar* and the independent Theatre on the Balustrade. He founded the Charter 77 human rights movement and spent four years in prison for subversion. After the Velvet revolution, he became president of Czechoslovakia, subsequently the Czech Republic.

Geoffrey Hosking is Professor of Russian History at the School of Slavonic and East European Studies, University of London.

Ivan Klíma was born in Prague in 1931. He edited the journal of the Czech Writer's Union during the Prague Spring. In 1969 he was visiting professor at the University of Michigan, but returned to Czechoslovakia the following year. His novel, *The Spirit of Prague*, and a collection of essays, *Waiting for the Dark, Waiting for the Light*, are published by Granta.

Leszek Kolakowski was Poland's best known Marxist philosopher before he emigrated to England, where he now teaches at All Soul's College, Oxford.

Sergei Kovalev was the head of the Presidential Commission on Human Rights until his resignation on 23 January 1996. He is currently setting up a human rights institution which will seek to consolidate all human and civil rights organizations in the Russian Federation.

Sally Laird was a former USSR Researcher for *Index on Censorship*, and edited the magazine from 1988 to 1989. Subsequently she became Director of the Central and East European Publishing Project (1989–92). She now lives in Denmark, where she works freelance as a writer, teacher and translator.

Irena Maryniak is *Index on Censorship*'s Eastern Europe researcher and editor. She is currently based in Budapest.

Adam Michnik is a former Polish dissident who spent a total of six years in prison for activities opposing the Communist regime. He was a member of the first non-Communist parliament from 1989 to 1990 and is now Editor-in-Chief of the biggest daily in Poland, *Gazeta Wyborcza*.

Bohdan Nahaylo is a writer and specialist in Russian affairs.

Nenad Pejic is a Bosnian Croat journalist and writer. He was Editor-in-Chief of the Foreign Affairs department of Sarajevo Television during the late 1970s and early 1980s and was elected by secret ballot as the first independently appointed Editor-in-Chief of Sarajevo Television in July 1989. He is also the author of a number of award-winning screenplays including *Trial*, *Masters of Darkness* and *Injustice*.

Lutz Rathenow is a poet and critic, as well as a writer of fiction and children's books. Always a dissident, he was never published in the GDR, and was only once given a travel visa to receive a prize in Vienna.

Vera Rich specializes in Belarusian and Ukranian affairs. She was the translator of *Like Water Like Fire* (1971), the first anthology of Belarusian poetry in English. Sponsored by UNESCO, the book was subsequently withdrawn under pressure from the Soviet censorship.

Salman Rushdie is the author of five novels. *Midnight's Children* was awarded the Booker Prize in 1993. *Satanic Verses* won the Whitbread Prize for the best novel, the German Author of the Year Award and the Italian Premio Pedrocchi. In 1994 he became the first president of the Strasbourg-based International Parliament of Writers.

Andrei Sakharov (1921–1989), Soviet physicist and dissident. He graduated in physics from Moscow State University in 1942 and was awarded a doctorate for his work on Cosmic Rays. He later worked on nuclear fusion and was responsible for the development of the Soviet hydrogen bomb. In 1953 he became the youngest ever entrant to the Soviet Academy of Sciences. During the 1960s he became estranged from the Soviet authorities because of his campaigning for a nuclear test ban treaty, peaceful international co-existence and civil rights within the USSR. In 1975 was awarded the Nobel Peace Prize, but in 1980 with the Cold War crackdown on dissidents he was sent into internal exile in the 'closed city' of Gorky. He undertook a series of hunger strikes in an effort to secure permission for his wife, Yelene Bonner, to receive medical treatment abroad. He was released in December 1986 and continued to campaign for civil rights. In 1989 he was elected to the Congress of the USSR people's deputies.

Andrei Sinyavsky is a Russian writer who survived trial, repudiation and long exile from the USSR in the 1970s and 1980s.

Svetlana Slapšak is a philologist and essayist. She teaches at the University of Ljubljana.

Leszek Szaruga is a poet, critic and former editor of the underground literary journal *Puls*.

Dubravka Ugrešić is a novelist living in Zagreb.

Judith Vidal-Hall has been Deputy Editor of *Index on Censorship* since 1994.

W.L.Webb writes chiefly on the literature and politics of Central and Eastern Europe. He was a research fellow at Nuffield College, Oxford, and for nearly 30 years literary editor of the *Guardian*, for which he also wrote about politics and ideas covering the Prague Spring and the rise of Solidarnosc in Poland.

Introduction

Irena Maryniak

In January 1968, just as the Prague Spring was preparing to gain momentum, two Russian civil rights activitists - Pavel Litvinov and Larisa Bogoraz - sent out an appeal to world public opinion to condemn the rigged trial, in Moscow, of two writers facing charges of anti-Soviet agitation and propaganda. The writers - Alexander Ginzburg and Yuri Galanskov - had been involved in producing and unofficially circulating work which would not have been passed by the Soviet censor: they had produced *samizdat* or do-it-yourself literary journals. Ginzburg was lucky enough to survive the 11 years he subsequently spent in prison camps. Galanskov proved less resilient and died in camp in 1972.

Litvinov's appeal was published in *The Times* and drew an immediate response from a group of 16 British and American writers, artists and musicians who sent back a telegram expressing support and admiration for the two imprisoned writers, and offering them whatever help was feasible. The signatories included W.H. Auden, Bertrand Russell, Igor Stravinsky and the initiator of the message, Stephen Spender. The telegram never reached its addressees, but it was read out on the BBC World Service. In August, five days before Soviet tanks rolled into Prague, Litvinov answered with a letter suggesting that an international council be formed in the UK to support the democratic movement in the USSR, to give it encouragement and assistance. A few days later he organized a small demonstration against the invasion of Czechoslovakia, and was arrested. Stephen Spender, meanwhile, took up his idea and, in 1971, a committee was set up to monitor violations of freedom of expression in the Soviet Union or wherever else they occurred. It was named Writers and Scholars International and, a year later, produced the first issue of its house journal *Index on Censorship*.

In the 25 years of its existence *Index* has documented, analysed and explored censorship and dissent worldwide. It has been a channel to the outside world for writers and intellectuals trapped in oppressive states and straitjacketed by stifling ideologies. Over that time it has witnessed the collapse of totalitarian regimes, in which all original intellectual activity was threatened with retribution, and their transformation into fledgling democracies or into neo-fascist states where whole peoples are targeted for liquidation and entire cities destroyed. In 1977 Milan Kundera called the countries of Central Europe 'a kind of crucible in which history has carried out incredible experiments both with individuals and with nations'. Today, the region - once the domain of competing empires and ideologies - is being tested again, this time for the viability of the nationally or ethnically based state.

Intellectuals, formerly harassed and persecuted by the Communist regimes they challenged, have emerged as national figureheads and sometimes as leaders. Václav Havel, the playwright, remains conspicuously at the forefront of democratization in the Czech republic; Adam Michnik, the historian, retains his role as a vital contributor to the development and maintenance of a free press in Poland. But a few hours drive further south, in Croatia and Bosnia, Franjo Tudjman, also a historian, and Radovan Karadic, a psychiatrist *cum* poet, have ruthlessly exploited their power as acknowledged custodians of the national spirit in a savage five-year conflict they helped to shape and guide.

Central and Eastern Europe have traditionally cultivated a view of the intellectual as a naturally qualified leader in the moral struggle against imperial or ideological oppression and as the guardian of the national ethos in times of foreign incursion or occupation. In 1948 most of the Czech intelligentsia, and many of their Slovak counterparts, supported a Communist take-over which promised to move people from their earthen-floored homes in impoverished villages into modern apartments, education and employment. Forty years on the intellectuals were at the centre of defiance to the political authority they had helped to install: having once called for greater economic equality on behalf of the poor, they now assumed the role of defenders of free and independent thought. Under Soviet-guided regimes, controls over literature of every kind were particularly stringent. Intellectuals had to make a political commitment, either to the existing regime (and by so doing expect to reap honours and money in exchange) or to opposition and take the consequences.

It may be that Marxism, with its own intellectual roots, naturally fostered a tendency to regard autonomous and critical thinking with a fear which was born of underlying respect. The Commission for the

Lost Literary Legacy of USSR has estimated, conservatively, that 1500 writers were killed on Soviet territory during the Stalinist purges; an additional 2000, at least, were imprisoned and hundreds vanished. But the venom with which the Soviet Union in particular treated its most talented writers may lie too in the role literature and publishing was known to have played in Tsarist Russia, when it became a vehicle for revolutionary ideas as much as a source of historical information, journalistic comment, and theological treatise.

As early as 1790, over seventy years before serfdom was finally abolished in Russia, a well-placed gentleman called Alexander Radishchev was condemned to death in St Petersburg for writing, printing and circulating in an edition of 31 copies of a book entitled *A Journey from St Petersburg to Moscow* which contained a stinging, if slightly pretentiously phrased, attack on the social injustices of his day. The sentence was commuted to ten years in exile, but a subversive voice was smothered and in 1802, within two years of his return from Siberia, Radishchev had committed suicide.

There is an emblematic quality about this story. It encapsulates the fortune which has since befallen countless writers and publishers - Russian and non-Russian - who tried to go their own way and were treated by the state with similar harshness. In Central and Eastern Europe writing and politics are linked by tradition. Since the eighteenth century, literature here has been the harbinger of social upheaval and political transformation. In Russia, the radical writers of the nineteenth century were the intellectual fathers of the revolutionaries of 1917. Literature can be dynamite. And that was something the Soviet leadership apparently had no difficulty in understanding: the system of censorship established after the Revolution was even more pervasive and effective than it predecessor in Tsarist times. From 1922, the state body for censorship, GLAVLIT, took a firm hold on the activities of writers and publishers to a degree which virtually ruled out the circulation of private manuscripts until after Stalin's death in 1953. It was not until the mid-1960s that unsanctioned publishing assumed a wider scale or that it acquired the acronym by which it became known throughout the world. *Samizdat* was a playful and challenging dig at *Gostizdat,* short for State Publishing House. 'I write it myself,' the veteran human rights activist Vladimir Bukovsky once said, 'I censor it myself, I print and disseminate it myself. And then I do time in prison for it myself.'

But, in the Soviet Union, it wasn't dissenting figures - like Bukovsky or Josif Brodsky or Alexander Solzhenitsyn - who alone defined the single voice of state ideology. During the post-Stalinist 'thaw', the ideas promulgated by suppressed authors also seeped timidly into officially published writing. Given the wide circulation of *samizdat* in the 1960s and 1970s, the influence, for instance, of Pasternak's *Dr Zhivago* can reasonably be assumed to have been considerable long before its official publication in 1988. And established authors began to draw on the curious reactive dialogue between established ideology and its opponents. It was here – in the work of writers such as Vasili Shukshin, Yuri Trifonov and Sergei Zalygin – that political 'restructuring', *perestroika*, germinated. Characters in their novels were typically preoccupied with independence and the exploration of the personality, the individual self as opposed to the collectively defined self. References appeared to pre-revolutionary culture and religion; individual experience seemed to present a challenge to ideological dogma.

After the arrival of *glasnost* in the late 1980s, the ideas expressed by so many underground writers in the 1960s and 1970s were suddenly splashed over the pages of Communist Party newspapers throughout the Soviet Bloc. A flurry of relatively unimpeded *samizdat* activity followed. The range of uncensored pamphlets, newspapers and journals was unprecedented. And the variety of views and persuasions in them pointed to the concerns of a whole spectrum of national, political and religious groups active at the time. With fewer restrictions on association and activity people were beginning to group together to deepen and expand their interests and ideas. Many of the clubs and societies which appeared in the Soviet Union were apparently wholly innocuous: stamp clubs, chess clubs, jogging according to the principles of yoga, ecology groups, literary societies and so on. But what they were doing, as much as the more politically orientated groups of the time, was paving the way for democratization and civil society. These were the forums for discussion, the groupings which would draw people into the democratic process, give them a sense of participating in the community and ultimately in the political life of the country.

Raids on unofficial publishers were still common though, as were short-term arrests of people campaigning for a multi-party system. But equally, in 1988, at least 200 unofficial publications were appearing regularly throughout the Soviet Union. The boundaries between 'official' and 'unofficial', between intelligentsia and bureaucracy, were beginning to shift perceptibly. People born and bred in the USSR were starting to ask questions in public even as they scurried down their local Lenin Avenue, past slogans proclaiming that the Party and the People were still united.

In the satellite countries of Eastern Europe the popular movements of national regeneration of the 1970s and 1980s had a significantly more defined political agenda. But here too they were upheld and guided by the 'intelligentsia' – that intellectually empowered class historically at the vanguard of social change in the region and unified, as never before, by its conclusions on the failures of Soviet state socialism. This is as true of the Prague Spring as it is of the Czech Velvet Revolution of 1981, the stifled Croat movement of the early 1970s, Solidarity in Poland, *Sajudis* in Lithuania, *Ruch* in Ukraine.

As Communism lost its ideological viability in the eyes of the reading classes, it vacated space for suppressed ethnic and national grievances along with concerns about long-standing and unrecognized human rights violations. To many people who belonged to ethnic communities which had fostered dreams of independent nationhood over centuries, nationalism must have seemed to offer a more honest ideological alternative, one that was closer to the heart and more in tune with popular self-perception and shared aspiration. And it was also a way for intellectuals to resolve the contradictory emotional pressures they were bound to experience as a culturally cosmopolitan, educated élite, at once tied to and alienated from its less well-read compatriots. The reappropriation of a common ethnic and religious past and the consolidation of independent political communities, in which intellectuals could apply their skills to the service of their own people, was a way of finding common ground with them and so resolving the conundrum.

But as Henn Bergson once said of religious practice, the spectacle of nationalism too often presents a puzzle and a humiliation for human intelligence. The bonds of historical memory, common ancestry, shared culture and shared territory can create political units which assert themselves with a ferocious and ruinous intensity. They did so in Germany in the 1930s, and have done so again in the former Yugoslavia in the 1990s in a way which apparently defies all logic. Technology, the sheer volume of industrial production and commerce, the speed of communications, the wider cultural and linguistic frame of reference so many people seem to enjoy – all these should surely be making national boundaries obsolete. Modernization, it has often been argued, erodes cultural differences, it starves would-be nationalists of the requisite fodder to transform ethnic identity into a principle of political loyalty. But apparently not, or not in some regions. If relatively peaceful transition to a more democratic form of policy in the historic cities of Central Europe gives reason to hope that civic responsibility is indeed being rediscovered here, wars in the Balkans and the Caucasus have confirmed that the once dampened embers of nationalist extremism can all too readily ignite. But under what circumstances? Are these manifestations of latent fury, as Frances Fukuyama maintained in the early 1990s, merely transitional birth pangs to a new and generally more democratic political order?

The response Ernest Gellner gave in one of his last essays points, first, to the unsynchronized movement of different societies into modernity and, second, to the new role of culture in developed industrial and technological societies where work and social activity consist not of manipulating and making things, but of composing ideas and messages, and controlling people. In London or Paris today, training in physical labour, or apprenticeship to trade and craft, continues to give way to education in an increasingly complex and technologically demanding idiom which provides the key to employability and social participation. The shift from experiential, personalized learning to a formal standardized public education has encouraged the growth of antagonistic attitudes between those initiated into the language-systems of modernity and those still excluded from them. Inevitably people relegated to the periphery of European economic development have resorted to seeking short-term psychological security in the recovery of group identity, political independence and moral or, more frequently, religious exclusivity. This often goes hand-in-hand with a profound ambivalence over the ethical fabric of life in developed countries: respect for technological achievement coupled with anxiety over the social fragmentation and moral breakdown it seems to carry with it. The lid of oppression has been lifted and communities, once isolated and held in check by totalitarian regimes, have been exposed to an incomprehensible and largely unsympathetic world. And with that, as Neal Ascherson has written, the suppressed enmities, held in check for decades by fear of cataclysmic intervention from an external and oppressive power, have been released. The demands of democratic politics, its calls for competitiveness and party choice, have split unsophisticated communities and societies into their prime units: tribes.

The boundaries have been most clearly marked by the renewed commitment of many people to religion, the revival of religious mythologies and reworkings of popular memory. Myth and religion provide the psychological power to resist the forces of modernity (as they sustained resistance to the threat of retribution by Turks or Cossacks in the Ottoman and Russian empires). They transform the marginalized into the chosen. They guarantee the redemption of the tribe and the preservation of its traditional values and way of life.

National myths offer territorial demarcation and affirm fraternity. Religion offers a symbolic focus for the political community to commune with and venerate itself.

Just how religion comes to nurture bonds of cohesion and group strength so effectively is a question for Emile Durkheim. Religious rites, he once wrote, express collective realities and aspirations, religious images or symbols provide an emblem or focus for these. Rite and symbol convey the essence of religious practice in its earliest form; Durkheim called it totemism. The totem was the symbol of the god but equally the symbol of the clan. It was the flag, the distinguishing mark of the tribe and a representation of the tribe itself. Because, Durkheim concluded, God and Society are the same thing.

The spirit of totemism is not exclusive to the nationalist ethos, of course. Communism too created it own totemic myth, expressed in terms of a community of builders of socialism. And it supported a cult and a literature through which that myth was sustained Images of Soviet leaders - Lenin and Stalin in particular - became the totemic emblems through which Communist society was to recognize itself; the symbolic representations which contained its collective identity and bound its energies.

By the 1960s, among some sectors of the intelligentsia, these images had given way to an interest in a more nationally based collective rooted in the traditions of the Russian Orthodox Church. The spectrum of ideas was broad: from a moderate 'conservationist' stance, at one end, which sought to retrieve Russian tradition from under the rubble of decades of destruction, to an *étatiste* or National Bolshevik position which promoted the establishment and maintenance of a strong Russian state capable of world leadership. The National Bolsheviks looked to the ideas of the nineteenth-century Russian ideologist of militant Panslavism, Nikolai Danilevsky, whose pseudo-scientific character analysis of different nations and theory of irreconcilable struggle between Slavic and Romano-German peoples (rather than between classes) could comfortably serve to vindicate state aggression, imperialism and racism.

Étatisme, absolute state supremacy, was also, in the eyes of many declared dissenters from state socialism, a characteristic feature of the Communist order. The word expressed the daily permeation of the state into every aspect of their lives, into the environment, and perhaps above all into their language. 'Formal distinctions between state and society have ceased to exist,' the Hungarian writer György Konrad wrote in *Index* in 1983, and continued:

> Our entire society consists of what I would call 'etatised men': they are dependent on the state, leading a life of all-pervading censorship ... Censorship resides in the lopsidedness of human bodies, in the lumpishness of clothing; mostly, of course, in the sluggishness of thinking, in the cowardice of imagination, in the insipidity of humour, in the dissembled thought dripping into words spoken aloud ... The etatised man is a political animal, even when he is completely a-political. He knows precisely what must not be said.

It is salutary to consider that, writing in March 1996 shortly before the Russian presidential election, the human rights activist Sergei Kovalev suggested that the principle of the supremacy of state was still the most potent political force in contemporary Russia. Along with moods of social apathy and xenophobia it overarches the political divide between democrats, communists and fascists, leaving human rights activists out on a limb. Not, of course as they once were, jobless and threatened with reprisal at every step, but excluded through the emphasis they have sought to give to human rights as the cornerstone of state and society.

Despite Kovalev's insistence that in Russia today human rights is a legal and political issue, his vision is not very different from that which Alexander Ginzburg conveyed when he visited London in 1980. The human rights movement in the Soviet Union was misunderstood in the West, he said. It was not, in origin, political; the spectrum of political views within it was too broad. Its foundation, and the ideological challenge it presented, was a belief in the individual and in moral self-sufficiency. 'We simply did certain things which we had to do and which it seemed proper to do,' Václav Havel had written from Czechoslovakia a year earlier.

But in the Soviet satellite countries, the European cultural emphasis on individual dignity and worth had not been fully erased by Communism. Dissent in Eastern Europe was, despite its moral and humanistic overtones, overtly political. It expressed opposition to Stalinist state socialism with its centralized single party system and to the Soviet veto directing all matters of policy. At its least sophisticated, Eastern European opposition was resistance to the political myth of the Russian 'elder brother' in the name of the supremacy of national kinship; at its best it was an acknowledgement of political responsibility for the defence of individuals' rights and for the associations or movements (such as Karta 77 or Solidarity) which sought to protect them.

What is less well known is that dissent within the Soviet Union itself bore a far more national hue than most Russian dissidents of the time may have been prepared to admit. The USSR was, to all intents and purposes, an empire run as a homogenous state, where minorities experienced discrimination and the erosion of their national identity. In 1980 the dissident physicist Dr Yury Orlov smuggled out a report from the labour camp where he was serving a lengthy sentence, estimating that 40 per cent of Soviet political prisoners were Ukrainians, 30 per cent Balts, with Armenians, Georgians and Crimean Tatars next in line. Imprisoned Russians were, he concluded, proportionally fewer. For all official claims that any nationalities' problems inherited from the revolutionary past had been settled for good, Soviet minorities linked their human rights grievances as closely to national aspirations as their Central European neighbours.

When the Soviet Union collapsed, the 15 nationalities which had the status of fully fledged republics of the USSR became independent nation states - some with long established historical identities, some (like Belarus) without. But there were well over 100 distinct ethnic groupings living within Soviet borders. And some of the people whose grievances are most self-evidently justified continue, unacknowledged, to struggle.

The story of the Crimean Tatars since the October Revolution, for example, has been a catalogue of atrocity and disaster. Massacres by the Bolshevik Secret Police (Cheka) in 1920, were followed by famine in Crimea and wholesale purges of the pre-revolutionary Tatar intelligentsia. By the mid 1930s, half the Tatar population of 1917 - about 150,000 people - had been deported or forced into exile outside the Soviet Union. And in 1944, after brutal reprisals for Tatar involvement in German-led village defence units, they were the first ethnic minority to face total deportation to Central Asia - in railway cattle wagons, with no sustenance or support.

The return of their children, born in Kazakhstan or Uzbekistan, to Crimea, since the dissolution of the Soviet Union, is a triumph of tenacity and faith. 'Crimea has been the geography of my spirit,' the exiled Crimean Tatar writer, Cenghiz Dagci, told *Index* in 1974. If, today, his people are hated and attacked and treated as unwelcome squatters by Russian and Ukrainian settlers on what was once their land, they remain faithful to their story and their ancestry, and to the myth which pronounces that this is indeed home.

'Tatar Crimea' is a myth of nationhood transposed back onto the historical platform; territorially based, fostered by a sense of difference and group loyalty, and above all by a story born of shared trauma. It is about the self assertion of the oppressed, about cultural renaissance and the space to breathe and to build. In other contexts a national myth such as this can become a vision in which the distinctions of ethnic and cultural identity are all important, and the barbarism of one's neighbour and of peripheral or migrant minorities is taken as read. It is a vision where a single public culture is demanded, where it is assumed, 'imagined' (Benedict Anderson would say) that a group of thousands or millions shares a culture, language, outlook and historical memory, and also that the sharing is supremely important. It is what the nation has in common that becomes its absolute and, by extension, what is different that can become its ultimate transgression. The national ethic leaves little space for outsiders to look in, with membership indicated above all by shared roots, sentiments and memories. It is less what *you* share in common with the next-door-neighbour, than the story of what your respective parents and grandparents shared, that counts.

And from all this can evolve a system of political symbolism where selected events, heroes, places and cultural artefacts are elevated into icons which affirm the isolation, genius and elect quality of the national tribe. Shared sentiment and memory contained in popular history, culture and religion become the tools by which a new and exclusively homogenous moral community is forged, worthy now of its mythical ancestry, with a new and cleansed breed of men and women to guide it. These are the common elements present in the work of the nineteenth century German *Volkisch* writers, of the Russian Slavophiles and, latterly, in Russia's *Pamyat* ('Memory') movement or in Romania's *Vatra Romaneasca* ('Union of the Romanian Hearth') a radical pressure group with formidable resources, which has liked to promote the idea of a pure community contaminated by foreign, cosmopolitan - read Jewish - elements. Croat and Serb nationalisms have also drawn on a popular hagiography of sages and saints, heroes and bandits, and on symbols resurrecting memories of epic battles, medieval kingdoms and religious conflict, all handed down for generations in small towns and villages incorporated for up to 500 years into two rival empires: Ottoman and Habsburg. Centuries of cultural divergence and social exclusivity - separating Serbs, Croats and more recently Muslims - form the backdrop to rifts now firmly woven into the fabric of life in the Balkans. But in the end, as Anthony Smith has so persuasively argued, the political potency of these divisions must lie in the relationship between the intentions of intellectual and professional élites, and the sentiments of the majority, in the way in which the symbols of ethnic identity are given social and political meaning.

If intellectuals were once seen as the victims of cultural terror, burdened by responsibility for the fortunes of their compatriots, they tend to be portrayed now (not inaccurately) as figures with neither influence nor lucre. But the intelligentsia, as a class of educated professionals, will remain a vital political player in those small countries of Central, Southern and Eastern Europe, concealed still behind a barrier of languages few outside the region know or study. And, indeed, in Russia too. Speaking at a Moscow colloquium organised by the weekly *Literaturnaya gazeta* in 1996, the writer Andrei Bitov declared that the role of the intellectual was to stand for moral and intellectual values, and to have nothing to do with power. Directed at a generation of thinkers absorbed in ideological and ethical issues, these may be wise words. The moralist and the visionary do not, on the whole, bring much security and stability to politics. But the children of writers who matured in the post-Stalinist thaw, as Bitov did, are now professional people with enviable linguistic skills and a clear awareness of the importance of information technology. These are the communicators of the future. The balance of their relationship and discourse with millions of people who have never had the benefit of a cosmopolitan, middle-brow education or been initiated into cyber-space, will most probably determine the social and political landscape of Central and Eastern Europe over the next twenty-five years.

Andrei Amalrik's Final Plea

Andrei Amalrik

In the Soviet Union the defendant in a trial has the right to a 'last word' or final plea. Andrei Amalrik, who was convicted in November 1970 for circulating 'anti-Soviet fabrications', declined to request anything from the court, but made the following statement.

The criminal prosecution of people for their statements or opinions reminds me of the middle ages with their 'witch trials' and indexes of forbidden books. But if the medieval struggle against heretical ideas could be partially explained by religious fanaticism, everything that is happening now is due only to the cowardice of a regime which perceives danger in the dissemination of any thought or any idea alien to the upper strata of the bureaucracy.

These people understand that the collapse of any regime is first preceded by its ideological capitulation. But, while holding forth about an ideological struggle, they can in reality oppose ideas only with the threat of criminal prosecution. Conscious of their ideological helplessness, they clutch fearfully at the criminal code, prisons, camps and psychiatric hospitals.

It is precisely this fear of the thoughts I have expressed, and of the facts I adduce in my books, which forces these people to put me in the dock like a criminal. This fear has reached such proportions that they were even afraid to try me in Moscow and brought me here [Sverdlovsk], calculating that here my trial would attract less attention.

But it is just these manifestations of fear which prove best of all the strength and correctness of my opinions. My books will be none the worse for the abusive epithets with which they have here been described. The opinions I have expressed will not become less correct if I am imprisoned for a few years because of them. On the contrary, this can only impart greater strength to my convictions. The trick which

Vol. 2, no. 1, 1972

says that people are tried not for their convictions but for circulating them seems to me to be empty sophistry, since convictions which do not manifest themselves in any way are not genuine convictions.

As I have already said, I shall not here enter into a discussion of my opinions, since a court is not the place for that. I wish only to answer the assertion that several of my statements are directed against my people and my country. It seems to me that my country's principal task at present is to throw off the burden of its hard past, for which, above all, it needs criticism and not eulogies. I think I am a better patriot than those who loudly hold forth about love for their country, meaning by that - love for their own privileges.

Neither the 'witch-hunt' conducted by the regime nor this trial - an individual example of it - produces in me the slightest respect, nor even fear. I understand, of course, that trials like this are calculated to intimidate many, and many will be intimidated - but I still think that the process of ideological liberation which has now begun is irreversible.

I have no requests to make of the court.

Interview with Swedish RTV

Andrei Sakharov

Translated by Hilary Sternberg

This is the full text of the interview that Sakharov gave to Olle Stenholm of Swedish Radio and Television. It was the first broadcast on 2 July, 1973.

... The most natural thing for any person in this situation is to regard his own system as the best. So that any deviation from the line is already something in the nature of a psychological process.

When I wrote my essay [Reflections on Progress, Peaceful Coexistence and Intellectual Freedom] in 1968 the process was still in its early stages, even my approach was more abstract. My life has been such that I have grappled in the first instance with global problems and only later come to the more concrete, personal, human ones. You have to understand this when you evaluate my 1968 treatise, you have to bear in mind anyway the path I have come to take – from my work on thermonuclear weapons, from my alarm at nuclear tests, at the destruction of people, at the genetic consequences, at all these things.

And I was very remote, so to speak, from the basic problems of the people as a whole, the country as a whole. I was in a very privileged position materially, isolated from people.

But then later on?

Later on my life somehow altered on a purely personal level, psychologically, it was simply a further stage in the development of the process.

But what is socialism? I started out, as it were, by thinking that I understood what it was and that I saw it as a good thing. Then I gradually ceased to understand a great deal. I found that I failed to understand the very [bases] of the economy, failed to understand if there was anything more to it than mere words or propaganda for domestic and foreign consumption. The [Soviet] state represents an extreme concentration of economic, political and ideological power, that is, extreme monopolisation. It stares you in the face. You could say, as Lenin did at the start of our revolution, that it is simply state capitalism, that is, the state acting as sole proprietor of the entire economy. But in that case there's nothing new at all about this socialism. It's simply capitalism developed to its extremes, the sort of capitalism you have in the United States, for example, and other western countries, but with extreme monopolisation. We ought not to be surprised, then, that we have the same problems, qualitatively speaking, the same criminality, the same alienation of the individual, as the capitalist world. With the difference that our society is an extreme instance, as it were, extremely unfree, extremely constrained ideologically and with a kind of ... And – what is probably the most characteristic feature – it's the most pretentious society; it's not the best society but it claims to be far better than all the others.

What do you see, in concrete terms, as the greatest defects in Soviet society today?

The absence of freedom, almost certainly. The absence of freedom, the bureaucratisation of the administration, the utter irrationality and the dreadful egoism of it, a class egoism, if you like, concerned in essence only with preserving the existing system and maintaining a facade of decency to cover up what is a very unpropitious internal state of affairs. A society very much on the decline. I've said all that in my writings. And that it must be widely known, common knowledge to all careful observers, that all our social services are more for show than matters of fact. That applies to education, to the way it's organised, and to the health service. People in the West often say this: 'Yes, you do have many shortcomings, but on the other hand you have free medical assistance!' Well, it's no freer here than in most western countries, in fact it's frequently less free, as they say, and the general standard is very low.

Do you regard Soviet society today as a class society?

Well, that's another theoretical question, a question that has to be treated theoretically. A society with a tremendous lack of internal equality, at any rate ... But can it be said to be a class structure? In a sense it *is* a peculiar kind of society. Whether one can call it a class society is hard to say. To a certain extent it's a question of definition.

It's a little like the argument we had last time about what society can be called a fascist society. That's a question of definition too, a question of terminology.

But the inequality, then?

There is inequality at many, many levels. Inequality between the rural and urban populations, where you have the collective farm worker with no passport, to all intents and purposes chained to his place of residence, his collective farm. He can only leave the farm if they agree to release him (which they usually do, I grant them that). There's inequality between different areas: Moscow and the large cities, which are privileged in terms of supply, life-style, cultural facilities, and all the other places. And the passport system reinforces, as it were, these divisions, this territorial heterogeneity.

You said earlier that you yourself were a privileged person?

I am privileged, of course, and these days I'm privileged from force of inertia too. I *was* privileged, supra-privileged because I worked at the very top of the arms industry. It meant - by Soviet standards - a colossal salary and bonuses.

What privileges do you think party workers enjoy in the Soviet Union?

They have enormous extra-financial privileges. All sorts of things - a network of sanatoria, a medical service ... enormous privileges. There are very real privileges arising from [personal] connexions, various personal factors. Privileges in one's work, one's career. All managerial posts of any standing are either ... well, a factory manager or a chief engineer, for example, only a party member can get the job. Exceptions are very rare. So your career depends very much indeed on your party membership, your position in the party structure, and your official ...

But as well as this, there's the traditional attitude to party cadres implied in the concept of *nomenklatura*. According to this, even if a person is a failure in his job, so long as he has been a leading party worker, he is transferred to some other job with very similar material advantages. The whole business of nomination and promotion in one's job is very closely linked with certain interrelationships within this system. Every big administrator has, of course, people who are his personal associates and who transfer with him from one place to another when he moves. There is absolutely no way of overcoming this; it's obviously become a sort of law in the state structure.

But talking of material perks, the main ones form an isolated and more or less clearly defined group which applies especially to the administration. They are assigned on the basis of party membership, but there are very big internal distinctions within the party itself also. It looks as though something rather like Orwell's inner party does exist in our country in a certain sense.

The people who belong to this inner party, then, enjoy tremendous material privileges. There's a system whereby they are paid extra wages in [special] envelopes. It's a practice that comes and goes. I don't know what the situation is at the moment, but it looks as if the custom has been revived in some places. Then there's the system of closed retail distribution shops where the goods are not only more varied and of higher quality, but even the prices are different, which means that the same currency buys these people goods at a different price in a different shop. In other words, the real amount of their wages is not particularly indicative either.

We have talked a great deal about the defects [in society]. Now, of course, there is the problem of what can be done to rectify them.

What we *can* do and what we should *aspire* to are different matters. I feel there is hardly anything that *can* be done, but ...

Why not?

Because the system is intrinsically a very stable one. The more unfree a system, the more intrinsically it is preserved, as a rule.

But can external forces not do anything?

We don't understand sufficiently well what the outside world is doing. It looks perhaps more as if the outside world is accepting our rules of the game. Which is a very bad thing. But there is another side to the matter. The fact that we are now breaking out of our fifty years of isolation may in time even have a beneficial influence. But it's very difficult to forecast how all this will come about. As far as the West is concerned, we can never make out whether it is a desire to help us or, on the contrary, a sort of capitulation, a game based on western domestic interests, where we are merely the small change.

But those are forces acting abroad. What about inside the Soviet Union?

There are certainly some processes at work inside the Soviet Union, but for the moment they are so indistinct and so deeply hidden that it's almost impossible to forecast anything positive, any changes at all, any positive ones ... We realise that a state as huge as ours can never be internally homogeneous, but in the absence of information, in the absence of contact between different groups of people, it is almost impossible to understand what is going on inside it. We know that nationalist tendencies in the peripheral areas of the state are very strong. But whether they are positive or not in each individual case is rather difficult to say. In some cases, the Ukraine for instance, they have become very closely interwoven with democratic trends. It's the same in the Baltic states: religious and nationalist matters merge easily and naturally with democratic ideas. But perhaps in other areas this is not so. We don't know the details.

So you are in fact extremely sceptical although you yourself ...

On the whole I'm sceptical about socialism in general. I do not see that socialism offers us anything new on the theoretical level, so to speak, for a better way of organising society. It simply seems to be that although there may even be a few positive variants - life is diverse enough - the development of our state as a whole has exhibited more destructive than constructive features. Or rather, the constructive features have been due to general human factors: there may have been quite a number of them, but they were general human factors which could have arisen in any other environment; while in our society there has been such an accumulation of fierce political struggle, destruction, and bitterness, that we are now reaping the sad fruits of exhaustion, apathy, cynicism, a kind of ... which we are having the greatest difficulty in shaking off, in shaking off at all. In what ways our society will develop is very hard to forecast from inside. Perhaps it's easier from outside, but one must do so with the minimum of preconceptions.

But Andrei Dmitrievich, you say you doubt whether anything at all can be achieved in the way of reforming the Soviet system, and yet you yourself go on doing what you do, writing statements, protesting. Why?

One always needs to create ideals for oneself even when one can see no direct way of realising them, because if one had no ideals one would no longer have any hopes, and then one would really feel one was groping in the dark, in an impasse.

Moreover, we are not sure if there are any possible ways in which our country can interact with the outside world. If we don't get any indication that this situation in our country is unfavourable ... then we shall not even be able to take advantage of the chances we may have, because we shall not know what it is that needs rectifying, or if there is any need at all to rectify anything.

Then there is another factor, the history of our country, which ought to serve as a warning. It ought to restrain the West and the developing countries from making mistakes on the scale of those our country has made during its historical development. A man may not keep silent, but that doesn't mean he hopes to achieve anything. The two propositions are not synonymous. He may not hope to achieve anything at all, but he speaks out all the same because he simply cannot, cannot remain silent.

In almost every concrete instance of repression we never expect to achieve anything, and almost always we have been sadly lacking in any results whatsoever.

But what are you yourself aiming to achieve?

In what sense? Socially?

Yes

Well, as an ideal, I tried in my *Memorandum*, and particularly in the *Postscript* to it, to delineate an ideal of a kind, but there were a lot of things I ought to have emended myself in the *Memorandum* because I wrote it a long time ago, in 1971, and it was published [almost] a year and a half later with no changes. For instance, I wrote about the Chinese problem in a tone which I would perhaps have refrained from adopting now. In fact I would have refrained in the sense that I wouldn't have written anything, because I am no nearer than I ever was to understanding our relations with China, and when you don't understand something it's best not to write about it. I wouldn't have the slightest desire now, for instance, to accuse China of aggression. But I didn't say it there clearly either; perhaps, though, there was an element of exaggeration in my view of the Chinese threat. China in fact represents simply an earlier stage in our own social development; she is more concerned with revolutionary self-assertion both at home and throughout the world than with, for instance, securing prosperity for her people or expanding her territory. They probably don't yet regard this problem *as* a problem. China is very like Russia in the twenties or the early thirties.

But if you think that socialism in the Soviet Union has not displayed its advantages, does that mean you think that in order to remedy the situation here the whole state must be reorganised, or can something be done within the existing system to improve and eliminate its defects?

I really don't feel able to answer that question. To reorganise the state completely would be unthinkable, there must always be some continuity, some gradualness, otherwise there would be a repetition of the dreadful destruction that we have already gone through several times, total collapse. So naturally I seek gradual change, I'm a liberal, a 'gradualist', if you like.

Well, what is the first thing that must be done?

What has to be done? Well, I realise that our present system can do nothing, or at least very little, about its own intrinsic qualities. What ought to be done? The ideological monism of our society should be liquidated. It's an ideological structure which is essentially anti-democratic and it is a tragedy for the state. Our isolation from the outside world, for example, the absence of the right to leave the country and return to it, is having an extremely pernicious effect on domestic life. In the first instance it is profoundly tragic for all those people who wish to leave for personal and national reasons. But it is also tragic for those who stay in the country, because a country which cannot be freely left or returned to is, for that reason alone, defective, it's a closed volume where processes develop in quite different ways from those in an open system.

You know that the right of free exit ...

... is one of the most important preconditions for return, free return.

And what else?

It is one of the necessary preconditions for our country somehow to develop along more healthy lines. Then there are things of a more economic nature which are also certainly very important. The extremely developed state socialisation in our country has led to a situation in which private enterprise has been closed down in the very spheres in which it is most effective, as it has in large-scale industry and in transport, where state control is perhaps the rational [form of management].

And as well as this, it has simply placed severe constraints on the individual initiative of citizens, as it has upon their personal freedom. This is having a bad effect on the living standards of the population and merely makes life more drab and dreary for many people than it might otherwise be. I'm thinking of private initiative in the fields of consumer goods, services, education, medicine. I am quite certain it would all play a very positive role in loosening the extremely monopolistic structure of the state. There are things relating to the administrative monopoly; the fact that the party's monopoly of the administration has reached such proportions here that . . . it must be apparent even to the party bosses that the whole thing is intolerable in principle. It has begun to affect the efficiency of the administration.

Well, what do we need? We need a great deal of openness and publicity in the work of the administrative machinery. And the single-party system is probably excessively and unnecessarily rigid. Even in the conditions of a socialist economy it is possible to do without the single-party system. As a matter of fact some elements of the multi-party system do exist in some of the people's democracies, though admittedly they look very much like half-caricatures.

We need elections with large numbers of candidates for the organs of state. Generally speaking, a series of measures which would have very little effect individually but which when combined might be able to shake the monolith we have created here, this fossilised structure that oppresses the life of the entire country.

The press must change its character. It's so standardised now that it has lost most of its information value. And when it does reflect any facts this is done in such a way that they are intelligible only to the initiated and give a distorted picture of the realities of life in this country; as for the intellectual life, it just doesn't exist, so it's not really something that can be distorted, there's no variety in intellectual life.

One thing in particular I must comment on is the role of the intelligentsia in society. The intelligentsia is kept down in a way that is quite unlawful. Materially it is very badly provided for. Badly provided for, even compared with manual labourers. But its absolute living standard is very low, of course, if you compare it with western countries which have reached roughly the same stage of economic development. This oppression of the intelligentsia – it is economically depressed too – means ideological depression as well, creates a sort of general anti-intellectual atmosphere in the country, in which the intellectual professions – teachers, doctors – don't enjoy the respect they should.

And another expression of this anti-intellectualism is the way the intelligentsia itself is beginning to retreat either into a narrow professional specialisation or into a dual intellectual life at work and at home; in the narrow circle of their friends people begin thinking in different ways, and this split mentality leads to hypocrisy and further moral and creative decline. Of course, it's the artistic, not the technical intelligentsia that is most distressingly affected by this. They already feel that they have reached a total impasse. And as a result the literature that does come to the surface is terribly grey, conventional, and generally tedious; literature, art, the cinema are beginning to ...

Can I put one final question to you? You have been very active indeed [in the human rights movement] over the last few years. Have you never feared for your own health and liberty?

Not very much, I personally have never been afraid for myself, but that's partly my nature, and partly because I started out from a very high social position; such fears would have been quite unjustified and irrelevant. What I fear at the moment are the kinds of pressure that don't affect me personally but may be exerted on the members of my family and my wife's family. That is the most painful thing, because it's very real and it's already happening, getting closer and closer to us. Things like what happened to Levich, his son[1] being picked up; it shows you how they go about these things.

Note

1. Corresponding Member of the Academy of Sciences Veniamin Levich, whose son Evgeny, an astrophysicist, was picked up on the street by the military authorities on 16 May 1973 and called up into the army.

The Orlov Tribunal

Lyudmila Alexeyeva and others

On 12 May, 1976, Professor Yuri Orlov, a Soviet physicist, founded a Group to Promote the Observance of the Helsinki Agreements in the USSR. This was the first of many such similar groups in Eastern Europe and had nine members to begin with. On the day of its foundation, Professor Orlov was warned by representatives of the KGB that his action was unconstitutional and illegal, but no evidence was offered to support this accusation. In the course of the following year the Group issued 19 major reports on violations of the Helsinki Accord in the Soviet Union, and on 10 February 1977, Professor Orlov was arrested on unspecified charges. In May 1977, Professor Orlov's wife retained the English barrister, Mr John Macdonald, to act as her husband's defence lawyer, but Macdonald was refused a visa to enter the Soviet Union. He then hit upon the idea of conducting his case for the defence of Orlov in the form of a special tribunal, at which evidence was heard from several dozen expert witnesses, including some former members of the Helsinki Group now in the West. The tribunal was held at the Institute of Physics in Belgrave Square, London, on Monday 13 June, and the evidence subsequently transcribed and submitted to the Soviet courts for consideration. What follows here is a condensed selection of some of the testimony that was offered.

Formation of the group: Lyudmila Alexeyeva

Yuri Orlov and his wife Irina Valitova live in a small two-room flat in Moscow near the University. Orlov is a scientist. He is a very quiet, capable man; he listens carefully to what people have to say and that is why people like talking to him.

The Helsinki Declaration which Mr Brezhnev signed in 1975 was widely publicised throughout the Soviet Union. Many of us who had taken an interest in human rights were disappointed that the provisions of the Helsinki Declaration were not more specific; Orlov thought it

Vol. 6, no. 6, 1977

would be helpful to establish groups in the countries which had signed the Helsinki Declaration to see how far the citizens of those countries enjoyed the rights set out therein.

The Group to Promote Observance of the Helsinki Agreements in the USSR was formed in May 1976 by ten people who had been participants in the human rights movement. I was a founder member. The formation of the group was our own idea. From the beginning we made no secret of what we wanted to do, and announced our intentions at a press conference on 13 May at the home of Andrei Sakharov, whose wife, Elena Bonner, was a member of the group.

From the beginning the Soviet authorities knew exactly what we were doing. On 13 May Orlov was interrogated by the KGB about the formation of the group. He was told that no one could doubt the Soviet Union's sincerity in implementing the Helsinki Declaration, and was warned that the formation of the group was unconstitutional. Orlov's response was that it was absurd to suggest that a group designed to promote the undoubted policy of the Soviet government could be unconstitutional.

Between 12 May 1976 and 10 February 1977 (when Orlov was arrested) the group issued 19 major reports on questions of human rights as well as a number of shorter statements on particular problems. During this period I was in constant touch with Yuri Orlov and knew precisely what Orlov was doing, as I was responsible for much of the secretarial work of the group.

The work of the group quickly became well known. People wrote to us, telephoned us, and came to see us from all parts of the Soviet Union. Some of them were individuals who felt they had been badly treated. Some of them, like the Pentecostals, the Crimean Tartars, or the Meskhetians, were representatives of wider communities, who wished us to consider whether the way they were being treated accorded with the principles of the Helsinki Declaration.

Orlov spent most of his time seeing people who came to him with their problems, examining their documents and questioning them to test the accuracy of the statements they made. When people came without documents, or when the documents they brought were unsatisfactory, members of the group travelled to the places from which they had come to find out whether the information we had been given was correct.

We sent all the reports to the Soviet government by registered post and received an official acknowledgement. We sent the first six reports by registered post to the embassies of the countries which were signatories to the Helsinki Declaration, but received no notification that these reports had been delivered. We also gave our reports to the foreign correspondents in Moscow, usually at a press conference held at the home of one of the members of the group.

In lieu of notification that the six documents posted to the embassies had been received, we decided to send the subsequent documents to the governments of the USA, the United Kingdom and Canada. We also sent some of them to the government of West Germany. I was responsible for delivering these documents and did it quite openly; I was the only member of the group who delivered them.

Prison conditions: Vladimir Bukovsky

I am 34 years old. I have been arrested four times because I expressed opinions which were not acceptable to the Soviet authorities. In all I have spent more than eleven years in prison, camps and psychiatric hospitals.

I spent a long time in Vladimir prison. The normal cells there have iron screens on the window so that no ray of light can penetrate. The cells are of different sizes, with three, five or ten men in the same cell, locked up all through the day except for half an hour of exercise, which takes place in a small courtyard, like a room without a roof. Only people who are in the same cell are allowed to exercise together.

The walls of the cells are made of rough concrete so they cannot be written on. They are damp. There is a heating system, but part of the punishment is to keep it deliberately low even in wintertime. The guards shove food through a trap door.

Sometimes the cells have no lavatories at all, only a bucket. Sometimes there is just a hole in the floor without any separation from the sewage system; all the stench from the sewage system thus comes back inside the cells, which have no proper ventilation system.

In punishment cells the conditions are worse. You are kept in solitary confinement in a room which is about $2\frac{1}{2}$ sq.m. The only light is from a small bulb in a deep niche in the ceiling.

At night you sleep on wooden boards raised a few inches off the ground without any mattress or blankets or pillow. You are not allowed to have any warm clothing. Often there is no heating at all in winter. It is so cold that you cannot sleep, you have to keep jumping up and running round your cell to keep warm.

At 6 o'clock in the morning your wooden bed is removed and there is nothing for you to do for the rest of the day, no newspaper to read, no books, no pen or pencil or paper - nothing.

According to the regulations a prisoner can only be put in solitary confinement for 15 days, but quite often when one 15-day period ends prisoners are put back for another 15 days. I was lucky, because although I was in solitary confinement several times, I only had 15 days at a time. Others were not so fortunate. It is quite customary for people to spend 45 days in solitary.

In solitary confinement prisoners get a specially reduced diet. This is part of the punishment which I received in Vladimir prison in 1976 after Mr Brezhnev had signed the Helsinki Declaration. On alternate days I had nothing to eat or drink except a small piece of coarse black bread and some hot water. On the other days I had two meals - in the middle of the day some watery soup with a few cabbage leaves, some grains of barley, sometimes two or three potatoes. Most of the potatoes were black and bad. In the evening I had gruel made from oatmeal or some other cereal, a piece of bread and several little fish called kilka, which were rotten. However hungry I was, I could not eat them. That was all.

The shortage of food, the poor quality of the food you are given, and the appalling living conditions mean that almost everyone who has endured imprisonment suffers from stomach ulcers, enteritis or diseases of the liver, kidneys, heart, and blood vessels.

When I was first arrested I was very healthy, but after I had been in prison I too began to suffer from stomach ulcers and cholecystitis. This did not make any difference to the way I was treated. I was still put in the punishment cell on a reduced diet.

I was in the same cell with Yakov Suslensky, who suffers from a heart condition. He had a severe heart attack in an isolation cell, but was not taken out of isolation. After we had protested he was moved, but only to another isolation cell. After he came out of isolation he had a stroke. This was in March 1976.

I was also in Vladimir prison with Alexander Sergienko who had tuberculosis. Notwithstanding this he was put in solitary confinement on a reduced diet. The details which the group issued on the punishments which he and I endured are correct.

I was also in prison with Mikhail Dyak, who suffers from Hodgkins' disease. He was released early, but not until three years after confirmation of his diagnosis. I knew many other people who were not released even though they had cancer and other serious illnesses.

In Vladimir prison I knew Zinoviy Antonyuk, Vladimir Balakhonov, Nikolai Budulak-Sharygin, Georgi Davydov, Gabriel Superfin, Leib Knokh, and Bograt Shakhverdyan. All of them were ill and the state of their health would have justified their early release.

In prison you are allowed to send out one letter a month, but the authorities can deprive you of that. If prisoners try to describe their state of health or the lack of medical help in prison, their letters are confiscated.

In prison hospitals essential medicines are often not available. For example, they have no blood bank. I remember in 1973 a man named Kurkis who had an ulcer which perforated. There was no blood available to give him a transfusion. He lay bleeding for 24 hours and then he died.

When you come out of prison or camp you are still subject to surveillance. You have to live and work where you are told. You are not allowed to go out of your house after seven at night and before eight in the morning. You are not allowed to visit public places like restaurants, cinemas, churches. You have to go to the police station to report every week. That is normal, it is part of life in the Soviet Union.

I left the USSR in December 1976, eighteen months after the Helsinki Declaration was signed.

Andrei Amalrik

I was arrested on 21 May 1970 and for thirteen months was held in investigation and transit prisons in Moscow, the Urals and Siberia. From June 1971 until April 1973 I was in a strict regime camp at Kolyma in the Magadan region of North-Eastern Russia. I then spent eight months in an investigation prison in Magadan, and was subsequently in exile there. I left the USSR in July 1976.

The strict regime camp of Kolyma is 300 kilometres north of Magadan, where the winter lasts eight months and is very harsh; the temperature varies between 20 and 60 degrees centigrade below zero.

The camp is surrounded by several rows of wire. Inside the wire are two wooden fences, and dogs patrol the space between them. The camp is divided into a living compound and a work compound. In the living compound are four barrack huts accommodating 800 prisoners.

All the prisoners have to wear uniform made of thin grey cloth and very thin boots. Everyone has their name and number sewn on their clothes. You march everywhere in columns.

Prisoners are fed three times a day. Breakfast is a sort of thin porridge, dinner is soup. Those who have fulfilled their work norm get extra porridge. The soup is very poor and has very few vitamins. That is why most of the prisoners are ill. Every minute of the day is planned and prisoners get less than an hour to themselves.

Prisoners work in the machine and furniture factories where the dust fills your lungs, or outside cutting wood and in the construction brigades.

It is difficult enough to work outside when the temperature is less than minus 20 degrees centigrade; at minus 50 or 60 degrees the conditions are almost unimaginable. When it is as cold as that there is a sort of dry fog, which means that if you extend your arm, you cannot see your hand. Yet every day you have to go out and work (with the exception of only one day when I was in camp). It is so cold that many prisoners suffer inflammation of the ear, which can lead to loss of hearing. You are not allowed to wear extra clothing or a fur cap. I made a band to go over my ears out of some socks, but the guards believed that I must be wearing this so I could listen to the BBC, which of course was nonsense.

I was put in a punishment cell on two occasions. Once in prison and once in camp. I was in a cell by myself. The cell was 1½ m. wide and 2½ m. long. The bed in the cell was made of wood. It was attached by hinges to the wall. In the daytime it was raised up and locked against the wall. The only thing to sit on was the concrete block on which the bed rested.

When I was put in the punishment cell my usual clothes were taken away and I was made to wear specially thin clothes. There were no books. You were not allowed to smoke. I was given warm food only every other day and then it was of very poor quality. On the other days I just had bread and water.

There was some heating in the punishment cell in prison, but there was no window and it was like living in a stone box. In the punishment cell in camp the heating was very low and there was a window, but it had no glass in it, so that the intense cold came right into the cell. It was impossible to sleep. You had to keep moving about all night in order to keep warm.

I was lucky. I only spent five days in the punishment cells. The usual period was 15 days. Frequently people spent 15 days in the punishment cells, were let out for one day and then put back for a further 15 days. Repeated solitary confinement means the slow destruction of the human body. Your personality is slowly destroyed.

Medicines are very poor and very few. In the camp where I was, there was one doctor who was not well qualified, one male nurse and one female nurse, whose objective was to see that people went to work.

I have spent two periods in exile. In 1965 and 1966, I was exiled to a small village and worked on a collective farm. You have no right to leave your place of exile and have to register and report to the militia once a month. The conditions of exile vary; they can be tolerable, or so bad that it is worse than being in camp.

All former political prisoners face restrictions. In most cases when you come out of prison or camp you are not allowed to return to where you used to live, or to your family. You are sent to a place where it is difficult to find accommodation, and very difficult to find work of the kind for which you are qualified. Usually, former prisoners are placed under administrative surveillance, entailing a curfew, a ban on public places, house-searches by the militia at any moment.

Psychiatric abuse: Lyudmila Alexeyeva

The day before Orlov was arrested, I was interrogated by the KGB. They had taken a number of reports which the group had published from my flat. They were particularly interested in the documents relating to psychiatric abuse and to prison conditions. They wanted to know how these documents had been compiled and what part I had played in preparing them. I told them that I had signed the documents, but I refused to answer any other questions.

They asked me about two documents relating to psychiatric abuse, which we issued at the beginning of October 1976, one of them being an appeal to the Supreme Soviet and the American Congress to establish a joint commission to investigate allegations of abuse in psychiatric hospitals in the USA and the Soviet Union.

This appeal had been prompted by an article in *Literaturnaya Gazeta* alleging that people in the United States had been placed in mental asylums for criticising White House policy. We said that we were prepared to present the information which we had in our possession about abuses in the Soviet Union to the Joint Commission.

In making this statement we had in mind the cases of Leonid Plyushch, Victor Fainberg, Natalya Gorbanevskaya, General Grigorenko, Esenin-Volpin, Krasivsky and Plakhotniuk. General Grigorenko was a member of the group and the others were all known personally to members of the group.

Dr Marina Voikhanskaya

I trained as a doctor at Leningrad and qualified in 1960. I took up psychiatry because I think mentally disturbed people are the most unhappy and the most melancholy in Russia and I wanted to help them.

For the first ten years I really enjoyed my practice and I loved my work. Of course I didn't like many, many things in my hospital. I didn't like the conditions in which my patients were kept. I didn't like the doors always being locked. The food was poor and the diet very limited. Relatives were able to bring food with them when they visited, but the patients who had no visitors simply went hungry.

There were other things I didn't like. The strong patients beat the weak ones. Sometimes the nurses stole from the patients. Sometimes the nurses beat the patients. Sometimes alcoholics beat other patients.

Once we wanted to bring a court case because some of the nurses beat a boy so badly that they damaged his liver, but we couldn't do it because the only witnesses were mentally ill people. I didn't like the fact that the patients only had a bath once in ten days, and that only once in ten days were they able to have clean clothes.

For the first ten years I really didn't know about the abuse of psychiatry in the Soviet Union. The first serious abuse that came to my notice was at the end of 1973. Ivanov, an artist and a completely sane man, was in my hospital and had been there for six months in another department before I found out about him.

The head of that department was a friend of mine. When I asked her about Ivanov, her whole manner changed. She became very angry and told me not to concern myself about him and refused to show me his file. But I could visit Ivanov because doctors are allowed to visit all patients in the hospital. I visited him every day for five months. Poor man – he was very gentle but was in a ward with dangerous patients. He didn't have any toothpaste or soap, books or pen and pencils, or paper. He was completely normal and he did not need to be in a psychiatric hospital at all.

When I started visiting Ivanov the attitude of the other doctors towards me changed. They pretended not to notice me. They wouldn't talk to me. The head of Ivanov's department said to me: 'He is sane but don't tell anybody about it'.

I was very angry that there was a sane man in my hospital. I tried to speak to the other doctors about it, but they thought I was crazy and urged me not to make a fuss: 'Sometimes it happens, but it doesn't matter'. After a few months I started being watched by the KGB and Ivanov was transferred to another hospital.

Then there was the case of an engineer called Kamerov. He was transferred to my department from another ward. He had been treated with high doses of a very strong drug haloperidol, which we only use for mentally ill people. When I first examined him I didn't know whether he was mentally ill or sane, but I thought something was wrong. His records showed that he was suffering from schizophrenia.

When I first saw him he didn't know me and didn't want to talk to me. It was very difficult to know what to do, but I decided to stop the drugs. So I did, and two days later, when their effects had worn off, he was completely normal, and we became friends. He is completely sane, but he is still in a psychiatric hospital.

There were other cases in my hospital of completely sane people being treated with drugs.

Haloperidol is a very useful drug when it is properly applied and it can help people who are mentally ill. It has unpleasant side-effects and it has to be administered with correctives to counteract them. There is, however, no justification for giving it to people who are sane, and if it is given without the correctives, it is a form of torture, for it induces appalling reactions. This happens in the Soviet Union. It happened in my hospital.

Another drug which was used in my hospital was sulphazine. It isn't really a medicine at all. Injections of sulphazine were given as a punishment. It is only supposed to be given on the directions of a doctor. Some doctors prescribe it because they are very badly trained and think it is a useful drug. Others give it because they know what the KGB expect of them.

For the last seven or eight years, whenever there is a public holiday, or when the head of a foreign state visits Moscow, all the sane people who have been in psychiatric hospitals are rounded up and kept in hospital over the holiday so that they cannot cause any disturbance. The hospitals become overcrowded with too few beds, people lie on the floor in the corridors.

When I started to complain about the abuses I had discovered in my hospital I was transferred to the geriatric department. I was not allowed to continue the work I wanted to do.

Leonid Plyushch

In January 1972 I was arrested and accused of anti-Soviet propaganda and in January 1973 I was tried *in absentia*, behind closed doors, at which neither my relatives nor the medical expert representing them, were present. (This in itself was illegal.)

From July 1973 to January 1976, I was in the Dnepropetrovsk special psychiatric hospital. It was hell. I subsequently found out that I was supposed to have been suffering from sluggish schizophrenia from an early age.

On the first day I was taken to the quarantine ward, where we were given underclothes that were torn. There were more patients than beds. I was put as the third person on two bunks that had been pushed together. The next morning I woke up and saw two orderlies beating up my neighbour, simply because he wanted to go to the lavatory. All the orderlies are criminals serving out their sentences.

Much of my time I spent in Department 9, which is the worst in Dnepropetrovsk. I was put in a supervised ward with the violent cases.

Other political prisoners warned me that one shouldn't complain. They said if you did you were given intensified treatment with neuroleptics and injections of sulphazine.

When we were allowed to go to the lavatory we went in groups and it was awful. People were fighting for a place and searching for cigarette stubs among the used lavatory paper. Some of the patients ate their excrement or masturbated. I don't want to blacken the picture, so let me add that this did not happen every day.

Sulphazine was never given as a genuine treatment but only as a punishment. It was usually given by injections in the thigh or the shoulder-blade, which is worse. When sulphazine is administered the patient's temperature becomes very high and after a course of injections of this sort the person is not able to sit, stand, or walk. I myself saw a patient who was practically dying from the effects of this treatment.

I was never given sulphazine myself. I was, however, given neuroleptics - both haloperidol and triftazin. I was also given two courses of insulin, over three-month periods.

The first course of insulin was given to me for shock purposes and it was administered in very large doses. I was told this by one of the nurses. I remember that I was tied down to the bed and my muscles were bulging. The second time I was given much smaller doses and they did not tie me down.

When I first went to Dnepropetrovsk I was given haloperidol in large doses without correctives to reduce the side-effects. For me this was absolute torture. I writhed and couldn't sit down, I couldn't sit still, then when they took me back to the ward I continued to writhe in pain. The physical effects of the drug make your tongue loll out and your eyes bulge. I simply couldn't do anything, there was no way I could get any relief. I just kept asking for correctives.

I think they gave me haloperidol because they wanted to frighten me and to break my will. I was in constant fear of becoming insane. I couldn't talk, my intellectual capacities decreased drastically. The doctors said that I didn't want to talk and that I was just hiding my anti-Soviet feeling, although this was not the case at all. I felt that I was becoming like an idiot who couldn't think, who couldn't do anything. I was terrified. I lost my memory, I lost my power of thought.

In the beginning, I wrote letters, but as the drugs began to take hold of me I found it more and more difficult to write until I got to the point when I stopped writing altogether. I couldn't see properly, when I tried to read the letters seemed to be floating around. When my wife visited me, I couldn't see her properly.

There were periods when I was not given any drugs. This happened when a rash broke out on my face and they didn't give me anything while that condition lasted. I felt my willpower returning to me and my mind improved a lot. Then I was put back on the drugs again and everything was as before.

There were about 60 political prisoners in Dnepropetrovsk.

I was not given any warning I was going to be released. The morning in January 1976 on which I was set free I was given drugs as usual. Later on, the senior doctor in the hospital told me that I had become well during my stay and that I would be going where my wife wanted to take me.

Even today I still feel the effects of the treatment I was given in Dnepropetrovsk. From the emotional point of view I can say that I'm not the same person I was before going into psychiatric hospital.

Struggle to emigrate: Emilia *Elina*

On the ninth day of my hunger strike Vladimir Slepak and Polishchuk came to Leningrad from Moscow on behalf of the group to visit me.

At eight o'clock that day I sent a telegram to President Podgorny saying I was on hunger strike because I had not been granted a visa. I sent a copy to Orlov. This had considerable effect. Two days later I was rung up by Inspector Pilin of the Visa Department, who was very polite. She told me that they had received an invitation for me to go to Israel.

When I went to the Visa Department they showed me the invitation. It was on a clean sheet of paper. It said the Literary Union of Israel request that a visa for the well-known Soviet writer Emilia *Elina* should be granted quickly. I am not a writer. I have only ever written one or two stories for my own amusement. These have never been published, although manuscripts which I lent to a friend were confiscated by the KGB when my friend's house was searched.

I explained that I had no relatives in Israel. I said that I wished to go to Canada. I made it clear that I was not going to produce an invitation to go to Israel and that I was not prepared to pay to renounce my Soviet citizenship.

As the authorities were not prepared to let me emigrate to Canada, I decided to continue my hunger strike.

After 22 days I was very weak and my daughter was ill. Members of the group in Moscow asked me to stop my strike. I took their advice and applied to emigrate to Israel. I did not, however, produce any invitation from people in Israel. This time my application was granted.

The Visa Department told me that I should have to pay to renounce my citizenship. I said that as they had provided me with a fictitious invitation to go to Israel perhaps they could provide me with fictitious money to pay the heavy fine for the renunciation of my citizenship.

A few days later I was informed that the Finance Department had decided that it would not be necessary for me to pay the fine.

I left the Soviet Union in April, 1977.

Religious persecution: Lidia Voronina

In the summer of 1976 a deputation of Pentecostals came to Moscow to ask the group to help their communities emigrate from the Soviet Union. The deputation was led by Nikol Sedenko and Vasily Patrushev, who came from the town of Nakhodka on the Pacific Coast and the village of Starotiterovskaya in Krasnodar region. I met members of the delegation.

The delegation asked Yuri Orlov whether it would be possible for a representative of the Group to visit their communities. On 2 December 1976, the group held a press conference in Moscow at which the members of the delegation presented the dossier, and Orlov announced that I would be visiting the communities.

I was away from Moscow for about three weeks. All the time I was kept under very close surveillance by the KGB. On the way to the airport I was followed by two cars with eight people in them. When we arrived at Krasnodar we were met by about 30 people, all in civilian clothes, who took over the surveillance.

Starotitorevskaya is a very remote village. When I arrived I was met by Nikolai Petrovich Goritoy, who is the spiritual leader and ex-pastor of the community. My work consisted of listening to what people had to say. Many, many people came and told of years of oppression by the authorities.

I visited people in their homes and attended Church meetings. While I was there several people were summoned by the KGB and told not to try to emigrate and not to have any contact with dissidents.

During my short stay I was able to see for myself how they were persecuted, and how life was made difficult for them by the authorities.

The community numbers about 100 people. They find it difficult to find jobs for which they are qualified. Their children are mocked at school and beaten up, and the teachers do nothing to stop this.

Most of the Pentecostals have large families, but even mothers who have ten or twelve children do not get the benefits to which they are entitled.

I also observed for myself the way in which the Pentecostals are ostracised by other people living in the village. The whole time that I was in the village the building where I was, was surrounded by police cars and motorcycles.

When I left the village I had to return to Moscow before I could fly to Khabarovsk. From there I went to Nakhodka by road. Again I was followed by the police. Again most members of the community came to talk to me and ask me for my help and advice.

All the documents, including names, addresses and data relating to court hearings, surveillance and other illegal actions of the authorities, were confiscated during the search of Ginzburg's flat.

Yevgeniy Bresenden

I am 36 years old. I was born in Barnaul in Siberia. My father died during the Second World War. My mother was a Pentecostalist. In 1949, she was arrested, charged with being an American spy and sentenced to ten years' imprisonment. Our home was confiscated. Almost all other church-goers in Barnaul received similar treatment. When my mother was released after six years our home was returned to us.

During the time that my mother was in prison I was at a State orphanage. My grandmother had wanted to look after me, but this was not permitted by the authorities. At the first orphanage I stayed in, I would pray and sing religious songs with the other religious children. As a result, we were separated and I was bullied and mocked by other children at the orphanage.

I went to live in Nakhodka, which is near Vladivostok, and worked there as a cabinet maker. I became known as a Christian and was dismissed from a succession of jobs. On several occasions I was beaten up by gangs of youths known to be recruited by the Militia. The Militia always denied this.

In November 1962, I was arrested. The official reason was that I had refused to perform military service despite an official medical report exempting me from military service on grounds of health.

I came out of a prison camp after a three-year sentence. I then worked as an electrician, which gave me an opportunity to travel. I was very active in the Pentecostalist Church and acted as a courier between Pentecostalist Churches in Siberia, the Far East and the Ukraine. On several occasions I visited Moscow. As a result, I became acquainted with Yuri Orlov.

In 1974, I applied for permission to emigrate after the authorities had informed me unofficially that it had been decided to take my three children away from me. I did not want them to go through what I had been through. They were then aged three years, two years, and seven months. I was summoned to appear before a committee of the Nakhodka Regional Council and said that I did intend instructing my children in religious education. Rastigaeu, the deputy chairman of the committee then informed me officially that my children would be taken away from me. The next time I was in Moscow I protested through the foreign correspondents and the decision to remove my children was not acted upon, although it was never formally withdrawn. At another meeting with the Council I was told by Rastigaeu that I had been officially diagnosed as insane. I also lost my job in September 1974. For three months I was unemployed and then found only menial work. Eventually I was allowed to emigrate in September 1975.

Religious repression takes many forms. Christian children are mocked at school, beaten up, forced against their will and that of their parents to join the Pioneer Youth Organisation, given deliberately low marks, refused references upon leaving school, or given poor ones. Students are expelled from university if they are found to hold religious beliefs. Adults lose their jobs or are deprived of State benefits. They do not get proper hospital treatment. I know of a number of pregnant women who have left hospital before giving birth because they are receiving no proper treatment. Christians are fined for holding prayer meetings. They are allowed to emigrate only after great difficulty and at considerable personal risk of the consequences of applying for permission to emigrate. All of this is so commonplace as to be taken for granted in Soviet society.

Searches and arrests: Lyudmila Alexeyeva

From November 1976 onwards Orlov, Ginzburg, myself and other members of the group were kept under constant surveillance by the KGB. Cars were parked outside our homes, we were followed wherever we went. We suspected that telephones were tapped and that our homes were bugged. This was unpleasant, but it did not affect the work which we were doing because we had nothing to hide.

On 4 January 1977 there was an official search of our flats.

My husband and I were expecting a friend to visit us that morning. At 8.30 there was a knock on the door and I opened it thinking it was our friend. He was there, but eight people burst into the flat with him.

We had a small flat with two rooms and a kitchen. One of the men produced a search warrant and told me that if I had any anti-Soviet literature I should give it to him straight away. From the start it seemed as if they knew where everything in the flat was. They went straight to those places where I kept my papers. They didn't touch any of my husband's papers, but confiscated most of mine.

At 7 pm they finished the search and asked me to sign the warrant to show that they had conducted the house search. I refused and they left the warrant on the table.

When they left I went out to a phone box and rang up the Associated Press correspondent to tell him what had happened. He said that Orlov's flat was still being searched and that an hour previously Tass had announced through their foreign language broadcasts that the house searches had shown that Orlov, Ginzburg and I were members of a Russian émigré organisation.

The search of Orlov's flat did not end until 10 pm and that of Ginzburg's flat until 3 o'clock the next morning.

We held a press conference the next day.

The search of Orlov's flat was similar to the search of my flat, except that they broke the door down because he refused to open it. In Ginzburg's flat the KGB planted 1,000 German marks and 100 US dollars in a cupboard.

Ginzburg was arrested on 3 February. The previous day Orlov had left Moscow for a few days' rest in a tiny village not far from Moscow, where he had once lived.

When Orlov heard that Ginzburg had been arrested, he decided to return to Moscow to make a statement. He did not wish to be arrested at once, and as he knew that I had been given permission to leave the USSR and therefore thought that my flat might no longer be watched, he came to my flat instead of going home. No one saw him arrive. I was not there because I was being interrogated by the KGB.

When I returned home I opened the door and saw Orlov. He put his finger to his lips and we did not speak because we knew that the flat was bugged. We started writing notes to each other.

Orlov wrote that he would like to make a statement to foreign correspondents, so I left the flat and rang up some foreign journalists and told them to come to my flat without telling them why. At 5 o'clock three correspondents arrived. Orlov made a very short statement. During this conference my telephone was disconnected.

I was worried. I told Orlov not to leave with the correspondents. I left with them. When I opened the door I saw that KGB officers were waiting. They had rushed there as soon as they heard Orlov's voice. I went back and told Orlov he could not leave as the house was surrounded. He decided he would stay there and that we would not talk to each other. We would act as if he was not there. He started making plans for helping me in the house, as we thought that he was likely to be there for a few days.

At 5 o'clock in the morning I sent my son outside. When he returned he told us that there were KGB agents outside the door.

In the morning I took some rubbish out. There were two more agents standing there. It was clear that our plan had not worked.

At about 10 o'clock there was a knock on the door. We thought it was Orlov's wife. We asked who was there. The answer came: 'The procurators'. I went back, told Orlov, and asked him whether I ought to open the door. He was not in his own home and he said they should be let in. He put on his jacket.

I opened the door. The minute I did so my tiny entrance hall filled with officers from the Militia. One was a civilian. One of the men in uniform had been in the group which searched my home. The procurator's office was therefore just a cover. There were about eight or ten in the entrance hall. The uniforms were brand new. They were all probably KGB officers in new uniforms. I asked whether this was another search. They said no. I asked why they had come then. They answered that different people had come to my flat. Special people. People who think alike.

The one in civilian clothing started opening cupboards in my room. I asked for his search warrant. I invited them in but did not take them into the room where Orlov was. One of them however opened the door and found Orlov. An officer said: 'What is he doing here while your husband is not at home?' They asked for Orlov's documents. He showed them his passport. They did not say whether they were arresting him or taking him for interrogation. Orlov did not ask for their warrant as he probably did not think it right as he was in someone else's home. He wanted to be as non-violent as possible. Therefore he put on his coat and left. Orlov is a very small man. All the KGB officers were very tall. They surrounded him. I waved over their heads. Then he was taken away. That was the last time I saw him.

The Future of Soviet Dissent

Roy Medvedev

To many superficial observers political and social life in the USSR appears rather monotonous, unlike the turbulent and frequently dramatic events and changes that occur in the West and the so-called 'Third World' countries. But appearances are deceptive. It is not difficult to demonstrate that during many critical periods in our history - 1928–31, for example, 1935–38 or 1953–57, not to mention 1941–45 or 1964–65 - the political and social atmosphere, indeed the entire socio-psychological climate in our country, altered virtually from month to month. However, even during relatively stable and peaceful periods the internal political situation may change rapidly in many respects. This applies to the balance of forces in the leadership, which so preoccupies Western Sovietologists; it also applies to the moods of vast sections of the Soviet people, including the intelligentsia and those working in the economic and cultural spheres. And, of course, to the so-called dissident movement.

Less than a year ago a book on the Soviet dissident movement and its history was published in Italy; it was called *Intervista sul dissenso in URSS* (Laterza, Roma-Bari, 1977). The authors were myself and P. Ostellino. I do not think the arguments and ideas we put forward are yet out of date. They do, however, need further commentary, for the situation has altered substantially since the well-publicised trials of dissidents in Moscow, Kaluga, the Baltic republics, and the Ukraine.

The dissident movement in the USSR has long since been not merely an object of close attention by the press and public opinion in the West, but also a subject for scholarly study.

Dissent in the USSR: Politics, Ideology and People, (edited by Rudolf Tökes and published by The Johns Hopkins University Press, Baltimore) is just one of the recent books which I have had an opportunity to read. Almost every book by a Western writer about the

Vol. 8, no. 2, 1979

Soviet Union published in the last few years contains a section or sections on the dissident movement - not to speak of the diverse examples of émigré literature in which dissidence has become virtually the basic theme. This is understandable, for it is precisely through the dissident movement with its wide range of differing currents and views that one can gain an insight into many crucially important deep-seated processes that are at work in our country. Although the number of active dissidents in the USSR at the present time is small (and still diminishing), it is this movement which will in many respects sooner or later determine the future of a country like the USSR. As the contemporary American philosopher Eric Hoffer writes: 'The discarded and rejected are often the raw material of a nation's future. The stone the builders reject becomes the cornerstone of a new world. A nation without dregs and malcontents is orderly, decent, peaceful and pleasant, but perhaps without the seed of things to come'. (E. Hoffer, *The True Believer*, New York, 1962, p. 40; Russian edition, Praeger)

The present article makes no claim to exhaustive scholarship. It consists mainly of my observations on recent events.

A dissident movement in one form or another has always existed in the Soviet Union. In the twenties, for example, there were a great many extreme oppositionist currents: the 'left' opposition and the 'right' opposition within the party was only one current, but it is the one that has been most extensively written about. A considerable number of other opposition groups and currents also existed in the first half of the thirties, although by this time they often took the form of clandestine organisations. Furthermore, the Stalin Terror did not so much liquidate dissidents as generate them, even though between 1936 and 1952 it was mainly directed against entirely loyal Party members and citizens of the Soviet state. Did not millions and millions of these people become dissidents in the prisons and the camps? Was it not those few survivors of the ordeals of the Archipelago who, 20 or 25 years later, made up an important part of the new generation of opposition? I need only name A. Levitin-Krasnov, D. Dudko, A. Solzhenitsyn, E. Ginzburg, A. Voronel, P. Yakir, M. Baitalsky - men and women of the most disparate convictions. And there were many, many others. Various forms of both right and left opposition existed, too, throughout Khrushchev's 'great decade'. Some people were incensed and disgusted at Khrushchev's destalinisation measures; others felt compelled to protest at events such as those in Poland and Hungary, or at the inconsistent and inadequate exposure of Stalinist crimes.

During the sixties the Soviet dissident movement acquired many new features. It embraced comparatively large (under our conditions) sections of the intelligentsia and the younger generation, and it began to be reported more regularly, and in significantly more detail, in the Western mass media. It was chiefly owing to this that Soviet society too became incomparably better informed about the various forms of protest and dissidence in the country. By the second half of the sixties, however, the dissident movement was already beginning to decline, and this trend has continued in the seventies, although there have been various international processes, which we may bracket under the general term of détente, which have periodically revived one or another form of opposition or even sparked off brief outbursts of public protest. Still, the temporary collapse of the dissident movement is a fact. This was perhaps inevitable, for the initial phases in any opposition or revolutionary movement almost always end in defeat.

Notwithstanding all this, the movement has not ceased to exist entirely, although in many respects it has acquired different qualities and characteristics from those it had only a year or two ago. What are the changes it has undergone? Let me list the main ones as I see them.

1. There is more debate and argument - some of it heated - among dissidents of differing schools and opinions. There were of course substantial differences between currents of dissident thinking in the sixties too. Disagreement and discussion became more intense during the first half of the seventies. This was natural, for there comes a time when emotional protest begins to be accompanied by various, increasingly elaborate, political, social, religious, ethical and cultural programmes and doctrines. Whenever a social movement enters a period of decline, however, these differences frequently degenerate into bickering and squabbling, which is encouraged - and often even instigated - by interested organisations. The last few months, for instance, have seen an extraordinary increase in the number of anonymous letters of various kinds containing the vilest slander and obscenities and presenting a distorted picture of the private life of certain dissidents. Books are appearing such as that by the Czech journalist Tomáš Rezáč, *The Spiral of Solzhenitsyn's Treacheries*, published by the Soviet publishing house Progress and only distributed in official circles. In the book's foreword, 'heartfelt gratitude' is expressed to the Soviet dissident writer Lev Kopelev who spent many years, together with Solzhenitsyn, in the same labour camp. Not a single one of the 'witty remarks' and opinions on Solzhenitsyn's lack of literary talent was ever uttered by Kopelev either orally or in writing, nor did he give interviews to the journalists whose names, with excerpts from their 'interviews', appear in the book. It is true that Kopelev has

criticised Solzhenitsyn's political stance and political platform, both in private conversations and in his published writings.

2. Repression has noticeably intensified against those dissidents (of whatever school of thought) whom the authorities evidently regard as incorrigible. Some are being exiled abroad - the prominent Soviet scholar Alexander Zinoviev, for instance, and certain others. Zinoviev, a Doctor of Philosophical Sciences as well as author of the satirical *Yawning Heights* and *Bright Future*, had already been subjected to various forms of persecution and restriction. In 1977 he was stripped of all his Soviet academic titles and even of the military decorations he had been awarded for bravery in action in the Second World War. When he applied for permission to travel abroad to take up a teaching appointment, there was no reply for a whole year. Then, in the summer of 1978, he was offered the chance to go abroad and, once there, was stripped of his Soviet citizenship.

Quite a few well-known dissidents were brought to trial in the spring and summer of 1978 and were sentenced to long terms of imprisonment or exile. They included Orlov, Ginzburg, Shcharansky, and some 20 others in various cities and republics. The Western press has already devoted a fair amount of comment to these trials. Trials of this kind deserve to be resolutely condemned, as does the way they were conducted. Foreign correspondents were not admitted to the court sessions; nor were many friends and relatives of the defendants, who had far greater reason to attend the trials than those members of the specially invited 'public' who filled the courtrooms. One cannot help wondering why, if the charges brought against Orlov, Ginzburg and the others were entirely justified and easily provable, they were heard at what amounted virtually to closed political trials.

Ironically, the Soviet press confined itself to brief articles on the trials, and the more thoughtful reader could not glean from them why exactly the defendants had been sentenced to such long terms of imprisonment. Thus, for instance, Orlov was charged with having compiled lists of political prisoners that were insufficiently precise. Can this be regarded as a crime? Orlov had informed Western correspondents about a strike in the port of Riga. But he had got his information from a Riga port worker, and there is no crime in that either. And anyway it is well known that short strikes take place every now and then in various industrial centres in the USSR. Even the fact that a parcel of clothing Orlov had received from friends abroad had contained underpants and vests was referred to as a fact discrediting Orlov! Also unconvincing in the extreme was an article on the

Shcharansky trial which appeared in all the main newspapers. The trial of Ginzburg was reported only in the local Kaluga paper, and then only two weeks after the event.

3. Repressions of various kinds have been directed in the first instance less against 'individual' dissidents than against the small dissident organisations which began to spring up. By these I mean the Helsinki Groups, the Russian Social Fund for the Relief of Political Prisoners, the committee to investigate the abuse of psychiatry, the editorial groups putting out the *Chronicle of Current Events*, the *Bulletin of the Lithuanian Catholic Church*, *Jews in the USSR* and certain others. The [Soviet] Amnesty group led by Valentin Turchin has been virtually wiped out; so have many other groups set up in the Union republics with a nationality, or, as the Soviet press puts it, a 'nationalist' programme. All this is clear evidence that the authorities are concerned to nip in the bud any attempts to create an *organised* political, religious, national or ideological opposition in the USSR. In doing so, however, they make no mention of the article in the Soviet Constitution according to which *all* public organisations in the USSR must recognise the 'leading and guiding role of the Soviet Communist Party' nor of article 200 of the Criminal Code on 'arrogation' [*samoupravstvo*], which prohibits Soviet citizens from 'the unwarranted exercise, in violation of the legally established order, of one's actual or supposed right, causing substantial harm to citizens or to state or social organisations'. Obviously, any reference to these articles from the Constitution and the Criminal Code would expose the anti-democratic nature of many aspects of Soviet legislation.

4. The new wave of emigration – by no means exclusively Jewish – has now begun to have a noticeable influence on political life inside the USSR. New émigré organisations and journals have started springing up abroad: journals such as *Kontinent*, *Vremya i my* (Time and We), *Tretya volna* (The Third Wave), *Echo*, *Khronika prav cheloveka v SSSR* (Chronicle of Human Rights in the USSR), the literary almanacs *Glagol* (Verb), *Pamyat* (Memory), *Perekrestki* (Crossroads), and several others. The emigration of many popular writers, publicists and academics has also noticeably enlivened the activity of already existing émigré organisations, publishing houses, journals and newspapers – *Novy Zhurnal* (New Journal) in the USA, for example, the papers *Russkaya Mysl* (Russian Thought) and *Novoye Russkoe Slovo* (New Russian Word) in Paris and New York, the journal *Vestnik russkogo khristianskogo dvizheniya* (Herald of the Russian Christian Movement) and even such small periodicals as *Possev* and *Chasovoy* (Sentry). Many

of these journals and newspapers which had hitherto been completely unknown in the USSR have now begun coming into the country, although of course in very limited quantities. The creation abroad of many new émigré organisations and journals staffed by people well known to or even highly popular with the *present* generation of Soviet citizens, especially the intelligentsia (such as [the late] Alexander Galich, Alexander Solzhenitsyn, Vladimir Maximov, Viktor Nekrasov, Oscar Rabin, Mstislav Rostropovich, Ernst Neizvestny, Alexander Voronel, Viktor Perelman, Andrei Sinyavsky, Zhores Medvedev, Alexander Nekrich, Pyotr Grigorenko, Natalia Gorbanevskaya, and many others), irrespective of the diversity of political, religious and ethical platforms of these representatives of the so-called 'third' emigration, has indubitably been an important catalyst in the spread of internal opposition in the USSR.

5. As the opposition, or simply the liberal movement, in the USSR has shrunk from its former massive scale to a much narrower base, so the flow of so-called *samizdat* has practically dried up. The hopes that were placed on this unique form of the uncensored press have been disappointed. The typescripts which used to spread like wildfire in thousands of copies in the mid-sixties have now all but ceased to circulate inside the country. Of course, *samizdat* has not completely disappeared. But very few people nowadays bother to type copies of manuscripts or articles that come their way or circulate them among their friends. On the other hand, the number of writers and publicists living in the USSR who have started publishing their books, documentary collections and articles abroad - in both Russian and foreign languages - is growing all the time. Furthermore, intellectuals, writers and academics of a rebellious disposition are publishing their works abroad quite on their own initiative, without begging official permission to do so. They include Lev Kopelev, Vladimir Voinovich, Viktor Kornilov, Georgy Vladimov, Lydia Chukovskaya, A. Gladkov, Vadim Erofeyev, Alexander Zinoviev, E. Gnedin, Natalia Mandelstam, Andrei Sakharov, A. Gladilin [some of these have now emigrated. Translator's note] and many others. The present author too has published several books abroad and entered directly into contracts with Western publishers for that purpose, including the Italian communist publishing house Riunita. A fair number of these books reach the USSR by one means or another.

6. Interest in twentieth-century Russian literature has led to the publication and reprinting in ever-increasing numbers of works by long, and not so long, dead Russian and Soviet writers who were

banned by the censorship in their day or were withdrawn from libraries and never again published, or simply books which lay for decades in the desks of departed writers and were preserved by their wives, children and close friends. I have in mind the works of such writers as Mikhail Bulgakov, Andrei Platonov, Mikhail Zoshchenko, Evgeny Zamyatin, Marina Tsvetaeva, Anna Akhmatova, Nikolai Gumilyov, Vladislav Khodasevich, and many others. Not only émigré publishing houses but also various commercial and academic publishers, as well as diverse charitable organisations and funds, are helping to get Russian and Soviet classics that are unknown to Russian readers into print; they are also publishing more and more Russian translations of works by Western authors - including books on Soviet themes by Sovietologists such as Harrison Salisbury, Stephen Cohen and Victor Serge, as well as other works. Books by such famous authors as George Orwell, S. Padover, Raymond Aron, Barbara Ward, Walt Rostow, A. Nevins and many others, even including Robert Kennedy's *Thirteen Days*, have been published in Russian translation.

7. More and more Soviet citizens are acquiring a good knowledge of foreign languages and thus gaining access to non-Russian political, historical, religious and artistic literature. Enterprises such as the holding of an international Book Fair in Moscow in September 1977 are adding a tremendous impetus in this direction.

8. The stepping up of the movement for human rights in the West - and especially the fact that the present American administration, and President Carter personally - have made the issue of human rights, and human rights in the USSR in particular, a cornerstone of American foreign policy and to a certain extent of domestic policy too. This has had a tremendous effect on a political life in the USSR and on the attitude to dissidents in our country. It is a matter, however, that merits special consideration. American policy on the human rights issue is a factor of crucial importance. There have been a fair number of positive achievements on this score, but equally there have been quite a few of the grossest miscalculations. If I appear to be putting Western policy towards the dissident movement in the USSR last in this section, this by no means implies that it is the least important factor. In certain respects it is the most important factor today, but it is also the most complex and cannot be dealt with in a few words.

I have enumerated here only what I regard as the most important influences on the character, aims and forms of the dissident movement in the USSR over the past year or two. These have also been observed by the most perceptive members of the Soviet intelligentsia who, though they may not even associate themselves directly with the movement, nevertheless take a close interest in its evolution. Let me therefore quote at length from an interesting letter I recently received and which I shall call for form's sake 'A Letter from the Provinces'. For understandable reasons I shall not reveal the author's identity.

> For about ten years now the dissident movement has concerned itself with defending those rights of the individual which have been trampled upon: the right to express one's opinion and to one's own free will. This is of course inestimably important. In a certain sense the right to freedom of expression, freedom of criticism and freedom to do one's own thing is the root of everything. If conditions are created for freedom of speech, all the other freedoms will automatically be retrieved. A society that criticises itself will be capable of development, of rapid repair of its dead parts, and there will be plenty of scope for the fresh and new. Many injustices and violations in many spheres of the economy and social life will disappear of their own accord simply in the free-floating interchange of opinions. But in practice almost all attempts to exercise freedom of expression have been harshly suppressed and many courageous individuals who have tried to practise the freedoms proclaimed in the constitution have been punished in one way or another. Even the human rights movement, caught up in the logic of events, has tended to concentrate more and more on rescuing its own members from victimisation or easing their fate. Just as the members of 'Narodnaya volya' (The People's Will) in their day were drawn imperceptibly into terror, into acts of vengeance for vengeance's sake, so many dissidents have gradually reduced the human rights struggle to a struggle, however noble, for the release of their friends, for the right to go abroad, for the easing of labour camp regimes and so forth. Even Sakharov, who set out from the most broadly-based considerations for the future of civilisation, his country and the world, became caught up in the whirlwind of the struggle for the rights of persecuted dissidents; he has noticeably narrowed his horizons and is now almost completely bogged down in endless legal representations. People of lesser stature than he sometimes lose their head entirely; flushed with the heat of battle, they come to the rescue of 'one of us' with resounding, urgent appeals and protests across the ocean. Dissidence is now suffering from the disease which assails any movement that is hemmed in on all sides, not only from external

persecution but also from the self-delusions, illusions and sectarian passions that are inevitable in a group which is persecuted and artificially isolated.

Movements with a more popular base, which spill over into the dissident intelligentsia but are motivated by national and religious principles, are also fairly specific. It is understandable that the Jews and the Volga Germans should make frequent demands to be allowed to leave the country, or the Tartars to return to their homelands. But in a country as vast as ours, with its predominantly Russian population, these demands, although legitimate, do not carry a broad popular appeal. The same can be said of religious movements, which are for the most part engaged in defending the rights of particular sects and scarcely concern themselves with matters relating to the life of the Russian Orthodox church as a whole. Without denying the legitimacy of all these individual rights and interests, I nevertheless believe that, over the democratic movement in the USSR as a whole, there has been a shift in the direction of cliquishness, sectarianism and self-defence by a rebellious intelligentsia ...

To some extent, of course, this is an inevitable process. Because the regime has suppressed all forms of independent thought, because the masses have been cowed and confused, the country has slipped back a long way from the mood of social reform and moral revival which prevailed in the mid-sixties. The membership of the democratic movement was determined precisely then, however far removed they may now be from their former views. They emerged from *that* era, on the crest of *that* wave, and I cannot see that they have been joined by many people from the younger generations.

But time has passed. In the authorities' eyes the democratic movement has become increasingly unlawful, while to the liberal the ideas and aims of the movement have tapered off and narrowed to a point on the problem of rights as it affects the members of the human rights struggle. Meanwhile real life presents an abyss of the most fearful problems connected with the life of the nation. Agriculture is in a state of permanent crisis. The peasant's sense of being master of the land has been destroyed, and the industrialisation of agriculture is being carried out without proper preparation. The food situation is deteriorating throughout the country, even in the capital - let alone the provinces. Vast numbers of industrial enterprises are operating at a loss. Capital construction is poorly organised and leads to the irrational wastage of enormous quantities of the nation's manpower and resources. Trade is plagued by

> commodity shortages and theft, finance by chronic inflation. The people are paralysed by disillusionment, apathy, work-shyness, drunkenness. The government displays stagnation, a lack of bold decision-making, a fear of responsibility at all levels, self-deception and straight deceit ...
>
> Our dissidents, carried away by the struggle for human rights, scarcely take any notice of this. But surely, here too one can discover a host of illegalities - in the judgement of civil and criminal cases, particularly cases involving minors - and because of this the small number of 'political' cases appear only a drop in the ocean of the injustices that are perpetrated every day.
>
> Can we really ignore the fact that the most important social and civil rights which affect the life of the nation as a whole - its economic conditions, opportunities for education, legal right to defence and so forth - are frequently emasculated and reduced to the minimum? ...
>
> It goes without saying that the democratisation of society is bound up with its liberalisation. But the struggle for human rights will only be successful if dissidence extends its interest beyond mere problems of the persecution of dissidents to the life and the rights of the worker in Tula, the collective farmer in Vologodchina, the librarian in Tetyushi, and the trade and technical college student in Podolsk.

I can only endorse in its entirety the opinion of my correspondent.

What are the prospects for the dissident movement at the present time? Obviously the authorities will not succeed in completely crushing it simply by harassment, arrests, exile or expulsion from the country, although it has now visibly shrunk. At the moment clear attempts are also being made to cut off 'incorrigible' dissidents from what is currently their basic environment, i.e. the creative intelligentsia. Alongside a 'tightening of the screws' in some spheres, first and foremost in that of politics, a certain 'liberalisation' is going on in some branches of culture and art. Many cultural figures who have the reputation of being 'liberals' or at any rate freethinking, independent people, have been given far greater opportunity than before to publish their writings, stage plays, make films and write academic works. Whatever the authorities' intentions on this score, it is certainly a favourable development. However, even these 'indulgences' will have only a temporary effect so long as the basic problems of Soviet life remain unsolved. The dissident movement, today weakened, will sooner or later revive with new vigour. This is inevitable, for without it there can be no effective solution to the most important and most complex problems of social and public life in a country like the USSR.

All intelligent people are now speaking out against senseless terror and violence. But an intelligent opposition is essential in any well-ordered society. Particularly in such an intricately-ordered modern society, where almost any important decision requires free discussion and the study of different points of view and independent arguments. Nowhere and at no time in its history has mankind yet thought out a better way of enabling society to keep a check on the activities of the state power - or, for that matter, any power, political, trade-union, economic, etc. - than free criticism and the right of opposition.

In his little-known book *Otshchepentsy*, (Renegades; published in Saint Petersburg in 1866), the nineteenth-century Russian democrat and publicist Nikolai Sokolov wrote that the sound and living principles which at the present time govern not only the material world but also people's faith and the moral world of society, such principles fear no criticism, nor do they need defending by force and coercion. Sokolov reiterates again and again in his book that the persecution of those who reject and criticise society is an indication not of strength but of the weakness of a society that has ceased to believe in its rightness, its morality and its dignity.

We are convinced that socialism, although it may assume various forms under different conditions, is precisely one of those living and not decayed or moribund doctrines. However, nowhere yet has socialism been elaborated to perfection either in theory or in practice. For this reason also the persecution of freethinkers in socialist countries is doubly intolerable and unworthy.

Opposition and dissidence will inevitably continue to exist in the Soviet Union too, if only because many of the most important problems of society have not yet been solved in our country. If we attempt by violent or any other means to stamp out a legal and loyal opposition, it will rise again in the future, but this time in different forms - forms that may indeed be a real danger to society.

Christian Poland and Human Rights

Leszek Kolakowski

For a number of historical reasons, religious and national identity in Poland have over a long period become almost indistinguishable; nowhere else has the convergence been so strong (with the possible exception of Ireland). Since the definitive triumph of the Counter-Reformation in the seventeenth century, the Roman Church has enjoyed a virtually monopolistic position among ethnic Poles; the Lutheran and Calvinist communities have been reduced to tiny minorities (in the sixteenth century, Calvinism was well-established among the nobility); sectarian movements have not achieved any significant size; and Judaism has not become a spiritual rival to the Church as its influence was felt in a different social milieu. There were, of course, sceptics, atheists, anticlericals, freemasons and freethinkers, chiefly among the educated classes, and they grew in number. Yet until the second half of the nineteenth century Polish culture was emphatically Catholic. To be sure, some of the outstanding writers who in the nineteenth century contributed decisively to shaping the 'Polish spirit' could not – by any standards – be counted among ultramontanist bigots: some were philosophically highly unorthodox, and anti-Roman or anticlerical views were by no means exceptional in their writings. Yet the profoundly Christian inspiration of their thought was undeniable and their work hardly affected the Catholic loyalty and fidelity of the faithful.

An erosion of faith was slowly taking place, however, among the Polish intelligentsia in the last decades of the nineteenth century, supported and stimulated by the social and intellectual forces that were operating all over Europe in the wake of growing urbanisation and industrialisation. The general spirit of the Enlightenment, positivism, and enthusiasm for science, combined with the idea of social progress and the secularisation of morals, inspired attacks on the Church for its

Vol. 8, no. 6, 1979

obscurantism, its parochialism, and its enmity to human advancement. These attacks were part of the well-known patterns of conflict that were then tearing at the traditions in the Christian parts of the world. However, radical movements, socialist and agrarian, although often strongly anticlerical, could hardly be called anti-Christian, and the mordant militant atheism which did exist was but a marginal phenomenon in cultural life. At the outset of the twentieth century Catholic modernism was not absent, but its influence was very weak compared with a country like France.

The split between loyal Catholics and the others grew sharper once Poland - after well over a century - regained its dreamt of, and fought for, independence in 1918. Though the Church, in cultural terms, kept its sway over the overwhelming mass of the population, its domination over the intelligentsia was not only challenged but suffered serious harm. What was creative and new in literature, philosophy, and the social sciences, originated mostly (it would be unfair to say entirely) outside the Catholic sphere of influence, in those milieux which were either indifferent to religion or, in part, positively anti-religious. The Church in Poland gained a reputation of particular rigidity and conservatism, both in social and intellectual terms. Its defenders argued that it was the strength of the religious continuity and unity which had preserved Polish cultural identity through the trial of partition, and had enabled the nation, under the worst of conditions, to successfully resist its powerful enemies.

There was a good deal of truth in the contentions of both sides. It is indeed arguable that it was the very rigidity of Polish Catholic culture, from the seventeenth century onwards, that gave the country its power of resistance; if the Polish Catholic spirit had been torn by doubts, more open to self-questioning, more responsive to novelty, it would probably not have produced the strength which eventually helped Poland survive her ordeal. On the other hand, if Polish culture had not been able to resist the Church's claim to domination, if it had failed to produce a science, literature, and an art independent of a self-confident bigotry, it would have doomed itself to sterility and stagnation. In brief, there was no unequivocal distribution of rights and wrongs in this dramatic history; both opposing forces contributed to our survival. This could not have been seen at the time of the struggle between them, but only *ex post facto*, once the old cultural patterns had practically disappeared. Why this clash between secular and religious cultural expression became anachronistic and irrelevant to Polish life is one of the most curious phenomena in the contemporary Christian world.

It ought to be noted, in spite of what has already been said, that the stubborn rigidity of Polish Catholicism in the twentieth century was not really exceptional by the standards then prevailing. In social doctrine the Polish Church moved in a rut similar to the rest of the Catholic world, apart from very few exceptions. In philosophy it continued to maintain the tenets of a closed, traditional Thomism, as did the overwhelming majority of Catholic philosophers and theologians everywhere. One must also remember that insofar as there were new trends in Catholic philosophy and social thought open and sensitive to the political and spiritual anxieties of the twentieth century, these were limited before the Second World War to tiny groups who hardly shaped the general character of Catholic life. The importance of these groups was to become manifest only later, in the entirely different order that emerged after the war. In fact, somewhat similar currents did appear in Poland just before the war and were also confined to small groups of Catholic intellectuals.

Confrontation

Despite all the losses it suffered, along with the entire population, in the persecution and massacres of the occupation, the Church emerged as spiritually influential as it has been before the war. It was the confrontation with the Communist power that brought about formidable changes in all aspects of Catholic life. If the Polish process of totalitarianism on the Soviet model never reached the level of other socialist countries, this is largely due to the popular resistance which the Church itself symbolised. The extent to which it was subject to harassment and repression varied, depending on many internal and external political factors; yet all attempts to split the Church from within failed. The ruling party supported and organised - often using police methods - various pseudo-Catholic 'progressive' groups intended to break down the unity of the Church, but despite the enormous effort invested by the state, the outcome was meagre indeed. Throughout the post-war years the Church has been subjected to various forms of pressure, but it has remained the only powerful form of organised cultural activity that has escaped nationalisation, and has managed to preserve its independence from the state. Not surprisingly, it provided an outlet for all sorts of social and political discontent, and though it never encouraged any violent expression of opposition, it naturally absorbed - by the sheer fact of not being state-owned - both the feelings of national humiliation that resulted from the forcible incorporation of Poland into the Soviet empire, and the people's passive resistance towards such oppressive and mendacious a power system.

It cannot be denied that neither in the Stalinist period nor later, when a shaky *modus vivendi* between the Church and state had been reached (systematically infringed by the state though it was), the repressive measures intended to disable religion and the Church in Poland never reached the degree of brutality characteristic of the Soviet state. The forms they took were of a different order: chicaneries to prevent children from receiving religious instruction in proper centres outside the schools (religion is forbidden in the state education, of course); restrictions imposed on the Catholic press, including a particularly devastating and vicious censorship; numerous interdictions and limitations on the building of places of worship; persistent violation of the Church's autonomy to appoint bishops; systematic discrimination against avowed Catholics in all areas of social life.

The point is that no Communist nor, for that matter, any ideological state can afford the separation of Church from state because separation implies that the state is indifferent to citizens' religious views and that their social positions and careers are unaffected by allegiances to a particular denomination. A state that is ruled by a single party professing a particular *Weltanschauung* with all-embracing pretensions – even if no one takes its doctrine seriously any more – is unable, in principle, to treat its citizens as equals, irrespective of their faith. It cannot be a lay state in the true sense, nor can it give up the goal, hopeless as it may be, of converting its citizens to its creed. Those who openly profess a different belief are bound to remain second-class subjects even if they are not directly punished by law. Thus, Poland's citizens are not prevented from attending Mass, baptising their children and marrying in church (acts which might invoke the death penalty in Albania), yet, if they do so, their chances of participating in public affairs or reaching positions of importance are drastically curtailed. Apart from certain posts reserved for a few loyal Catholics in certain public bodies intended as window dressing, for the overwhelming majority of the population all avenues leading to participation in power are definitively closed. It is certainly possible for a worker or peasant to be a party member and a Catholic at one and the same time, but he will still remain one of the 'proles' like the rest of the believers, for it is not the party members but the salaried apparatchiks who wield power.

In assessing the function of the Church and of Catholic values in the anti-totalitarian opposition and in the struggle for human rights, two sides of the question have to be taken into account: the sheer presence of the Church as a non-nationalised crystallisation of spiritual life, and the actual content of its teaching and preaching.

The distinction is of importance: the totalitarian state (even when clumsily and inefficiently totalitarian, as in Poland) is propelled along by an unrelenting drive to nationalise everything, including culture and memory, feeling and thought, as well as by the need to destroy all forms of communal life other than those it sets up itself. All forces that withstand this voracity, whether in the economic or in the cultural field, automatically acquire an anti-totalitarian significance, irrespective of the degree to which their exponents have themselves adopted libertarian values. In other words, an independent Church, no matter how rigid or intransigent, would still have preserved, by the simple fact of being there, a priceless element of pluralism in an otherwise totalitarian situation.

In fact, the Church in Poland has sustained these elements of pluralism not only by the mere fact of its existence and by winning recognition and tolerance from the state, however grudgingly this was yielded. The Church has also changed - not in its doctrine, or fundamental moral teaching, but in becoming open, sensitive in its general attitude, tolerant, and intellectually fertile. These changes have come about as a result of a number of cultural factors. With the destruction of the propertied classes, all the threads and commitments which in former years tied the Catholic culture to the traditional social hierarchies were broken, and the Church found itself in a position of poverty among the poor. (Boorish party propaganda to the effect that the Church was a servant of the landlords and capitalists soon became meaningless.) On the other hand, throughout the post-war years, Christianity was not only being subjected to harassment and repression (which often acted as a double-edged weapon, both enfeebling and strengthening); it was also being corroded by the 'secularist' spirit, usually - but not always - associated with the processes of urbanisation, the rapid increase of social and spatial mobility, and the expansion of general schooling. Once it was no longer able to rely on its highly privileged (though not institutionally established) cultural position of the prewar period, Christianity made a great effort to survive under duress by using only its moral and intellectual resources.

And it succeeded as nowhere else, almost miraculously. It produced a new generation of intellectuals - open-minded, intelligent and tolerant, yet profoundly Christian in a real, not tactical or political, sense. The Church became active in all areas of cultural life. The independent Catholic press (leaving aside the spurious, government-sponsored variety), though incessantly in the grip of censorship and police restrictions, has been free of falsehood and has enjoyed general trust for this reason. It cannot print what it would wish to, but it does not lie. In the atmosphere of all-pervading mendacity which poisons and distorts the public language of the entire Communist world, the language of Christianity has remained honest. We all know that the Catholic press is muzzled but when we read it, we get the feeling of a breath of fresh air.

Transformation

The evolution of Catholicism in Poland has also been aided by various factors in the international, as well as the internal, situation. For one thing, the Church was actively involved in the process of change that affected Catholic life all over the world, both before and after the second Vatican Council. Above all, it was helped by the inexorable corruption and degradation, both moral and intellectual, of Communism.

Christianity, as embodied in the Catholic Church, thus emerged not only as Poland's main bulwark of pluralism but also served as a haven for the truth. Out of all this, it became a powerful agent in the struggle for human rights, carrying the fight well beyond its own particular cause.

For years this entire process was hardly noticed by the anti-totalitarian movement which developed within Communism in the mid-fifties, and which used to be known under the somewhat misleading label of 'revisionism'. The point has been admirably argued[1] that those critics who attached the Communist despotism from their leftist or socialist tradition failed to perceive both the anti-totalitarian potential of Christianity and the profound transformation of Catholicism itself. This lack of perception was to impair the effectiveness of the democratic resistance until the mid-sixties.

The 'revisionists' (and here I ought to use the first person plural, as I was actively involved in the disputes), for all their attacks on the Communist tyranny and the Leninist doctrine, remained the prisoners of various conceptual distinctions which had become utterly anachronistic. Even though they might occasionally laud the 'progressive' trends in the Roman Church, they more frequently attacked it on grounds that might have been valid decades before but had since then lost all significance.

Of course my point is not that the Church is immune to criticism or that its policy is infallible, but that the leftist clichés and categories - including in particular the left/right, progressive/reactionary, humanist/religious distinctions - were becoming increasingly and glaringly inadequate to deal with our crucial problems, and that all analyses that employed these distinctions as a basic system of reference were bound to lead to false conclusions.

Revisionism, effective though it might have been in wreaking havoc on Communist ideology, was a transient phenomenon, and its role naturally decreased with the collapse of Communism as a viable ideological force. By the sixties, it became clear that there was nothing to 'revise' any longer. Once Communism had been reduced to a matter of sheer power, and its doctrinal aspirations were no longer being taken seriously even by its own ruling parvenu class, attempts to wear it out from within became pointless.

Cooperation

This process reached its culmination in 1968, the year of a major cultural pogrom in Poland. After a period of inevitable disruption, the altered situation released new forms of democratic opposition, and the secular/Christian distinction finally, and deservedly, lost its meaning. The current anti-totalitarian movement does not operate in perfect unison, and the various groups tend to stress different aspects of their struggle against the dictatorial order. At times, they feud among themselves. But the division into Catholics and non-Catholics, believers and sceptics, is non-existent in political terms. Both in the legal Catholic press and in the numerous illegal (albeit not clandestine) journals, priests and former party members appear side by side. Many ex-Marxists, who are only rarely allowed to appear in print, find refuge there.

Thus in Poland Christianity has become the most unyielding repository of traditional libertarian values. If the authorities view the Church as a kind of rival party that they failed to destroy, this is because they are unable to imagine human actions other than those motivated by greed for power and privilege. Although the Church, due to its independent position, acts as an outlet for a variety of feelings and needs within the opposition, it only does so because the source of its strength lies ultimately in its faith and not in any political doctrine. It must be stressed that many of the young and old who are attracted to the Christian tradition were brought up in an intellectual milieu that was either irreligious or indifferent to the Church. Some find in it an irreplaceable vehicle of cultural continuity, the expression, *par excellence*, of historical national identity, and the only reliable source of moral guidance. Others return to Christianity in full response to its religious message.

By a cruel irony of destiny - or of Providence - the official, ruling ideology, once rooted in the ideas of the Enlightenment, has become host to all the vices formerly attributed to the Roman Church. It was the Church which used to be reproached with hampering independent thought, of stifling learning, of upholding indefensible social privilege, of employing massive untruths in order to promote its worldly interests, of persecuting heretics and Jews, of combating democracy. At various periods in history some of these charges were well-founded, some might have been exaggerated but still they contained a sufficient basis of truth. None of them can justifiably be raised against the contemporary Church in Poland today, all of them are true when applied to the ruling party. It is Communism that has become the incarnation of obscurantism, fear of enlightenment and truth, the persecutor of free cultural expression, the seed-bed of falsehood and anti-Semitism. Furthermore, even when the Church was rightly blamed for its intolerance and backwardness, it never had guns at its disposal (as Stalin aptly observed).

The Church in Poland has strenuously maintained its right to perform its evangelical mission, and has asserted man's universal right to spiritual liberty, but has been equally emphatic in its insistence that it does not issue prescriptions on political matters. No doubt it is difficult to clearly divorce the cause of human rights from constitutional questions. In fact, the latter is not in issue in Poland where the Declaration and Covenants of Human Rights are in principle legally binding (much as they may be made void by a number of specific laws or by the deliberate vagueness of other legislation). The concept of human rights suffices both for the democratic opposition to phrase all its claims, and for the church to struggle for its place in public life and for freedom of expression. Thus the moral foundation of both is essentially the same. Having taken up the cause of human rights as its own, and having given it universal meaning – by no means confining it to Communist countries – the Church does not need to desist from its condemnation of violence even for just ends.

In Poland, both as a matter of principle and for obvious circumstantial reasons, the Church has never endorsed, let alone incited, violent opposition to the regime. In critical moments, when violence was likely or indeed had erupted, the Church used its influence to promote calm. Neither the democratic opposition nor the Church are interested in violent clashes which could have disastrous consequences, including a Soviet invasion; and this is an interest they share with the ruling party. This common interest is strong enough to allow room for a limited agreement between Church and state, although it is insufficient to bring about the removal of various restrictions imposed on religious life, let alone to loosen the intolerable fetters of censorship. But the government, having lost all credibility among the population (even the qualified and shaky legitimacy it achieved by the economic improvements of the early seventies), is compelled to canvass for the support of the Church to avoid an uncontrollable explosion of popular wrath that could bring Soviet tanks on to the streets of Warsaw.

It is common knowledge that the government has lost the battle for what the Poles refer to as 'the government of the souls', and that the Church has remained the greatest, unquestioned authority in the country. This well-known fact was mentioned in a Vatican broadcast to Yugoslavia and this was described in an editorial in the London *Observer* as the 'Vatican's criminal folly' since the 'vital interests' of the USSR were at stake and thus the entire stability of Europe might be upset; it looked as though the Vatican had called the Poles to an armed uprising. I cannot remember similar strictures after the Pope in person had directly appealed to the poor Mexican peasants to organise themselves to fight for their rights; and indeed no 'vital interests' of the USSR were at stake on that occasion.

Cardinal Wojtyla's election to the Holy See and his recent trip to his native land enormously fortified both the Church's moral authority and the steadfastness of Polish Catholicism. By thus increasing the chances of anti-totalitarian resistance, dangers as well as hopes may breed, especially when the economic failures of the government provoke more and more fury. May we hope that the ruling party, under its self-imposed duress and just to avoid the worst, will seek a minimal consensus by letting the population voice its grievances and by enlarging, even slightly, the extent to which people can influence the way they are ruled? Thus far, experience has not been encouraging, but nothing is absolutely precluded.

Whatever happens, it is clear that the vicissitudes of Christian life in Poland have led to a situation the significance of which goes far beyond the confines of its own borders. This kind of coalescence of Christianity, in its worldly aspects, with the human rights movement and democratic values, has never before been achieved. It might herald dramatic changes throughout the entire Christian world.

Note

1. Adam Michnik, *The Church, the Left, the Dialogue*, published in Polish in Paris by Kultura, 1977.

Goulash Archipelago

Mark Frankland

Le Tremblement des Hommes by Paul Goma Editions du Seuil Paris
Le Rétablissement de l'Ordre by Milan Šimečka François Maspero Paris
Opposition = 0.1% ed. by Miklós Haraszti Editions du Seuil Paris
Etre Communiste en Allemagne de l'Est by Robert Havemann François Maspero Paris
Communism and East Europe ed. by František and Larisa Silnitsky and Karl Reyman Harvester Press
The Kremlin's Dilemma by Tufton Beamish and Guy Hadley Collins and Harvill

Alexander Ginzburg said in London recently that Soviet dissidents like himself often had difficulty making themselves understood when they came to the West. They were constantly asked political questions which they could not answer - 'What does Mr Brezhnev really think?' and so on - and in the end many Westerners went away disappointed.

The trouble, he said, was that people misunderstood the Soviet human rights movement. Its origins were non-political and its members had widely differing political opinions. Its unity lay in its moral principles, above all the belief in the individual. To make a political movement they would have had to temper their individuality which they had discovered and guarded at such cost.

It is hard to imagine a dissident in East Europe talking in this way. For one thing, the European cultural and religious tradition, with its emphasis on the individual, remains real enough in countries like Poland, East Germany, Czechoslovakia and Hungary. For another, most East European dissidents are self-confessedly political and in some cases even outcasts from their countries' inner communist citadels. Whereas Soviet dissidents, with rare exceptions like Roy Medvedev, have usually never had anything to do with the Central

Committee and the Kremlin, East European dissidents have included prime ministers, politburo members, and enough senior (and once loyal) academics and journalists to staff a party school and a newspaper.

What is more, dissent in East Europe can be analysed quite successfully in broad political categories like liberal, social democrat and Marxist socialist (the latter, of course, capable of infinite subcategorisation). These groups are also united by sharing a common enemy: the system of socialism imposed on East Europe by Stalin, the foundations of which are the concentration of power in a centralised communist party and the acceptance of an ultimate Soviet veto over policy (Rumania being partly an exception in this latter respect).

But that said, the dissidents of Eastern Europe and their successes and failures are remarkably different. Take Paul Goma, the Rumanian writer, and Milan Šimečka, the Czechoslovak teacher of philosophy: theirs are the experiences of two different worlds.

Goma's is that of the still brutal Balkans where his battle is almost a personal one against Nicolae and Elena Ceausescu. Some of Goma's interrogations at the headquarters of the Rumanian *Securitate* appropriately took place under one of those portraits of Ceausescu that show him holding in his hand the sceptre that is the traditional symbol of the ruler of the Rumanian lands.

Goma got into trouble in 1977 for trying to start a Rumanian human rights movement inspired by Charter 77 in Czechoslovakia. The police tried to scare him off with some peculiarly unpleasant methods. They sent a punch-drunk boxer round to his flat who once he got in refused to leave. Then they terrorised a sixteen-year-old boy and dispatched him to make a pass at the happily married Goma who, wisely, refused to let him through the door.

When Goma was finally arrested, he was beaten up by no less a person than the Deputy Minister of the Interior. One can't imagine that happening in Czechoslovakia, where the techniques used these days are, in Šimečka's words, rather those of 'civilised violence'. Šimečka is a world where people are brought to heel by nothing so crude as a beating (though there have been exceptions) but rather by 'civilised' pressures that can be maintained indefinitely. They include expulsion from the work for which one is trained and barring one's children from higher education, this latter probably the most painful blow that can be dealt the average East European intellectual.

Reading these books, it struck me that one way to approach the dissident movements in East Europe today is to classify them according to how hopeful they are. Hope, after all, is what they are about. So I started to make a list, beginning with the most hopeful, and was myself surprised by the result. I felt that I had to put at the top either Poland (no surprise there) or East Germany. In the end I decided that East Germany should come first. Then I put Rumania, followed by Hungary (scarcely an expected ranking) with Czechoslovakia bringing up the rear. (The remarkably different conditions in each country are conveniently summarised in *The Kremlin's Dilemma*.)

East Germany comes out on top because it is there, above all, that dissident intellectuals remain possessed by Marxist optimism. The Ulbricht and Honecker years, far from diminishing their Marxist enthusiasm, seem to have acted upon it like a pair of powerful bellows. Thus Rudolf Bahro gives his book *The Alternative* the subtitle 'A Contribution to the Critique of Real Socialism', consciously echoing the name of Marx's preliminary study for *Capital*. His declared aim is to dissect what passes for 'real socialism' in East Europe in the spirit of the master.

Few people in the West suppose any more that East Europe is waiting to be won back to pure capitalism. But it is one thing to accept the no longer so new socialist structure of their countries, as most East European dissidents do, and another to insist, as Robert Havemann does, that if only East Europe could democratise itself, it would become an irresistible example to the so-called capitalist world.

Havemann, an eminent scientist, was for many years, a loyal Stalinist. 'When Stalin died in 1953', he writes, 'I publicly declared that I was beholden to this man for my life, my liberation and my health'. As a Stalinist he was against the East German workers' revolt in June 1953, which prompted Brecht to write the words that mock the Marxist-Leninist's disenchantment with an ill-behaved, ungrateful working class:

Wouldn't it be simpler under these circumstances
For the government to dissolve the people
And elect another one?

Havemann is no longer a Stalinist and his belief in liberalisation has lost him his job and privileges. This, in a way, is fair, because Havemann now is an apostle of equality and abstinence. For him communism has nothing to do with a washing machine in every kitchen and a car in every garage. That, he says, is simply imitating capitalism.

He is an unabashed believer in a communist utopia in which people are not only free and equal but also follow high-minded pursuits – 'people must be liberated from the slavery of this cheap, vulgar music which invades our world'. The 'elaboration' of this utopia, he says, is 'an essential task of our times'.

This, in a sense, is what Rudolf Bahro has tried to do in *The Alternative*. Like Havemann, Bahro the ex-party functionary now exiled in West Germany, is a puritan with a vision of an austere, high-minded utopia. He too despises East Germany's 'moderate welfare, devoid of prospects, in which we vainly try to outbid late capitalism'.

His argument could easily be put in religious terms: man's obsession with material things at the expense of the spiritual. Bahro regards the chase after an ever higher standard of living as dangerous and in perhaps even the short run impossible. What is needed therefore is a 'cultural revolution', because civilisation can now only develop by the cultivation of 'inner freedom': 'This inner freedom is the precondition for a collective renunciation, based on understanding, of a continued material expansion which is both disastrous and subjectively purposeless. General emancipation is becoming an absolute historical necessity.' If Governor Jerry Brown of California were a Marxist he would talk like Rudolf Bahro.

It is, by the standards of the rest of worldly-wise East Europe, breathtaking stuff. One explanation for it is the relatively high standard of living in East Germany. It is easier (for a man at least) to despise a washing machine when you have had one in your house for several years. As important, though, must surely be the native German enthusiasm for abstract systems. While the rest of Eastern Europe has been learning lessons about power and human weakness, these Germans still go on about the perfectibility of man and society along rational lines. They seem to have no awareness of the sad message of our times: 'The world doesn't suffer because of bad ideas. It suffers from good ideas' (the words of Milovan Djilas).

The optimism of the Polish dissidents is of a quite different sort. It certainly has almost nothing to do with Marxism: of all the East European countries it is in Poland that Marxism seems most vigorously ridiculed. If the Poles are optimistic it is because they are strong. The combination of an extraordinarily solid Catholic Church, an active dissident movement, much of whose thinking is partly shared by a large section of the country's intelligentsia, and a working class whose outbursts of discontent have been able to overthrow governments, is matched nowhere else.

You cannot be a Pole and not have a sense of history. Adam Michnik's essay in *Communism and Eastern Europe* is a useful reminder of something that many of us forgot during the excitement of the

Pope's visit to Poland last summer: an alliance between the intelligentsia and church is not easy in Poland.

The left-wing Polish intelligentsia, traditionally hostile to clericalism, found it possible to support the communist party's attacks on the church in the 1940s and 50s. Matters have greatly changed now, not least because of the appearance of progressive Catholic currents. Michnik believes that the magazine *Wiez* under the editorship of Tadeusz Mazowiecki has done much to explain the church to people like himself.

Michnik also argues that, though the Polish church has certainly changed, even more important is 'the fact that the attitudes of the church and the Secular Left towards each other have converged ... Our attachment to human rights would be doubtful if we wanted them only for ourselves. That is why we have the political responsibility of defending the freedoms of the church and the human rights of Christians.'

It is a potent but uniquely Polish alliance, impossible to repeat elsewhere, because the Catholic Church in other parts of Eastern Europe is an intruder in the national sanctuary rather than its guardian. In a country like Rumania, where the main faith is Orthodox Christian, faith seems all too easily grafted on to official patriotism. The Rumanian patriarch is as fulsome in his public praise of Ceausescu as any of the poets in the court of King Nicu.

It may seem perverse to rank Rumania before Hungary in a table of optimism. Goma's story, for example, could scarcely be gloomier, not the least depressing part of it being the failure of other Rumanian writers to support him. But the justification is that, unlike Hungary or Czechoslovakia, Rumania still has all the hope of a reform movement before it. Rumania has passed from Stalinism to national Caesarism as though it were the most natural historical progression possible. How many visitors to the museum of party history in Bucharest stop to marvel at the inscription from Herodotus, at the very beginning of the exhibition, praising the courage of the Dacians (the ancestors - more or less, according to one's scholarly taste - of the modern Rumanians)?

The hope of change lies not so much with dissidents, of whom there are relatively few, while some of the strongest (the Baptists, for example) come from groups outside the mainstream of Rumanian life. It is, rather, with those Rumanians on whom Ceausescu depends to rule the country, men whose intelligence can only be insulted by the excesses of his personality cult with its immoderate nationalism and dated obsession with the forced development of heavy industry.

But what is there to hope for in Hungary, a country that has gone to the limits of the freedom that is tolerable to the present leadership in

Moscow? It is a country on quite a long leash, but it is a leash all the same. The frustration of this is caught in the epithet Hungarian *samizdat* writers have for their country - the Goulash Archipelago.

Unfair, perhaps, for most Hungarians enjoy the goulash without being even aware of the outlines of the archipelago. But they are there - in the impossibility of criticising the Soviet Union, in the absence of a home-grown foreign policy, and in the inevitable taboos that must exist in a one-party state, even when its ruler is as sensible as János Kadar.

Thus the small Hungarian samizdat literature is the only place for an essay on the real number of poor people in Budapest, although Hungarian officials are ready enough to talk about such tricky matters in private. But its chief function is to allow a critical debate, often from a Marxist point of view, of the unsatisfactory nature of Marxism-Leninism as it is officially proclaimed and practised in Eastern Europe. It strikes an English mind as far more realistic stuff than the utopia-building of Bahro and Havemann.

Take, for example, the thoughts of András Hegedüs about bureaucracy. There is nothing about a cultural revolution that is going to sweep away the bureaucrats and give every cook a hand in the affairs of state as Lenin once promised. (Did he really believe it?) Hegedüs's experience may have been a help - he was prime minister *before* the uprising of 1956. At any rate, he accepts that bureaucracy is here to stay and so concentrates on searching for ways in which it might be controlled. Other Hungarians, like Miklós Haraszti, have prodded such sacred cows as the supposed ideal condition of factory workers under East European socialism and found the reality to be shockingly different.

The Hungarian regime has treated its still rather small group of active dissidents with caution. They have been expelled from the Party, of course; some have been jailed (though usually briefly); and others encouraged to leave the country. The lack of hope in Hungary is not so much felt among this group as among ordinary intellectuals who lack the stuff dissenters are made of and yet are well aware of the limits of their freedom. They, perhaps better than anyone else, can understand the extraordinary gloom that reigns in Czechoslovakia. If Czech communists were unable to liberalise the system, what hope have the Hungarians?

I lent Milan Šimečka's *The Re-establishment of Order* to a Vietnamese refugee. He returned it to me with the words 'I understand now. I shan't ask you any more questions about communism'. It seems at first a low-key book for it does not deal with the stirring events of the Prague Spring and has none of the drama of the eye-witness accounts of that period. Its subject is in the title. It describes how Gustav Husák and the rump of the Czechoslovak communist party have been able to bring their kind of order to the country in East Europe most suited to liberal socialism. It makes profoundly gloomy reading, for it suggests that there is little chance of shaking off the grip of a cleverly directed all-powerful state.

A citizen in such a state, Šimečka points out, does not have to do so very much that is difficult in order to live quietly. He must accept the right of the party to rule; that this party possesses the only truth; that his well-being depends on the state and that it therefore pays to go along with the state. But the state only demands a passive loyalty. The good citizen must repeat the necessary slogans, but he need not believe in them (as long as he keeps quiet about his disbelief).

And if the state has its doubts about the grown-ups, it always has the new generation to work on. The state is obsessed with imposing a uniform education on its children. In a school, Šimečka writes, 'there are only defenceless children and teachers who represent the most malleable human material of real socialism', for they are not only almost entirely women but vulnerable to all sorts of 'recycling' and 'restructuring'.

Šimečka does, however, see one way in which this sort of state might lose its way. Part of the bargain with its citizens is that it delivers the consumer goods. Its persecution of the intelligentsia, he writes, has convinced the great mass of the population 'that one will only burn one's fingers if one plays politics and that no political idea is sufficiently attractive to be worth sacrificing the joys of consumption that real socialism assures in Czechoslovakia. But woe to the state that has nothing more to distribute!'

Austerity, slow-rising living standards or even falling ones, are becoming the order of the day throughout East Europe. But while in the West we have long been free to contemplate the possibility, even the desirability, of low growth, the parties of East Europe have always insisted that growth and communism go hand in hand. There is, though, no reason to suppose that a crisis of this sort will make the regimes any more liberal. If the goulash runs short, may not the defences of the archipelago simply be strengthened?

After Tito

Chris Cviic

As the Tito era drew to a close in Yugoslavia, not a few of those who were keen on change and reform entertained the hope that the post-Tito rulers would, in the interests of the consolidation of their power, allow a degree of liberalisation, especially in the country's cultural life. Others feared that, on the contrary, Tito's successors, nervous and unsure of themselves, would opt for a degree of tightening up and that in this course they might be backed by the majority of the ruling Communist party's two million members. In the event, neither has happened: the push for liberalisation that some had hoped for has not materialised. Nor has full-scale repression - though some pretty illiberal moves have been made by the authorities in the year since Tito's death on 4 May 1980.

President Tito's successors have embarked on preparations for the next - and the first post-Tito - party congress (due to be held in the early summer of 1982) divided and without a clear policy. In the economic field, there is a wide measure of agreement that the country needs to rely on market forces more than in the past. Even the leaders of the party's 'dogmatic' wing are backing the policy of a return to the 'market socialism' of the mid-1960s in the hope that this will help to get the country out of its serious economic difficulties quicker; those difficulties are: a large foreign trade deficit and a foreign debt which at the beginning of 1981 stood at $18 billion; 40% inflation; 13% unemployment with some 800,000 out of work in Yugoslavia and more than 700,000 working abroad and liable to lose their jobs owing to the recession in the West. But in the political field there is no clear consensus. This lack is clearly reflected in the debate conducted over the last year in the usual coded language.

In this debate, Alexander Grlickov, the Macedonian leader who in the party presidium looks after relations with other Communist parties, has emerged as one of the chief protagonists of change and reform, although of a pretty modest and limited kind. On the 'dogmatic' side, one of the frequent and prominent spokesmen has been Dusan Dragosavac, a Serb from Croatia, executive secretary of the party presidium with a two-year mandate expiring in May. Stane Dolanc, the energetic Slovene and one of the most interesting of the post-Tito leaders whom Mr Dragosavac replaced as executive secretary in May 1979, has taken up a middle position, sometimes inclining towards reform and sometimes towards the firm maintenance of the status quo. Tough and illiberal when talking to, say, the old partisans, he can present a more open-minded image when, for example, talking to *Nin*, Yugoslavia's leading weekly in Belgrade. The magazine which had been close to the liberal Serbian leader, Marko Nikezic, sacked by President Tito in October of 1972, has managed to retain some of its old liberal attitude through all the subsequent changes. In an interview on 18 January, published in *Nin*, Mr Dolanc spoke of the three drafts of the famous letter restoring democratic centralism in the party which Tito asked him to prepare in October 1972, and then rejected as 'too soft'. The fourth was, however, all right.

At a special briefing for magazine editors held in the party presidium early in February, Mr Grlickov came out with a strong plea for a 'triple' dialogue: within the party, with 'other socialist forces' and finally with the 'opposition' (*Politika* (Belgrade), 10 February). In his exposé, Mr Grlickov warned his party colleagues that if they did not take charge of that dialogue, it would start without them and somebody else would capture it. He regretted 'a certain tendency towards dogmatisation of our thought' and attempts by some 'state theoreticians' to grab a monopoly for themselves. He did not go as far as to suggest that anything the 'oppositionists' had written should be published and then polemicised with. That would be in an ideal world and 'we do not live on the moon', he said. He preferred a middle solution, a necessarily restrictive one, he added, which would involve providing an answer in the press to the 'strategy of the opposition', in other words reporting, even if indirectly, much of what the opposition is saying.

Mr Dragosavac made his own position clear in a speech delivered in Kosovo on 14 January in which he warned the Yugoslav press not to forget when writing (enthusiastically) about Poland that there are other, 'anti-socialist', forces at work there too. In an interview with *Politika* on 11 February, he bitterly attacked all those who, under the guise of a demand for an amnesty for 'verbal' political offences (see below) are seeking to 'fan religious, racial and national hatreds'.

A surprisingly outspoken plea for a more liberal publishing policy was made on 10 December in the Zagreb *Start*, a fortnightly that is the Yugoslav equivalent of *Playboy*, by Mitja Ribicic, a former federal prime minister and now president of the Socialist Alliance, the party's mass organisation, in Slovenia. As well as making many detailed criticisms of the work of the federal government and the prime minister Veselin Djuranovic himself (something Yugoslav politicians usually avoid), he advocated making available to all those in Yugoslavia who want it 'hostile émigré' press and other publications. It was, he argued, ridiculous to read in the Yugoslav press attacks on Djilas's books when nobody has had a chance to read them. Why should such literature always remain the sole responsibility of our security service and the men of the interior ministry, he said. But so great was the uproar that followed the remarks of Mr Ribicic, who has ironically never had a particularly liberal reputation, that on 19 December he published a 'clarificatory' interview in *Borba*. In this, and in a speech on 12 January, he made it plain that he was against the idea of an independent magazine being allowed to publish in Belgrade. But there are signs that the publication of a Slovenian magazine will be permitted later this year.

At a level below the top the debate about the desirability and degree of liberalisation has been conducted in *Borba* (Struggle), the daily which used to be the main party organ and has since become the organ of the Socialist Alliance while still retaining a slightly 'official' status; in *Komunist*, the party weekly which is published in eight editions for each of Yugoslavia's six federal republics and two autonomous provinces (compared with only two editions for *Borba*, the Belgrade edition in the Cyrillic script and the Zagreb one in the Latin script). In a remarkably outspoken series in January in *Komunist*, a Serbian party intellectual, Radovan Radonjic, called for a purge in the party of 'opportunistic and parasitic' elements which would give it a chance (echoes of Poland) to renew itself.

On the credit side, there has been, for example, the decision to screen on Zagreb television on 23 October a play about a strike in an engineering factory. Yugoslavia has had strikes since 1958, but they are usually of short duration and legally neither allowed nor forbidden. This play called *Obustava u strojnoj* (Stoppage in the Factory) upset a certain number of party hardliners who tried to have it stopped. Questions were even asked about it in the Croatian assembly in Zagreb, but the screening went ahead.

Even more important, perhaps, was the fate of *Karamazovi* (The Karamazovs) by the young playwright Dusan Jovanovic. The play deals with one of the taboo themes - the plight of the so-called Cominformists, party members who, when asked to declare themselves for Tito or Stalin in the great quarrel of 1948, opted for Stalin. Some 15,000 were sent to a concentration camp on an island in the Adriatic where they were very harshly treated. It was to have been put on in Belgrade in March 1980, but the theatre director got cold feet - reportedly because of scenes showing the interrogation and brainwashing of the Cominformists by their erstwhile comrades. He decided to take the play off a few days before its first performance. But later in the year it received a special prize from *Start* magazine in Zagreb and was eventually staged in Celje in Slovenia - albeit under a different title and with some changes in the script and production. The play received enthusiastic notices from the Slovene press but also a black mark from the *Borba* critic who called it a 'political diversion' (*politicka diverzija*).

Articles strongly critical of the Yugoslav system have appeared in magazines. One was 'A plea for a dialogue about the state in socialism' by Professor Neca Jovanov, the main Yugoslav expert on strikes. The article, which appeared in the main party monthly *Socijalizam* in Belgrade, argued that the decentralisation that had so far been carried out in Yugoslav society did not necessarily amount to democratisation. The study caused quite a furore but had no unpleasant professional or party consequences for its author. A radical critique of the whole Yugoslav system was published in 1979 in a sociological magazine called *Revija za sociologiu* (Sociological Review) in Zagreb by Professor Ljubomir Tadic, a member of a group of critical Marxist philosophers who have been a thorn in the authorities' flesh ever since the 1968 student demonstrations in Belgrade. The article was attacked in *Borba* on 3 March by Professor Fuad Muhic, a Party ideologist from Sarajevo in Bosnia, who has done hatchet jobs for the Party in the past.

Unlike Jovanov, Tadic *has* suffered professional consequences for his non-conformity. He and six other philosophers from Belgrade University were suspended (on two-thirds pay) when they refused to accept non-teaching jobs. Finally, the law was changed last year so that they could be removed altogether. This was done by a decision of the Serbian education minister on 8 December, delivered to the seven on 9 January. In a letter sent to the leading political and educational institutions of Serbia on 20 January (but, of course, not published) the seven defiantly recall their statement at the time of their suspension from teaching in 1975 on the grounds of 'spoiling the youth'. They had then declared that 'ideas cannot be defeated by preventing their proclamation from the professorial chair'. The present letter gives instances of how their work has systematically been suppressed - their books and articles were refused publication, (with rare exceptions like Tadic's), their lectures cancelled, their attempts to take their detractors to court frustrated. They end with the defiant words: 'Ideas can only be undermined by wiser ideas'. On 15 January a leading member of the group, Professor Mihailo Markovic, had his passport impounded by the authorities. But the magazine with which they were associated, the Zagreb quarterly *Praxis* which was suppressed in 1975, is likely to appear in Britain this spring with the help of a distinguished group of Western co-editors.

Further examples on the debit side in Yugoslavia - and they have been a good deal more numerous over the past year than those on the other side - have included the authorities' treatment of petitions for amnesty. Article 157 of the 1974 Yugoslav constitution provides for the citizens' right to initiate proposals for new laws and for squashing old ones. In June 1980, barely a month after Tito's death, a group of 36 Serbian intellectuals presented such a petition demanding a change of the law governing political offences, especially the so-called verbal offences for which it is possible under Article 133 of the penal code to get up to ten years. In October another petition demanding an amnesty for verbal offenders was presented by 102 intellectuals including some well-known writers like Dobrica Cosic, philosophers like Professor Ljubomir Tadic and lawyers like Srdja Popovic who has defended many dissidents. On 17 February the official Tanjug agency reported that the petitions had been rejected as 'legally and politically unacceptable'. Tanjug also revealed that in November 1980 a total of 172 people were serving sentences for political offences. (The real number is thought by some of the regime's critics to be much higher.)

The authorities also rejected a separate petition presented by 43 intellectuals in Zagreb. Its scope was broader - it demanded an amnesty for all political offenders - unlike the Belgrade one which confined itself to verbal offences. This demand is thought to have been prompted by the feeling of many intellectuals in Croatia that various trials for sabotage and terrorism in the past few years - particularly since 1976 - were rigged. But the broader scope of the Zagreb petition gave an opening for official attacks on it as a demand for an amnesty for terrorists, spies and saboteurs. The signatories, who included the former Rector of Zagreb University, Professor Ivan Supek, several members of the Yugoslav Academy of Arts and Sciences in Zagreb, prominent artists and writers, doctors, and three prominent Roman Catholic priests, were all questioned by the police. A student who helped collect the signatures, Dobroslav Paraga, was arrested on 21 November and has been in jail since, awaiting trial. On 24 November the police detained his friend, Ernest Brajder, having searched his flat for illegal material. Three days after his arrest, Brajder died in prison. The police appear not to have known that he was suffering from terminal cancer.

One of the most prominent signatories of the Zagreb petition, Franjo Tudjman, formerly a Tito general and director of the Party history institute in Zagreb, was sentenced on 20 February to three years' imprisonment and banned for five years from public activity, including publication. He too was tried and sentenced under the notorious Article 133 of the penal code for 'hostile propaganda with help from abroad'. His offence was that he had, between 1977 and 1980, given four interviews critical of the present political situation in Yugoslavia, and particularly of Croatia's position in it. Two of the interviews were never broadcast because the journalists Tudjman gave them to in the spring of 1980 - one working for German and one for French radio - were expelled after seeing him and had their tapes impounded. One interview was used on Swedish television. It contained the remark that the authorities appeared to mind particularly: that in Tudjman's view Euro-communists like Santiago Carrillo and Enrico Berlinguer could quite easily, in today's Yugoslavia, be arrested for their views. At the trial Tudjman said that in his view the strongest reason for his trial and sentence was the work he was doing as a historian on the atrocities committed between 1941 and 1945 by the wartime Pavelic regime in Croatia against which Tudjman was fighting as a partisan. His researches had established that only about a tenth of the victims officially claimed to have been killed had actually died. He argued that not 600,000 but some 60,000 perished and that the exaggerated figure was used to discredit the Croats in order to keep them in a subordinate position in Yugoslavia.

Tudjman's work on European nationalisms was published earlier this year by Columbia University Press in New York. In Yugoslavia, he has not published anything since his prison sentence for 'counter-revolutionary activity' in 1972, of which he served two years.

The Tudjman trial coincided with further attacks on the intellectuals who had signed a request for permission to publish an independent critical magazine in Belgrade under the title *Javnost* ('Public') - the name of the first Socialist magazine in Serbia in the nineteenth century edited by Svetozar Markovic, the father of Serbian socialism. The request was made in the name of Dobrica Cosic, perhaps the most popular Serbian writer today, and by Ljubomir Tadic, the philosopher mentioned above, and supported by some 100 writers, journalists, and university people. It was rejected in December, as had been earlier in the year a similar demand by a group of Slovene intellectuals in Ljubljana.

Meanwhile the sentences handed out for political offences continued to be harsh: on 30 December a Serbian Orthodox priest in Borik near Sarajevo, Nedjo Janjic, was sentenced to six years' imprisonment for singing at his son's christening Serbian chauvinist songs calculated to fan discord among Croats, Serbs and Moslems.

It is possible that the regime's calculation that it does not have to pay too much attention to the intellectuals demanding reforms may prove to be correct. Yugoslav intellectuals are divided along national lines, with a good deal of mistrust still existing not only between Croats and Serbs but also Serbs and Moslems. Unlike in Poland, they have no direct links with the workers, and the various churches have few links with each other. But at the end of 1980 this began to change. The Serbian Orthodox church remained aloof from the whole sphere of human rights - and was duly praised for it by the President of the Croatian Assembly, Jure Bilic, in a speech on 13 February. But the Catholic Archbishop of Zagreb Mgr Franjo Kuharic indirectly endorsed the Zagreb petition in his sermon on Christmas Day in Zagreb Cathedral, saying the government should listen when citizens make suggestions. He revealed also that he had not yet had a reply to his request made three months before for access to be granted to the priests to prisons, from which they have been barred since 1945. Another controversy centering on the personality and role of the wartime Archbishop of Zagreb, Alojzije Stepinac has brought the Catholic church into something resembling confrontation with the regime. Here perhaps is another example of how the Yugoslav leaders' nervousness exacerbates situations and reopens fronts which had hitherto been relatively quiet.

Poland's Lesson in Freedom

Adam Michnik

It was not preceded by a declaration of war. In the course of that December night functionaries of so-called Security rammed at the doors of our houses, broke them down and, distributing blows left and right, blinding us with tear gas, handcuffed us and took us into prisons as internees. We were the first prisoners of war - a war of the Communist establishment against its own people. That night was the first victorious battle of the General who, following in a rather curious way the directive of the Ninth Congress of the Communist Party forbidding anybody to hold more than one post, was at the same time Minister of Defence, Prime Minister, First Secretary of the Party, and now in addition had made himself Chairman of the 'CROW' (WRON, the acronym of the Military Council of National Salvation, in Polish happens to mean 'a crow'). And so his name is now for ever associated with that ugly and stupid bird, the caricature of the national emblem, the eagle.

The war took the nation by surprise. Future historians will appreciate the precision of that first blow, its excellent timing, the efficiency of the troops. Poets will glorify the famous victories of that army in the streets of Gdansk, on the shop-floors of factories in Warsaw, in so many foundries, coal-mines and shipyards. The brilliant stratagems which enabled them to take both the main building of Polish Radio and Television and the telephone exchange will forever be celebrated as great feats of Polish arms.

Since the time of King Sobieski none of our leaders can boast of such success as those who took control in mid-December 1981. Now musicians can compose symphonies, painters depict intrepid charges, film makers produce patriotic films, all to the glory of the leaders on that December night.

Let's stop joking. Despite the official propaganda imposing such

Vol. 11, no. 4, 1982

stylistic flourishes in its commentaries, we need to ask ourselves, even though we are still stunned and shocked, what the truth is about what has happened in Poland. To defend their power, privileges, and position as rulers, the Communist elite took desperate measures on 13 December. It's pointless reiterating the details but quite plainly the elite's security was endangered, and not only in Poland but in the whole Communist camp.

The December coup did not aim at implementing a Communist utopia. It was a classic counter-revolution against the working class, begun in order to defend the conservative interests of an *ancien régime*. Contrary to the official statements, it was *not* a reply to attempts to seize political power. Solidarity had no 'shadow cabinet', nor indeed any programme. The origins of the coup are primarily to be found in the insoluble conflict between a multi-million strong social movement, based within Solidarity, and the totalitarian structure of a Communist state. The essence of the conflict was the simple fact of the existence of an independent and self-administered institution supported by the nation.

Thus the problem was not power itself but its scope and nature ... Implementation of the reform programme would have undermined the basic maxims of Communist rule over both state and society. It was patently obvious that the Party would not benevolently yield even a scrap of its power, and so conflicts were inevitable.

However, we believed that the nature of those conflicts would be different. We never thought that the Party machine would resort to military force to resolve social issues. We did not believe they would choose the argument of force instead of the force of argument. This of course is not the first crisis in the history of Communist states, and those interested in comparing Hungary in 1956, Czechoslovakia 12 years later, and Poland's 15 months, will find specific features common to all, but some significant differences too. The common ground was the attempt to broaden national and individual rights. The differences are to be located in the dynamics of social change in each case.

In 1956 the reforms began in Moscow, stemming from the 20th Congress of the CPSU, when the party bureaucracy dismissed the lingering shadow of Stalin and removed the constant threat of the security police. This inspired moves towards change in the Polish and Hungarian states. In Poland Gomulka was just released from prison, and came to power with immense prestige, which was a sufficient guarantee for both Polish society and the Kremlin. In the Kremlin's eyes Gomulka was a Communist with whom they could communicate; for Poles he seemed a suitable mouthpiece for national and democratic aims.

In Hungary the resistance against change coming from the Stalinist remnants provided a spur towards change, imposed by street revolutionaries. The power machine collapsed like a house of cards, and the Soviet intervention was a simple consequence. In Czechoslovakia the changes were initiated by circles within the Party, who realised that change was essential to maintain economic efficiency, that without change the Communist system would drift into waste and obscurantism. The victorious liberal faction led by Dubcek was supported by the whole nation and aimed at commencing democratic reforms in central government, accompanied by a relaxation of the tight relationship with the Soviet Union.

The new Czech socialism had many faces, ranging from the moderate reformism of the Party to the pluralist vision depicted by non-conformist journalists. But the decisive factor was the open rebellion by the Czech leaders, who sought the removal of the blatant Soviet dictatorship, and asked society to give them a mandate to accomplish this. They sought their power in the Czech nation and not merely within the walls of the Kremlin.

Democratic movement

In Poland the situation is vitally different. It's difficult to call it 'socialism with a human face'. It's more like Communism with broken teeth, unable to bite a nation well organised to attack it. The constantly repeated cry that there was 'open counter-revolution' and 'fascist terror' is contradicted by the facts – no people were molested or killed, not one drop of blood was shed by people working for the Polish revolution ...

Our living conditions supply answers to the puzzle as to the limited nature of the Polish revolution. There were many democratic opposition groups widely supported by public opinion, sheltering under the protective umbrella of the Catholic Church. Such groups took advantage of the relatively tolerant nature of Gierek's regime to develop self-help and self-defence measures within society. Gierek's tolerance was due to the need for economic collaboration with the West, along with his regime's political weakness – it had nothing to do with liberalism.

Independent intellectual life was organised, and uncensored scenarios for the future struggle for freedom were available for wide discussion. Among the more important developments was the start of the Workers' Self-Defence Committee (KOR), established after the 1976 strikes. Its aim was the reconstruction of society and the rebuilding of social inter-action outside the domination of the official authorities. The vital question for us was not 'how to reform the regime' but how to defend ourselves against it ...

Solidarity was a democratic movement of workers born in an anti-democratic environment, among totalitarian structures which regarded the terms of the Yalta treaty as the only legitimate justification for any social activity. Poles need no reminder of the terms of that treaty, which has been interpreted recently by *Stern* as seeming to mean that human rights are only for people living west of the Elbe, and that the *knout* and barbed wire are sufficient for regulating the lives of Eastern savages. The problem for Poland's leaders was to translate the Yalta treaty into current language, and this was not easy. A powerful social movement with no precedent, which daily shaped itself afresh during the constant conflicts with the ruling Party. Solidarity had no clear certain aims and no concept of coexistence with the Communist regime. Naturally it was easily provoked and diverted into participation in unimportant side-issues ... Solidarity knew how to strike but it was unprepared to wait. It could attack directly but it could not withdraw. It had a general outline programme but no gradual means to implement it. It was powerful in factories among workers but weak at the negotiating table. It had to face an opponent who could not speak the truth, could not administer, could not maintain promises, but who could manage one thing - the crushing of social solidarity. Solidarity was a gargantuan with steel legs but hands of putty. It faced a regime which had practised the art of repression for 27 years.

The ruling elite was morally and financially bankrupt and, because of its political weakness, unable to carry through any policy. Its *political* weakness was mistaken by Solidarity for total weakness, forgetting that the security forces had been untouched by political corrosion. Solidarity forgot that these forces usually become efficient instruments in the hands of a dictatorship, especially if there is nothing to lose. The Communist regime in Poland was a giant with putty legs but steel hands. In calling for democratic elections to the Sejm and local government Solidarity seemed to forget that this would mean an emergency for the rulers whose power would inevitably, and rapidly, vanish. Let us repeat. Solidarity has never called for the abolition of Communist rule and the imposition of government by the Union. But this is how things were interpreted by the Party leadership ...

Wishful thinking

The December coup was their answer. Solidarity was caught off balance since it didn't expect a military attack; responsibility for this unpreparedness lies not with the workers but with all those, including myself, who were called on to assist in shaping the political vision of the Union. Theoretical consideration of changes to the system lagged far behind what was actually going on. As often happens in Polish history, practice was far in advance of theory. The main conflict within Solidarity concerned the entirely vague ideas as to the rate and range of changes to the system.

Initially the supporters of compromise within Solidarity had the upper hand, but gradually it became obvious that the authorities treated all moves towards compromise as indications of the weakness of Solidarity's will ... Some said 'enough of strikes, they lead nowhere' whereas others argued that inconsistent striking was futile and that a general strike was necessary to force the government to concede. It is difficult to say which view prevailed, but certainly the latter shouted loudest. It was usually these voices, frequently young workers from the big industrial plants, which forced Solidarity's leadership to take radical steps, which became increasingly more difficult to halt, although attempts were made to do this by both Walesa and Kuron. The authorities were held in contempt and their power was neglected; few thought that Polish troops would attack Polish workers, or that a military coup was possible. This was naive wishful thinking. The preceding months had formed a pattern of conflicts between the state and society in which there was no consideration of open violence. The image of the gallows and blacklists had existed only in the sick minds of certain Party leaders.

Solidarity had only one answer to the declaration of martial law – the sit-in strike. This was rendered useless by the military attacks but the problem now is that awareness of the inadequacy of peaceful tactics may well bring disastrous consequences for the future. The bloodshed at the Wujek mine may well become an example that should be remembered if in the future we talk to the authorities and hope to achieve anything.

What did the Communists think of Solidarity? The August 1980 crisis was naturally no shock to them but what astonished them was the maturity of the demands, along with the determined discipline and solidarity of the workers. Gierek's clique thought it essential to avoid confrontation with the workers, but this posture was not to be continued. The Union's swift spread across the country meant that the authorities could only hope and work to provoke a split within the Union. Solidarity became a deadly threat to them, precisely because it dissolved a basic principle of Communist ideology, that the Communist Party represents the working class ... Understood as a distinct coherent group of organised members, the Party was significantly absent during the August 1980 strikes, and as an instrument for breaking social solidarity, so efficiently used in this way in the past, it no longer existed. In trying to revive the Party its leaders unclasped a Pandora's box. On the one hand in its search for victims and scapegoats it revealed shocking evidence of the extent of the corruption amongst the Gierek cliques. On the other hand Party members were returning their cards *en masse*, or worse still, organising themselves into 'parallel structures' which called for reform of the Party along democratic lines, rejecting the Stalinist model of hierarchical authority.

This indeed was the biggest difference between the Polish events and those of 1956 and 1968. The Communist leaders then - Nagy, Gomulka and Dubcek - began to regain social confidence and the reformist groups within those Communist parties were backed by society as a whole. In Poland itself the Party was left behind in 1980, and was overtaken by social pressures seeking changes. The Party, the PZPR, changed under pressures external to itself, and the PZPR's reform programmes lagged far behind those presented by Solidarity. Furthermore the Party reformers were not one homogeneous group, but they contained a wide diversity of personalities with different backgrounds. Among them were Andrzej Werblan, former ideological dictator in Gomulka's and Gierek's times; Stefan Bratkowski, journalist and one of the organisers of the 'Experience and Future' group and Chairman of the Polish Journalists Union; Wojciech Lamentowicz, a 36-year-old tutor at a PZPR college; Zbigniew Iwanów, a leader of a strike during August 1980 at one of Torun's major factories. All of them, no matter their differences, were victims of a paradox which befalls all Communist reformists across the world. In aiming at the reform of a totalitarian system in the name of human rights and social justice, trying to restructure a bureaucratic machine which stifles creative freedom and instead favours mediocrity and mendacity, they are able to attack the machine with efficiency only so long as they present a corporate face, only whilst they remained a faction struggling for power. The moment they became this they were placed outside the Party and forced to act in such a way that could be strictly condemned as hostile.

In order to solve this insoluble problem they developed the 'parallel structures' but, too weak to force the approval of the Party's machine, they were quickly crushed by its conservative apparatus. The Polish Party reformers were a pathetic parody of their colleagues in 1956 and 1968, even though their reformism was apparently more deeply rooted in everyday reality and was less abstract. There were no discussions of the Young Marx, instead there were heated talks about economic reform. But it was only an illusion; the movement had no support in intellectual circles in general ... Society now speaks with a common voice, and besides that the Party reformers still expressed their ideals in the peculiar language of the old Marxist-Leninist style. For the Party reformers the vital question was how to make the Party more democratic, which for them was synonymous with how to make society democratic. For society the issue was how to save democratic processes from the Party's dictatorship ...

The Party machine accused Solidarity of seeking political power instead of being a pure trade union. Solidarity's suggestion was that the PZPR should become a political party gaining its legitimacy through social support, instead of being a trade union for the rulers, which is the most precise definition of the ruling Communist Party. And that was what it was all about. The considerably democratic change brought about by the PZPR 9th Congress changed nothing. As a result of the democratic elections there were elected to the highest Party posts people under intense suspicion, such as Albin Siwak, called the 'Polish Stakhanov' - a leading worker with a security forces membership card. With Siwak in the Politburo the PZPR could not possibly count on social confidence being granted, and the new statutes and programme approved at the Congress were still-births. The PZPR machine could still only count on hopes that Solidarity would split, and that the mediation of the Church would influence this.

The front of national agreement, symbolised by the meeting between Jaruzelski, Walesa and Glemp, was based on the Party machine, Solidarity and the Church, and was the final attempt to eliminate Solidarity from national issues without bloodshed. The Catholic Church, the highest moral authority in Poland, supported by the Polish Pope, was at that time inclined to favour compromise and tried to build bridges of social understanding to appease the tension between the rulers and Solidarity. But this was intended as a genuine compromise and not merely a withdrawal of Solidarity's aims and principles. Such a withdrawal was implied when the rulers suggested that the front of national agreement should draw up common lists of candidates for the coming local elections, a solution not acceptable to the Church. This was a climax, since it appeared that a conflict was again inevitable, and for the authorities it was clear that they could not achieve the kind of compromise they sought ...

It was followed by the Radom meeting of the Komisja Krajowa (Solidarity's national body), and then the military coup. Solidarity expected a conflict but thought it would focus not on a struggle for power but how power was to be executed and used ... We have to admit that the night attack of 12 December was carried out in splendid military fashion, with complete lack of scruples by its participants.

Solidarity was 'pacified' with tanks and bayonets and the resistance of the workers was crushed. This triumph of the machine may well bring unexpected results, since it may establish the true nature of the machine's political myopia. Bayonets frighten and kill, and win battles against unarmed people, but you cannot sit on a bayonet. You cannot erase 15 months of freedom with a bayonet . . .

'Here we have time to reflect'

Here, in my new home guarded by armed men in uniform, with its iron bars and barbed wire, only fragments of news reach me. Here, we have more time for reflection. Those 15 months of the Solidarity period were a lesson in freedom. Solidarity may be erased from walls but not from memories. Its example will continue to operate under different circumstances, perhaps not only for us Poles but also for others in the same geo-political region.

Here behind the bars any gesture of Solidarity and 'solidarity' is like breathing fresh air. Every piece of good news helps us to go on living, but there are some bad moments too, such as when I hear the Vice-Premier of Poland (Rakowski) speaking to West German magazines about the satisfactory condition of his imprisoned political opponents. He cuts a grotesque figure when he performs that role, and his German interviewer is either cynical or naïve.

A few more words on the internees. We are jailed without warrants from a prosecutor. Each of us can be released providing he signs the loyalty declaration and agrees to act as a police informer. Our guards think that in our state of prostration we have no strength to resist. All of us, workers, farmers, intellectuals, are hostages. Our fate is an example to our colleagues. Our status is something to show to foreigners. It is far worse for those sentenced for striking. It is too early for us to develop any formulas yet. We each have to try and answer the questions for ourselves, decide for ourselves how to resist the evil, how to defend, how to behave in this strange war which is an everlasting struggle of truth against falsehood, of freedom against violence, of dignity against humiliation. I'm reminded of a philosopher who said there is no final victory in this struggle, though no final defeat either. Writing these reflections is my part in the war. I will surely be silenced for some time to come and that is why I would like to greet my friends, especially those who are in hiding and are struggling against the regime, and wish them enough courage and strength to walk across the empty darkness between despair and hope and enough patience to learn the difficult art of forgiving.

Rumania: A Simple Solution: a feuilleton of advice for the Rumanian leader

Ivan Kraus

Dear Mr Ceausescu, I have for some time now been following your political career with great admiration because I know that you alone decide what is and what isn't good for Rumania. This in an age when in many countries politicians still waste a lot of time by indulging in lengthy and fruitless debates in parliaments and legislative assemblies. I'm therefore convinced it is no exaggeration to say that there is no statesman in the world today who would show so personal an interest in his citizens as you do.

I have just learned about your latest measures from the daily press. Having ascertained that the Rumanians eat too much and that, as a result, a full third of the population suffers from diseases due to obesity, you have proposed a diet consisting of ten eggs, ten dekagrams of butter and a kilogram of meat per citizen per month.

You have also decreed that room temperatures should not exceed 15 degrees Celsius, being well aware that citizens of a socialist state must not be too delicate.

Your order that lifts should only operate from the third floor up will likewise help to improve the physical fitness of your people, just as the decision not to use refrigerators in winter and to switch the TV off at ten p.m. every night, except on special occasions such as the days when the nation is celebrating a birthday – yours, your wife's, or that of some other member of your family.

It is to be regretted that some of your citizens seem not to understand the wisdom of these measures you have decided to take, so that it is necessary for the police to step in and keep a watchful eye to make sure that people don't overheat their homes, use their fridges in winter, or consume too much energy on illumination, cooking, ironing, or watching TV. It is only the irresponsible attitude of a few individuals that makes it necessary to resort to blocking up their points.

I, however, am an optimist and believe that before too long everyone will realise that they can only hope to see a brighter tomorrow if today they switch the lights off early. It is no secret that you and all your family have to work very hard. Your son Nicu is Minister for Youth, your brothers Ion and Ilie are in charge of the Ministries of Planning and Defence respectively, another brother, Nicolae, heads the Ministry of the Interior. Moreover, your wife is your First Deputy.

It is well known that altogether 50 members of your family have to devote all their time, energy and talents to the job of running Rumania, with its 22 million inhabitants. That makes it almost half a million citizens per member of your family, and that is a record that cannot be equalled anywhere in the world today. Not even Flick in West Germany, Heineken in Holland, Grundig or Ford can measure up to you in effectiveness. Duvalier achieves only minimal output with his employees, Idi Amin has gone bankrupt, and Khomeini has too many shareholders and still cannot make a go of it.

I mention all this only because I think that your latest idea - to register all typewriters in the country - requires a little more elaboration. Allow me therefore to discuss this interesting measure and to make a few suggestions as to how it could be improved.

First of all, it is absolutely essential also to register chalks, pens, crayons, pencils, brushes, as well as ink, varnishes and sprays (insofar as these are obtainable in your country), and other material such as paper, note-pads and exercise-books. And talking about paper, you mustn't forget wrapping and toilet paper. Also all kinds of material used to cut out, stick on or otherwise position letters of the alphabet. I am referring to newspapers, sacks, textiles, scissors, glues, drawing pins, needles, pins and nails.

However, people can use other means too to express anti-State or otherwise harmful sentiments. By means of the Morsecode, for example, which can be transmitted with the aid of light. For that reason I would recommend the registration of lamps, chandeliers, torches, bulbs, batteries, spotlights, lanterns, fireworks, as well as mirrors.

More primitive methods such as smoke signals can also be used to convey anti-State slogans, for which reason I would restrict the sale of matches, candles, lighters, as well as cigars and cigarettes.

Furthermore, you must not forget all the objects that can be used to transmit sound signals. No citizen should thus be in a position to obtain without permit bells, whistles, and musical instruments (percussion, wind and string - for short distances). The number of musical instruments owned by all orchestras and ensembles should be checked without delay, and reliable musicians issued with music passports.

All this, however, is still not enough.

People wishing to express some anti-State thought can be extremely ingenious, as I discovered in Prague in 1968, when the arrival of Soviet troops gave rise to what I might call a festival of anti-State creativity.

The lesson we learned then was that citizens can make use of empty tins, dustbins, boxes, barrels, as well as tyres and building materials such as bricks, breeze blocks, beams and planks. Tools to be found in any storeroom must also be included in this category: pliers, picks, hoes, shovels, drills, scythes, even sickles.

Furniture, too, can come in handy. All you need is a few tables, chairs, hat-stands, benches or wardrobes and you can put together a slogan.

Nor should farmers and farm labourers be left out. They can achieve the same result with the aid of sugarbeet, potatoes, marrows, any kind of vegetable and also all larger - i.e. legible - species of fruit. Even the smaller fruits, such as red currants, blueberries and raspberries, can be made use of for writing, if not on walls, then certainly on tables.

Similarly, pots and pans, saucepans, lids, plates, in short all kitchen utensils, crockery and even cutlery offer similar possibilities.

And, alas, we cannot exclude medicine bottles and pills, including vitamins, while foodstuffs too can be misused. Sausages, salamis, hams, loaves of bread, rolls, butter, yoghurt, ice-cream, beer and other bottles - all this is potential communication material, just as various personal items such as lipsticks, compacts, make-up kits, purses, watches, and chewing gum.

Finally, I must draw your attention to yet another object - the book. Or rather books. I know that these are carefully censored before they ever get to the bookshops, libraries, schools or scientific institutes. But it is not their content which concerns me here.

The very shape of a book makes it an ideal tool for the compiling of words or whole sentences, so that all an inventive anti-State person needs, for instance, is a pile of your own, ideologically absolutely innocuous autobiographies, or some other officially sanctioned works, from which to compose an unsuitable slogan.

I am well aware that any systematic measures to prevent the spreading of anti-State ideas in the way I have outlined above would be extremely costly.

I realise that it would require the appointment of special censors in every office, factory, institute and cooperative. They would also have to be sent to other sectors, such as the railways, road transport, and district and regional administration, and above all every street and house. Not to mention the armed forces and the police.

If I take into account the cost of the reporting and systematic registration of all individual objects, to which has to be added the expense incurred in setting up and operating the central censorship offices and control commissions, it occurs to me - as I sit here typing on what is as yet a free, unregistered typewriter - that there would be a far simpler and cheaper solution, which I take the liberty of offering for your consideration.

I suggest that we solve the problem rationally and simply by *abolishing the alphabet.*

That is the only way we can achieve socialism quickly and without risk.

USSR: Hope for Dissenters?

Sally Laird

It takes no special percipience or cynicism to detect the motivation behind some of last year's 'big name' releases. Shcharansky, whose fame had long been a thorn in the Soviet flesh, was profitably traded as a 'spy'. Orlov benefited vicariously from another such deal. Irina Ratushinskaya's release was announced just before the superpower summit in Reykjavik. All of these releases were, in the words of dissident Valery Soifer, 'gifts to the West' rather than to 'democracy inside the Soviet Union'.

Sakharov presents a more complex case. Mr Gorbachev's involvement in his release might be read as a mark of personal respect for his country's most famous prisoner. Sakharov's support for the government's nuclear strategy, his positive remarks about Gorbachev's foreign policy initiatives and drive for greater 'openness' – *glasnost* – at home, may well have earned him a measure of trust from the Soviet leader. The fact that the Nobel laureate's release was publicised at home as well as abroad, and that he has been interviewed by Soviet as well as foreign journalists, lends credence to the view that Gorbachev may have decided to treat Sakharov as a kind of one-man 'loyal opposition'. On several occasions the Soviet leader has openly suggested that Soviet society has suffered precisely from the absence of such sanctioned opposition – a view not shared, apparently, by all his 'loyal' colleagues. Possibly Gorbachev was blocked from releasing Sakharov earlier by conservatives and hard-liners of the kind who spoke so contemptuously of the exiled physicist only a week before his release, and who doubtless fear that 'openness' may be getting out of hand.

If so, what almost certainly tipped the balance in Sakharov's favour was not a spontaneous change of heart, but a more traditional concern for Western public opinion. The timing of Sakharov's release suggests an obvious propaganda motive. It came within days of the news that writer Anatoly Marchenko, who had spent twenty years in jail for his human rights activities, had died in prison at the age of 48. According to Cronid Lubarsky, editor of *USSR News Brief*, the Munich-based human rights bulletin, the authorities had been planning to use Marchenko himself as a bargaining chip in negotiating for political concessions from the West (in particular, they hoped to secure recognition for Soviet trade unions from their Western counterparts in exchange for Marchenko's release). Marchenko's death upset these plans. More importantly it tarnished the self-confident, 'goodwill' image which Soviet officials had been cultivating at the opening of the Helsinki follow-up conference in Vienna. Urgent action was needed if the planned Moscow conference on 'humanitarian issues', announced with great bravado in Vienna, were not to prove a fiasco.

By itself, then, Sakharov's release does not provide evidence for an unequivocal shift in policy. Even the favourable treatment he has received might be interpreted only as an attempt to isolate him as a special case whose fate has no relevance for other imprisoned dissenters. But this is not to say that there has been no change at all, or that there are no prospects of change in the future.

For a start, whatever the motivation behind the release, Sakharov's return to Moscow has had an electric effect on all those in the Soviet Union who have been hoping that Gorbachev's policies will lead to the real democratisation of their society. The release of a famous dissident may or may not be proof that such hopes are justified, but it will certainly inspire renewed efforts to test the scope for change. Not only Sakharov himself, but others too are unlikely to remain fettered by gratitude to his 'liberators'. It is in the nature of 'openness' that Gorbachev and his government cannot retain a monopoly over its interpretation.

By encouraging the intelligentsia to speak openly on 'approved' issues, Mr Gorbachev has unleased their opinion on human rights issues as well. Several prominent writers, including the popular poets Bulat Okudzhava and Yevgeny Yevtushenko, recently spoke up in protest at the 3-year camp sentence given to writer Pavel Protsenko, convicted of 'anti-Soviet slander' for writing and circulating religious literature. The effect, if any, of this particular protest is not yet known. But a strategy of selective deafness is unlikely to win respect from intellectuals who have found their voice under the new regime, and whose favour Gorbachev has been courting.

Even more significant, from the human rights point of view, are the effects of 'openness' within state institutions such as the judiciary. In response to criticism by prominent Soviet lawyers, a new codification of Soviet laws is currently being drafted. The aim is to strengthen the rights of the individual against the State, to ensure that these rights are known, and to increase the role of defence lawyers during pre-trial investigation as well as in court. Professor V. Kudryavtsev, a legal expert at the Soviet Academy of Sciences who is involved in drafting the new code, has been an outspoken critic of improprieties in current legal procedure, and has argued in particular for official recognition of the 'presumption of innocence' principle which, he says, has repeatedly been flouted. In the pages of *Pravda* Professor Kudryavtsev has expressed the hope that the new code will 'establish guarantees of legality and strong protection for the rights of the Soviet people' (see The *Guardian*, 3 September and 8 December 1986).

There is some evidence that criticisms such as those expressed by Professor Kudryavtsev have already begun to take effect. Over the last year, close observers of the Soviet human rights scene, such as Cronid Lubarsky and Yury Orlov, have discerned at least the outline of a more favourable pattern. Lubarsky's bi-monthly *USSR News Brief*, meticulously compiled from reliable sources both within and outside the Soviet Union, gives detailed documentation on the persecution, arrests and trials of dissenters. Together, his reports for 1986 suggest that changes are afoot which may be attributed not just to a concern for image, but to the influence of Gorbachev's more generally open policy.

Amnesty International confirms that over the past year altogether twelve 'prisoners of conscience' have been prematurely released from imprisonment. They include not only the 'big names' previously mentioned, but less well-known figures whose cases have been reviewed under normal judicial procedure. Vladimir Poresh, an Orthodox Christian, was released after his latest sentence was overturned by a higher court. He had been re-arrested in prison while serving a previous sentence for 'anti-Soviet agitation and propaganda', and charged under the infamous Article 188-3 of the Criminal Code ('maliciously disobeying the administration of a penal institution'). Article 188-3, known as the 'Andropov' article because it was introduced under his leadership, has been widely used to facilitate the re-arrest and further sentencing of troublesome political prisoners. It is perhaps not accidental that this article – or its improper use – has been singled out for public criticism. Helsinki monitor Tatyana Osipova, likewise sentenced under Article 188-3, was also prematurely released from her term in camp, possibly as a result of a similar review (she is now in internal exile with her husband). And the Crimean Tatar activist Mustafa Dzhemilev, whose release from camp was announced almost simultaneously with that of Sakharov, had been charged under the same article. None of this amounts to evidence that the 'Andropov' article is about to fall into disuse (indeed there is plenty of evidence to the contrary). But is does confirm that criticisms emerging under *glasnost* may have given greater room for manoeuvre to more liberally-minded members of the legal profession.

There is evidence of this in other cases too. A striking example was that of Latvian peace activist Mikhail Bombin, who was given a relatively lenient suspended sentence (for 'anti-Soviet slander') after an unusual trial in which the prosecution effectively took up his defence. The trial was open to all who wished to attend. Both the prosecutor and Bombin's attorney pointed out gaps and inconsistencies in the investigation of the case, and the prosecutor went to the lengths of - illegally - pleading Bombin's intoxication at the time of the alleged offence as a mitigating circumstance. Later, a court of appeal resisted pressure from the procuracy to punish him more severely.

These are isolated cases, but they offer some encouragement. As Cronid Lubarsky pointed out (in a telephone conversation with *Index*), confusion and ambiguity are at least better than monolithic certainty. Under the new regime, power in the Soviet Union has become more diffused. The KGB may carry on unabashed, but it can no longer count absolutely on the cooperation of the judiciary.

Moreover, the overall rate of political arrests does appear to have decreased. Of course, this impression may simply be due to lack of information: the KGB has always concentrated on destroying the internal information network in the Soviet Union and its links with people like Lubarsky abroad. But new informants constantly emerge, and Lubarsky is sufficiently confident of his sources to confirm this favourable trend. The 'List of Political Prisoners' which he compiles annually contains 150 fewer names this year than last.

None of this gives grounds for complacency. There are still over 650 known cases of people imprisoned or exiled in the Soviet Union for expression of political, religious or national dissent, and the actual figure is certainly higher than this. Conditions within the camps and prisons fail to meet the most elementary standards. Over the past two years several well-known political prisoners - including the poet Vasyl Stus, journalist Valery Marchenko, mathematician Mark Morozov, and now Anatoly Marchenko - have died as a result of long-untreated illness, malnutrition, and brutality. The persecution of religious believers from 'unregistered' sects continues unabated. While some of the activists in the unofficial peace group have been allowed - or even encouraged - to emigrate, those that remain behind have suffered continual harassment. Despite concessions here and there and promises of 'greater flexibility' in the future, thousands of would-be emigrants still await permission to leave.

Cronid Lubarsky, Yury Orlov and others all stress that the plight of those still suffering imprisonment or harassment must not be forgotten. Continued pressure must be applied if the positive spin-offs from *glasnost* are to emerge into a real pattern - let alone a full-blown policy - in the realm of human rights. Campaigns launched from abroad on behalf of individual prisoners have proved very effective in certain cases. On its own, however, external pressure is not enough. Moreover, in the context of superpower politics, such pressure is all too easily subsumed under political game-playing, alas providing ammunition for the Soviet authorities' own interpretation of all unsanctioned criticism as a form of anti-Soviet propaganda. So long as human rights remain hostage to propaganda - in both East and West - we are unlikely to see large-scale change.

This certainly doesn't mean that campaigners in the West should cease to speak up on behalf of Soviet political prisoners. But they must be careful not to ally pressure for their release with specific prescriptions for political change, or with claims to a monopoly of virtue in the realm of human rights. As in the past, real change will come only as a result of pressure from within the Soviet Union - which is why we should draw most encouragement from small signs that such pressures have already begun to take effect.

It is clear that Mr Gorbachev has not yet made up his mind about the human rights issue. But his willingness to take calculated risks has been amply demonstrated, not only in such acts as Sakharov's release, but in the much larger gamble of sanctioning hard-hitting criticism in the interests of a more efficient and prosperous society. Calculated risks can have incalculable consequences. Mr Gorbachev needs encouraging in the belief that even the unplanned consequences of his gamble - such as we have begun to see - will ultimately benefit rather than destroy the society he is trying to create. He is more likely to be persuaded of this, not by those who crow at the potential unravelling of the Soviet state, but by those who maintain that the identity of the state could survive even the mass amnesty of all political prisoners.

This may sound naively optimistic. But it is the view held by Yury Orlov and Andrei Sakharov, among others. Like other human rights activists of the seventies, both have maintained - in a manner now echoed by certain Soviet officials - that huge improvements could be made if only the Soviet authorities would abide by their own laws and constitution. Arguably, even the most pernicious laws - those prohibiting 'anti-Soviet slander' and 'anti-Soviet agitation and propaganda' – would lose much of their sting if they were legally applied. As Sakharov has pointed out, in most if not all cases in which dissenters have been convicted under these articles, it was never proved that the 'malicious fabrications' that they circulated were either malicious or fabricated, or that the statements they made and actions they took were designed to undermine the Soviet state.

Soviet leaders would do well to listen to those, such as Orlov and Sakharov, who have been unwilling to make themselves a party to political propaganda on either side of the East/West divide. Mr Gorbachev shows no great willingness to do so yet, at least so far as human rights are concerned. But it would be nice to think that, with Sakharov back in Moscow and on the telephone, he may yet take up the opportunity.

Czechoslovakia: Stories and Totalitarianism

Václav Havel

Translated by Paul Wilson

Written in April, 1987 for Revolver Review *and dedicated to Ladislav Hejdanek on his 60th birthday.*

A friend of mine who is heavily asthmatic was sentenced, for political reasons, to several years in prison where he suffered a great deal because his cellmates smoked and he could scarcely breathe. All his requests to be moved to a cell of non-smokers were ignored. His health, and perhaps even his life, were seriously threatened. An American woman who had learned of this and wanted to help out telephoned an acquaintance, an editor on an important American daily. Could he write something about it, she asked? 'Call me when the man dies,' was the editor's reply.

It's a shocking incident but in some ways understandable. Newspapers need a story. Asthma is not a story. Death could make it one.

*

In Prague there is only a single Western news agency with long term accreditation. In Lebanon, a country far smaller than Czechoslovakia, there are reporters by the hundred. This is understandable since 'nothing's happening here', as they say, whereas Lebanon is full of stories. It is also, of course, a land of murders, wars, death. But the two are connected: as long as humans can remember, death has been the point at which all the lines of every real story converge.

Our condition is rather like that of my friend: we are unworthy of attention because we have no stories and no death. We have only asthma. And why should anyone be interested in listening to our commonplace cough?

Vol. 17, no. 3, 1988

After all, one can't go on writing forever about how hard it is to breathe.

*

I'm not bothered by the fact that terrorists are not on the loose here or that people are not being murdered in the streets or that there are no big scandals over corruption in high places and no violent demonstrations and strikes.

What bothers me is something else: the fact that this remarkable absence of newsworthy stories is not an expression of social harmony but merely the outward consequence of a dangerous and profound process: the destruction of 'the story' altogether. Almost every day I am struck by the ambiguity of this social quiescence, which is essentially only the visible expression of an invisible war between the totalitarian system and life itself.

It is not true, therefore, to say that our country is free of warfare and murder. The war and the killing merely assume a different form: they have been shifted from the sphere of observable social events to the twilight of an unobservable inner destruction. It would seem that the absolute, 'classical' death of stories (which for all the terrors it holds is still mysteriously able to impart meaning to human life) has been replaced here by another kind of death: the slow, secretive, bloodless, never quite absolute yet horrifyingly ever-present death of 'non-action', 'non-story', 'non-life' and 'non-time'; the strange collective deadening - or more precisely anaesthetising - of social and historical nihilisation. This nihilisation annuls death as such, and thus it annuls life as such too: the life of an individual becomes the dull and uniform functioning of a component in a large machine and his death is merely something that puts him out of commission.

All the evidence suggests that this state of things is the intrinsic expression of an advanced and stabilised totalitarian system, and even that it grows directly out of its very essence.

*

Visitors from the West are often shocked to find that Chernobyl and AIDS arouse no horror here, but are rather a subject for jokes.

I must admit this doesn't surprise me. Because it is utterly immaterial, this totalitarian nihilisation is, on the one hand, even more invisible, ever-present and dangerous than the AIDS virus or radioactivity from Chernobyl. On the other hand it touches each of us even more 'physically', more intimately and more urgently than either AIDS or radiation does, since we all know it directly from everyday, personal experience and not just from newspapers and television.

Under the circumstances is it any wonder that the less menacing, the less insidious and less intimate threats are relegated to the background and made jokes of?

Invisibility triumphs here for another reason too: the destruction of the story means the destruction of a basic instrument of human knowledge and self-knowledge. Totalitarian nihilisation denies people the possibility of actually observing and understanding that process 'from outside'. There are only two alternatives: either you experience it directly, or you know nothing about it. This menace permits no reports of itself.

The foreign tourist can therefore form the legitimate impression that Czechoslovakia is a poorer and duller Switzerland, and that press agencies are right to close their bureaux here: after all, how can they be expected to report on the fact that there is nothing to report?

I will attempt to make a few observations on the origin and nature of our asthma.

I will attempt to show that the disappearance of the story from this corner of the world is a story in itself.

*

In the 1950s there were enormous concentration camps in Czechoslovakia filled with tens of thousands of innocent people. At the same time the construction sites were swarming with tens of thousands of young enthusiasts of the new faith singing songs of socialist construction. There were tortures and executions, dramatic flights across borders, conspiracies, while at the same time, panegyrics were being written to the chief dictator. The President of the Republic signed the death warrants of his closest friends but you could still occasionally meet him on the street.

The songs of idealists and fanatics, political criminals on the rampage, the suffering of heroes – these have always been a part of history. The 1950s were a bad time in Czechoslovakia, but there have been many such eras in human history. It still shared something with those other periods, or at least bore comparison with them; it still somehow resembled history. I could not have said that nothing was happening or that the age did not have its stories.

The basic blueprint for political power as it was installed in Czechoslovakia after the Soviet invasion in 1968 was a document called 'Lessons From the Years of Crisis'. There was something symbolic in this: the powers that be really did learn a lesson. They discovered how far things could go when the door to plurality of opinions and interests was opened: the very totalitarian essence of the system was jeopardised. Having learned this lesson, political power began to focus entirely on self-preservation. In a process that had its own, mindless dynamics, all the mechanisms of direct and indirect manipulation of life began to expand and assume unprecedented forms. Henceforth nothing could be left to chance.

The past nineteen years in Czechoslovakia can serve as an almost textbook illustration of how an advanced or late totalitarian system works. Revolutionary ethos and terror have been replaced by dull inertia, pretext-ridden caution, bureaucratic anonymity and mindless, stereotypical behaviour, the sole point of which is to become, ever more fully, exactly what they are.

The songs of the zealots and the cries of the tortured have fallen silent; lawlessness has donned kid gloves and moved from the legendary torture chambers into the upholstered offices of faceless bureaucrats. If the President of the Republic is seen in the streets at all it is behind the bulletproof glass of his limousine as it roars off to the airport under police escort to meet Colonel Khaddafi.

The advanced totalitarian system depends on manipulatory devices so refined, complex and powerful that it no longer requires murderers and victims. Even less does it require fiery utopia builders spreading discontent with their dreams of a better future. The epithet 'Real Socialism', which this era has coined to describe itself, points a finger at those for whom it has no room: the dreamers.

*

Every story begins with an event. This event – understood as the incursion of one 'logic' into the world of another 'logic' – initiates what every story grows out of and draws nourishment from: situations, relationships and conflict. The story has a 'logic' of its own as well, but it is the logic of dialogue, encounter and the interaction of different truths, attitudes, ideas, traditions, passions, human beings, higher powers, social movements and so on – in other words, of a number of autonomous, independent forces which have done nothing in advance to define each other. Every story, therefore, assumes a plurality of truths, of 'logics' and of subjects, of decisions and forms of behaviour. The logic of a story resembles the logic of games, a logic of tension between the known and the unknown, between rules and randomness, between the inevitable and the unforeseeable (for example the unforeseeable outcome of whatever provokes a confrontation with the inevitability of a different order). We never know with any certainty what will emerge from the confrontation, what elements may yet enter into it and how it will end; it is never clear ahead of time which of the potential qualities in one 'player' it will arouse and what action he will be led to perform by an action on the part of his 'antagonist'. For this reason alone mystery is an essential dimension of every story. What speaks to us through a story is not a particular agent of truth; instead, the story manifests the human world to us as an exhilarating arena where many such agents come into contact with each other.

The fundamental pillar of the present totalitarian system is the existence of a single, central agent of all truth and all power (a kind of institutionalised 'rationale of history') which also becomes, quite naturally, the sole agent of all social activity. This activity ceases to be an area in which different more or less autonomous agents square off, and becomes no more than the manifestation and fulfilment of the truth and the will of a single agent. In a world governed by this principle, there is no room for mystery; proprietorship of complete truth means that everything is known ahead of time. And where everything is known ahead of time there is no soil for the story to grow out of.

Obviously the totalitarian system is in its very essence (that is, in the essence of its basic principle) directed against the story.

When the story is destroyed, the feeling of historicity necessarily disappears as well. I remember the early seventies in Czechoslovakia as a time when something like a 'cessation of history' took place: public activity seemed to lose its structure, its impulse, its direction, its tension, its rhythm and its mystery. I can't remember what happened when, or what made one year different from another one, or even what was actually going on, and I don't think it matters very much, for when the unforeseeable disappears, the sensation of meaning itself disappears along with it.

History was replaced by pseudo-history, by a calendar of rhythmically recurring anniversaries, congresses, celebrations and mass gymnastic events; in other words, by precisely the kind of artificial activity that is not an open-ended play of agents confronting one another but a one-dimensional, transparent and utterly predictable self-manifestation (and self-celebration) of a single, central agent of truth and power.

And since human time can only be experienced through story and history, the very experience of time itself began to disappear: time seemed to stand still or go around in circles, disintegrate into fragments of interchangeable moments. The march of events that came out of nowhere and went nowhere lost its story-like character and thus lost any deeper meaning as well. When the horizon of historicity was lost, life became nonsense.

Totalitarian power brought bureaucratic 'order' into the living 'disorder' of history and thus effectively anaesthetised it as history.

In a sense the government had nationalised time. And as a result, time encountered the same sad fate as many other nationalised entities: it began to wither away.

*

As I've already suggested, the revolutionary ethos in Czechoslovakia has long since vanished into thin air. We are no longer governed by fanatics, revolutionaries or ideological zealots. The country is administered by faceless bureaucrats who may profess their adherence to a revolutionary ideology but in reality are only looking out for themselves: they no longer believe in anything. The original ideology has long since become no more than a formalised ritual that gives them a legitimacy in space and in time and provides them with a language for internal communication.

Oddly enough this ideology has only now begun to bear its most important fruit; only now, it would seem, has the full extent of its deepest consequences begun to appear.

How are we to explain this?

Simply: by old age and the deeply conservative (in the sense of preserving) nature of the system. The further away it is from its original revolutionary fervour, the more slavishly it clings to all its constitutive principles, which it sees as the only certainty in an uncertain world. Gradually, through it own dull automatic motion, it slowly, mindlessly and inevitably transforms those principles into a monstrous reality. The ceaseless strengthening, developing and perfecting of totalitarian structures have long since come to serve only the naked self-preservation of power, but this is precisely the best guarantee that what was genetically encoded and hidden away in the original ideology may also flourish undisturbed. The fanatic whose unpredictable zeal for the 'higher cause' might threaten this automatic process has been replaced by the bureaucratic pedant whose reliable lack of ideas makes him an ideal guardian of the vacuous continuity of the late totalitarian system.

I think that the phenomenon of totalitarian nihilisation is one of the late fruits of an ideology that has already gone to seed.

*

The totalitarian system did not fall from the sky as a fully developed, pure 'structure in and of itself'. Nor is it the work of a pervert who has stolen a scalpel designed to remove malignant growths and begun killing healthy people with it.

We need only penetrate the tissue of various dialectic sprouts to discover that the germ of this nihilisation lies dormant in the very heart of the ideology upon which this system is based: in its self-assured belief that it has fully understood the world and revealed the truth about it. And if the main terrain of its self-assurance is history, is it any wonder that its nihilising intention radiates most clearly from how it approaches history?

It began with an interpretation of history from a single aspect of it; then it made that aspect absolute and finally it reduced all of history to it. The exciting multiplicity of history was replaced with an easily understood interaction of 'historical laws', 'social formations' and 'relations of production', so pleasing to the order-loving eye of the scientist. This, however, gradually expelled from history precisely what gives human life, time, and thus history itself a structure: the story. And banished to the kingdom of unmeaning, the story took with it its two essential ingredients: uniqueness and intrinsic ambiguity. Since the mystery in a story is merely the articulated mystery of man, history, having lost the story, began to lose its human content. The uniqueness of the human creature became a mere embellishment on the laws of history, and the tension and thrill inherent in real events were dismissed as accidental and so unworthy of the attention of scholarship. History became boredom.

The negation of the past negates the future as well: when the 'laws of history' were projected into the future, what would be and what had to be suddenly became obvious. The bright glare of this certainly burned away the very essence of the future: its openness. Plans to make an earthly paradise the final end of history, to rid the world of social conflict, of negative human qualities and even, perhaps, of human misery as well, climaxed the work of destruction: the petrification of society as a fiction of everlasting harmony, and of man as the permanent proprietor of happiness – these were the silent consummations of an intellectual execution of history.

Yet by presenting itself as an instrument of the ultimate return of history to itself, ideology unwittingly admits to its own destructiveness. The claim is that through ideology, history finally understood itself, understood where it was going and how it had to proceed: that is, under ideology's guidance. So ideology revealed the historical necessity of what must happen, and at the same time it revealed the historical necessity of itself as that which has come to fulfil that necessity. In other words, history has at last discovered its final meaning. The question is, however, does history which has discovered its own meaning still have any meaning at all? And is it really history any more?

Ideology, claiming to base its authority on history, becomes history's greatest enemy.

The hostility is double-edged: if ideology destroys history by explaining it completely, then history destroys ideology by unfolding in a way other than that prescribed by ideology.

Ideology, of course, can destroy history only ideologically, but the power based on that ideology can suppress history in real ways. In fact it has no choice: if history, by unfolding autonomously, were allowed to demonstrate that ideology is wrong, it would deprive power of its legitimacy.

By negating history, of course, power is not just defending its ideological legitimacy, but its very identity as totalitarian power. And we have seen how incompatible that identity is with a sense of history.

But that identity too, of course, has a firm ideological anchorage of its own: the principle that there is a single central agent of truth and power - the backbone of the totalitarian system - could scarcely have come into existence at all, let alone develop and grow strong, had it not initially drawn power from the self-assurance of ideology which so smugly disdains any viewpoint other than its own, and so proudly declares its own historical mission and all the prerogatives this mission endows it with. After all, totalitarian power has been fed and weaned and nourished and is imbued to this day with the intolerant spirit and mentality of this ideology, which sees plurality only as a necessary evil or a mere formality. In fact it is the very embodiment of this spirit. And its central principle can be justifiably understood as nothing more than the consistent working through of the original ideology and the perfect incarnation of its vanity; as its legitimate product, it draws on ideology's nihilising energy, so that it can successfully put the theories of ideology into practice.

It can be said that what the asthma society is now suffering from is only a natural continuation of the war that intellectual arrogance once declared on the story, on history and thus on life itself.

Boredom has jumped out of the history textbooks and into the real life of the nation.

*

Drawing on the assurance that it is totally right and therefore has a claim to total power, any fledgling totalitarian power first tries to limit and ultimately to eliminate altogether its main competitors: other sources of power. The first to go is political plurality. But along with it, or shortly afterwards, intellectual and economic plurality necessarily disappear as well, since any power that respects these pluralities would not be total.

First of all, then, the story is driven out of public life.

By virtue of its own specific weight - the weight of its own totalitarian essence - this power naturally tends to deepen its totality and extend its range; it recognises no authority over itself, one that might limit it. In other words, once the claims of central power have been placed above law and morality, once the exercise of that power is divested of public control and once the institutional guarantees of political plurality and civil rights have been made a mockery of or simply abolished, there is no longer any reason to respect any other limitations. And so the expansion of central power does not stop at the frontier between the public and the private, but instead, arbitrarily pushes back that border until it is shamelessly intervening even in areas that were once considered exclusively private. (For example, a club of pigeon-fanciers that had once enjoyed a kind of autonomy now suddenly find themselves scrutinised by the central power: the borders of what can come under surveillance shifted from political parties to pigeon-fanciers. And of course it didn't stop there: today that power walks through my bugged bedroom and distinguishes my breathing, which is my own private matter, from what I say, which the state cannot be indifferent to.)

With the banning of opposition parties and the introduction of censorship, the attack on the story and thus on life itself is not over; on the contrary, that is just the beginning.

Because they are more hidden, indirect interventions are in some ways even more dangerous. Everywhere today, public life is no longer as sharply distinguished from private life as it used to be. The countless phenomena of modern civilisation bind these two spheres together by thousands of mutual ties and so they are essentially only two faces, two poles or two dimensions of a single and ultimately indivisible life. Everything that takes place in the public sphere inevitably - though sometimes through complex and hidden routes - penetrates the private sphere, influencing it and in many cases directly shaping it. When public life is negated, this inevitably deforms, distorts and ultimately negates private life as well: every measure taken to establish more complete control over the former has a pernicious impact on the latter.

The attack on plurality and on the story and on public territory is therefore not merely an attack on a single side or area of life; it is an attack on life as a whole.

The web of direct and indirect instruments of manipulation is a straitjacket that binds life and necessarily limits the fundamental ways it can appear to itself and structure itself. And so it languishes, declines, wastes away. It is cheapened and levelled. It becomes pseudo-life.

*

While I was in prison, I realised again and again how much more present - compared with life outside - the story was. Almost every prisoner had a life story that was unique and shocking, or moving. As I listened to those different accounts, I suddenly found myself in something like a 'pre-totalitarian' world, or simply in the world of literature. Whatever else I may have thought of my fellow-prisoners' colourful narratives, there is one thing they were not: they were not documents of totalitarian nihilisation. On the contrary, they testified to the rebelliousness with which human uniqueness resists its own nihilisation, and the stubbornness with which it holds to its own and is willing to ignore this negating pressure. Regardless of whether crime or misfortune were the predominant motifs in any give story, the faces in that world were very specific and personal. When I got back from prison, I wrote somewhere that in a single cell of twenty-four people you can probably encounter more unique stories than in a high-rise development housing several thousand. People truly afflicted with asthma – those colourless, servile, obedient, homogenised, herd-like citizens of the totalitarian state – cannot be found in large numbers in prison. Instead, prison tends to be a gathering place for people who stand out in one way or another, the unclassifiable misfits, highly individual people with all sorts of obsessions, people who are scarcely able to adapt.

There is probably always a greater concentration of people in prison who stand out in some way than there is on the outside. Nevertheless, I'm convinced that what I observed bears a direct relationship to conditions under totalitarianism. The nature of many of the stories directly confirmed this.

On the whole, it's logical: the wider the scope of those instruments by which the system manipulates, de-individualises and circumscribes life, and the more powerful its embrace, the more thoroughly everything truly unique is pushed to the periphery of 'normal' life and ultimately beyond it – into prison. The repressive apparatus that sends people to jail is merely an organic part and, in fact, a culmination of the general pressure totalitarianism exerts against life: without the horizon of this extreme threat many other threats would lose their weight and their credibility. In any case it is certainly no accident that, proportionally, Czechoslovakia has many times more prisoners than the United States. And clearly criminality – I mean real criminality – cannot be that much higher in Czechoslovakia.

What is in fact higher is the demand for uniformity and its inevitable consequence: the criminalisation of difference.

*

If the subjects entering into a story can fully manifest and realise their uniqueness only through the story itself, in other words if uniqueness requires a story to become what it is, then by the same token a story assumes and requires uniqueness. Without unique - mutually distinguishable - subjects to appear in a story and create it, the story could never get off the ground. Uniqueness and the story are therefore like Siamese twins: one is unthinkable without the other, and they cannot be separated.

They also have a common abode: plurality. Plurality of course is a precondition not only of the story but also of uniqueness, since uniqueness is only possible alongside another uniqueness with which it can be compared and contrasted; where there are not many uniquenesses, there is no uniqueness at all.

An attack on plurality is therefore an attack both on the story and on uniqueness. And if the totalitarian system sees plurality as its chief enemy, it must repress uniqueness as well. Indeed, the world of advanced totalitarianism is outstanding for the remarkable decline of uniqueness; it is as though a veil of vague, expressionless indistinguishability clung to everything, colouring it the same shade of grey. Paradoxically this veil clings to its source as well: in banishing all other comparable unique agents from its own world, the central agent divests itself of its own uniqueness as well. Hence the strange facelessness, transparency and elusiveness of power, hence the blandness of its language, the anonymity of its decisions. Hence too its irresponsibility, for how can a subject be genuinely responsible when its identity is so blurred and when, moreover - because it is so alone - it has no one left to be responsible to?

This antipathy to uniqueness is not something the individuals who rule plan deliberately, but an intrinsic expression of the system's totalitarian essence. Its centralism cannot co-exist with uniqueness or individuality: in destroying plurality this system inevitably destroys all forms of autonomy, particularity, unpredictability, independence, multiplicity and variation. If we mix all the colours together we get a dirty grey. The intention of totalitarianism is to make everything totally the same. Its fruit is uniformity, *gleichschaltung* and the creation of a herd mentality.

And so gradually the great multiplicity of personal traditions, habits, lifestyles, attitudes, the uniqueness of localities and their climates, human institutions and communities, products and objects disappear forever.

Standardised life creates standardised citizens with no individual wills of their own. It begets undifferentiated people with undifferentiated stories. It is a mass producer of banality.

Anyone who resists too much, despairs too much or insists too much on having something of his own that exceeds the general norm or who tries to escape the standardised nothingness - either by going abroad or on a 'trip' - in other words anyone who disturbs the prescribed appearance of this standardised world and thus 'sets himself apart' from society, as it were, is inevitably headed to a place where he will no longer be a blotch on the surface of social life: to jail.

Once a place where crimes were punished, prison is now a 'correctional institute': a refuse bin for human peculiarities and their bizarre stories.

*

Whenever I found myself in a new cell I was always asked where I was from, and when I said I was from Prague, the question always came back: 'Whereabouts in Prague?'

It would never have occurred to me to say I was from Dejvice, so at first the question surprised me. But very quickly I understood it: in this old-fashioned world of individual stories a thing as old-fashioned as the uniqueness of a city quarter still plays a role. Obviously there are still people for whom Dejvice, Holesovice or Liben are not just addresses but a real home. People who have not capitulated to the standardising and nihilising pressure of the modern housing estate (where you can no longer tell what city you're in) and who still cling to the uniqueness of their streets, the pubs on their corners, the former grocery store across the road - and to the mysterious and secret meaning of the stories connected to these localities.

It seems sadly symbolic to me that I have heard the most natural of questions - 'Where is your home?' - asked most often in prison.

*

The history of the system I live in has demonstrated persuasively that without a plurality of economic initiatives and those who participate in them, without competition, without a market place and its institutional guarantees, an economy will stagnate and decline.

Why then does this system so stubbornly resist all attempts to restore these proven instruments of economic life? Why is it that all such efforts have so far either been hopelessly half-baked or else repressed altogether?

The deepest reason for this is not the leaders' fear that it will conflict with the ideology, nor their personal conservatism, nor even the fear that limiting the economic power of the centre inevitably leads to a limiting of its political power.

The real reason, in my opinion, lies - again - in the totalitarian essence of the system itself, or rather in its overwhelming inertia. The system must control everything or it is not total. It cannot release from its sphere of control such an enormous and vital part of life as the economy without losing its identity. Were it to recognise institutional guarantees of economic plurality and undertake to respect them, it would be acknowledging the legitimacy of something else, something other than its own total claim to power, something that placed legal limits on that power. This would be tantamount to denying its own totalitarian nature and it would thus cease to be itself. So far, overwhelming inertia has always prevented the totalitarian system from carrying out this kind of ontological self-destruction. (I have no reason not to believe that sometime in the future a stronger power might arise to oppose this inertia and compel the system genuinely to relinquish its totalitarian essence. I'm only saying that this has never yet happened, anywhere.)

I mention this now because although the standardising and therefore nihilising impact of political and intellectual centralisation is immediately clear, the analogous impact of economic centralisation – as one of the indirect methods of manipulating life in general – is far from being so obvious. But that is precisely what makes it more dangerous.

*

Where there is no natural plurality of economic initiatives, the interplay of competing producers and their competing, entrepreneurial ideas disappears, and along with it the interplay of supply and demand, the labour and commodity markets, voluntary labour relations disappear too. Gone as well are the stimuli to creativity and its attendant risks, the drama of economic success and failure. Man as a producer imperceptibly ceases to be a participant or a creator in the economic story and becomes a mere instrument whose stereotypical functioning can no longer give time a genuinely human structure. Everyone is an employee of the state, which is the one central proprietor of economic truth and power, and as such, everyone is buried in the anonymity of the collective economic 'non-story'.

With the loss of his uniqueness as a relatively autonomous participant in economic life, man loses some of his social and human uniqueness and thus, as well, part of his hope of ever creating his own human story.

When economic plurality disappears, the motives for competition in the marketplace of consumer goods naturally disappear along with it. The central power may of course talk about 'satisfying differentiated needs' but the economic pressures of a non-pluralistic economy compel it to do exactly the opposite: to integrate production and standardise the choice of goods. In this artificial economic world, diversity is merely an economic complication.

As a consumer then, a person has no choice, and once again therefore he is manipulated in far-reaching ways: not only does he have to depend (like all who live in modern industrial societies) almost exclusively on commodities he himself did not produce, he does not even have a choice of different commodities and thus cannot even realise his own uniqueness at least in this limited way. All he has is what he has been allocated by the monopoly producer: the same things that have been allocated to everyone else.

A centralised designer of furniture may not be the most typical representative of the totalitarian system, but as one who unconsciously realises its nihilising intentions he may have more impact than five government ministers put together: millions of people have to spend their entire lives surrounded by the furniture he has invented.

Let me exaggerate deliberately: it would be to the greatest advantage of a centrally-directed system of production if only a single type prefabricated panel were produced from which a single type of apartment building would be constructed; these buildings in turn would be fitted with a single kind of door, window, toilet, door handle, washbasin and so on, and together this would create a single type of housing development constructed according to a single, standardised urban development plan, with minor adjustments for several different categories of landscape, given the regrettable irregularity of the earth's surface. (In each apartment, of course, there would be the same kind of television set showing the same programme.)

Imperceptibly but irresistibly, not deliberately but inevitably, given the form of economics engendered by the totalitarian system, everything begins to resemble everything else: the buildings, the clothing, the workplaces, the public decorations, public transport, the forms of entertainment, the behaviour of people in public and in their own houses.

This general standardisation of public and private spaces is a faithful reflection of the deep intentions of the totalitarian system and it necessarily has a standardising effect on the way of life and its rhythms, narrowing the range of alternatives and the sphere of desires and aversions, of sensual experience and taste. It flattens the world in which people live.

In such an environment, uniqueness languishes and stories become interchangeable.

Is it any wonder that an ambitious reporter would rather risk his life in Lebanon?

*

If a citizen of our country wishes to travel abroad, get a new job, exchange his apartment or his stove, or organise an amateur event, he is usually compelled to undertake a long and exhausting march through various offices for the necessary permits, certificates, recommendations, and he must frequently demean himself or at least bite his tongue when confronted with the swollen and indifferent monster of bureaucracy. It is tiring, boring and debilitating. Many people, out of disgust or a mental inability to submit themselves to all this, or for fear that it will simply drag them down, quickly give up on many of their most personal ideas, desires and plans.

In doing so of course they also renounce something of their own potential story. It may be something of secondary importance. But the process of surrendering something of oneself always begins with small matters.

Another indirect instrument of nihilisation is the bureaucratic regulation of the everyday details of people's lives. It is that special sector in which public matters infiltrate into everyone's private life in a way which is very 'ordinary', but at the same time extremely persistent. The sheer number of small pressures that we are subjected to every day in this sector together create a kind of horizon that is more important than it may seem at first: it encloses the space in which we are condemned to breathe.

There is very little air in that space. Not so little, however, that we might suffocate entirely and thus create a story.

*

These examples, of course, do not exhaust the range of ways in which the totalitarian system directly and indirectly, negates life.

The elimination of political plurality deprives society of a basic means of structuring itself because it does not allow a variety of interests and opinions and traditions to proclaim their presence and make a contribution. The elimination or drastic curtailment of intellectual plurality makes it hard for a person to choose a way to relate to Being, to the world and to himself. Culture and information controlled from the centre narrow the horizon against which man matures into his own uniqueness. The demand for general and unquestioning loyalty forces people to become bit players in countless empty rituals and leads them to despair of any kind of public self-realisation. Man ceases to be an autonomous and self-confident participant in the life of the community and becomes a mere instrument by which the central agent realises itself. The ever-present danger of punishment for any kind of original expression compels one constantly to make certain one is moving cautiously enough across the quicksand of one's own potential, and this is a process that pointlessly wastes one's strength. An extensive network of bureaucratic limitations affects everything from one's choice of profession or study, the possibility of travel, the limits of admissible creative initiative, right down to the extent and kind of personal ownership, and all of this shrinks to an uncommon degree the space one has to act in. The total claim of the central power - respecting only those limits it imposes upon itself for practical reasons in any given moment - creates a state of general uncertainty: no-one is ever sure of the ground he stands on, or what he may venture to do, and what he may not, or what may happen to him if he does. The sway this power exercises over the executive power of the legislature and the judiciary, coupled with the actual omnipotence of the police, makes people feel uncertain and insecure. The imperious vanity of the administrative apparatus, its anonymity, and the extinction of individual responsibility in the faceless pseudo-responsibility of the system (anyone may offer excuses for anything or be accused of anything, since the will of the centralised power recognises no arbitrator in any dispute with an individual) creates a sensation of helplessness and cripples the will to live one's own life.

All of that together - and much more that is even more subtle - lies behind our asthma.

On the surface of things, everything goes on just as it does anywhere else: people work, have fun, make love, live and die. Beneath this surface, however, a destructive disease is gnawing away.

'Call me when the man dies.'

In this case the patient will not die. Nevertheless to keep his disease a secret amounts to encouraging it, and encouraging its spread.

*

In recent years, several very good film comedies have been made in Czechoslovakia that were successful at home and abroad. One or two of them were even nominated for Oscars.

However much I may enjoy these films, I can't shake the depressing feeling that there's something not right about them. American audiences, who do not have to suffer daily the kind of asthma that prevails here, naturally see nothing wrong with them.

What do these films have in common?

One important thing, I think: the stories they tell lack historical background. No matter how many superficial and essentially ornamental techniques these films employ to suggest a particular locality and a particular moment in time, essentially they seem to exist outside space and time. The stories they tell could have taken place anywhere and any time.

There are two immediate ways in which totalitarian pressure surgically removes their historicity: directly, in other words through censorship and self-censorship, both of which have an extraordinarily evolved sensitivity to anything that might capture, in any essential way, the historical dimension of life; and indirectly, by the destruction of historicity in life itself. It is, of course, extraordinarily difficult to grasp the historic quality of a moment when a global attack on the very notion of history is taking place, because it means trying to tell the story of the loss of story, the story of asthma.

This double pressure automatically forces a creative person to turn his attention to private life. And yet – as I've already said – private and public life today (particularly under totalitarianism) are inseparable; they are like two linked vessels, and one cannot very well capture one truthfully while ignoring the other. Private life without a historical horizon is pure fiction, a façade and ultimately a lie.

Indeed, the picture of life that has been artificially reduced to its purely private dimension (or provided with no more than superficial reminders of the public dimension, while carefully avoiding everything essential in that dimension) inevitably becomes an eccentric anecdote, a genre picture, a story told over the back fence, a fairy-tale or a fiction concocted from thousands of undeniably living individualities. In such a presentation, even the most private life is somehow strangely twisted, sometimes to the point where it becomes implausibly bizarre, a paradoxical outcome of some intense and paralysing desire for living verisimilitude. It is obvious what has made this desire so intense: the subconscious need to compensate for the absence of the opposite pole – truth. It is as though life in this case were stripped of its genuine inner tension, its true tragedy and greatness, its genuine questions. The more charmingly all of its superficial features are caricatured, the more seriously the work somehow misses the point of its innermost themes. Imitating life, it in fact falsifies it. Calligraphy replaces drawing.

In the films I'm talking about, what I miss of course is not this or that concrete bit of political detail. There are always some details from political reality present, sometimes even more than is good for the work. I miss something else: a free vision of life as a whole. This is not a matter of theme: I can well imagine a film about nothing more than love and jealousy, yet where this profound freedom would not be so lacking.

During the Nazi occupation several popular film comedies were made in Czechoslovakia. They were outstanding for a similar historicity and the untruths that flowed from that. Here again it wasn't the theme that was at fault: it wasn't images from concentration camps that I found lacking. I missed an inner freedom, and felt that their humour was only a slick way of making a virtue of necessity.

It's interesting how you can always tell in the end.

The domestic success of today's Czech film comedies has a problematic side to it. People find in them a rather strange kind of consolation: it confirms their illusions that the asthma does not in fact exist, and to the extent that it does exist, you can live with it; that it's not really so important; that their lives have not been ravaged to the extent they sometimes seem, in weaker (or more precisely: stronger) moments. It's a pacifying excuse.

These films tell unique stories. What they do not show, however, is the nihilising pressure against which these stories have been brought to life. People are thrilled to find that stories still exist. They are elated with them and end up kidding themselves: they forget that the story is only on the screen. That it is not their story.

I don't know if there is anywhere to hide from the AIDS virus.

It seems to me, however, that there is no hiding place, no reservation, where one is safe from the virus of nihilisation.

*

There is a sphere in which the symptoms of our asthma can, on the contrary, be observed better by a foreigner than by someone suffering from it. This sphere is the visible or public face of the daily life of society. We have long since grown accustomed to this face. But more than one observant visitor has been shocked by it.

All you have to do, for example, is ride the subway escalators and observe the faces of people going in the opposite direction. This journey is a brief pause in the daily rat race, a sudden stoppage of life, a frozen moment which may reveal more about us than we know. Perhaps it is one of those legendary 'moments of truth'. In this situation, a person suddenly stands outside all relationships; he is in public, but alone with himself. The faces moving past are all strangely empty, strained, almost lifeless, without hope, without longing, without desire. The eyes are expressionless, dull.

It is enough to observe how people behave towards each other in stores, in offices, and on the streetcars and subways: they tend to be surly, selfish, impolite, and disobliging; for the counter staff, customers often seem like an imposition, and they serve them while talking among themselves about their own private matters. When asked a question they reply with evident distaste (that is if they know an answer at all). Drivers yell at each other, people in queues elbow in ahead of others and snap at each other. Officials don't care how many people are waiting to see them, or how long they've waited. They make appointments and often are not there to keep them. They get no pleasure from helping people and have no regrets when they can't. They are capable of slamming the door in a supplicant's face, cutting him off in mid-sentence. It would not be so depressing were it not that these officials are often the final court of appeal in a given matter.

It's enough to look at people in the streets: most of them are in a rush, their faces are full of worry, they pay no attention to things around them. A sense of ease, cheerfulness and spontaneity has vanished from the streets. In the evening or at night the streets seem empty and hopeless, and if you do happen to see a group of relaxed, happy people, they are usually foreigners.

Warmth, openness, kindness and unassuming friendliness are gradually vanishing from everyday public contacts. Everyone seems to have a single thing on his mind: where to find what he happens to be looking for. Indifference and bad manners are spreading, even in restaurants people seem somehow buttoned up. Mindful of their own behaviour, they speak to each other in low voices, checking to make sure no one else is listening. Class four restaurants have become the last remaining oasis of natural companionship, and they tend to be in the suburbs rather than in the centre; these are the places one remembers in prison. But even in such places, more and more people come there just to drink intensively.

At the bottom of all such phenomena lies a vague stress: people are either nervous, irritated, somewhat anxious, or else they are apathetic. They give the impression that they expect to be hit at any moment from an unexpected quarter. Calmness and healthy certainty have been replaced by aggressivity.

It is the stress of people living under a constant threat. It is the stress of unfree, humiliated, and discouraged people who no longer believe in anything. It is the stress of people compelled, each day, to deal with absurdity and nothingness.

It is a stress of people living in a city under siege.

The stress of society which is not permitted to live in history. The stress of people exposed to the negating radiation of totalitarianism.

*

Life, of course, goes on. It resists manipulation in many ways, adapting to it or finding ways to live with it. In real terms, it has not been destroyed, nor is it ever likely to be. Cracks can always be found for it to penetrate, levels where it can go on developing, ways in which, even in this suffocating milieu, it can express itself and structure itself into stories. Somehow we will always manage to write our stories by the way we act.

I am not describing here anything like the end of humanity. I am merely trying to draw attention to the inconspicuous, unspectacular and undramatic war that life wages every day against nothingness.

I am merely attempting to say that the struggle of the story and of history to resist their own nihilisation is in itself a story and as such belongs to history.

It is our special metastory.

We do not yet know how to talk about it because the traditional forms of storytelling fail us here. We do not yet know the laws that govern our metastory. We do not even know yet exactly who or what is the main villain of the story (it is definitely not a few individuals in the power centre: in a sense they too are victims of something that transcends them, just as the rest of us are).

One thing, however, is clear: we must tell the story of our asthma not despite the fact that people are not dying from it, but for precisely that reason.

Only one small detail remains: we have to learn how to do it.

USSR: Why the Empire's Subjects are Restless

Bohdan Nahaylo

The Gorbachev leadership's inauguration of the policies of glasnost, democratisation and economic 'restructuring' (*perestroika*) has exposed quite a few hitherto suppressed truths about the Soviet system and simultaneously released numerous pent-up forces. In no other area have the results been so dramatic as in the sphere of national relations.

The riots in Kazakhstan at the end of 1986, the Armenian-Azerbaizhani conflict over Nagorno-Karabakh, the push by the Baltic republics for the restoration of their sovereignty, as well as numerous demonstrations by Crimean Tatars and the sinister activities of the russian ultra-nationalist *Pamyat* group, are but the most publicised of the recent manifestations of trouble with what the Soviet authorities euphemistically refer to as their 'nationalities question'.

Since censorship was eased, the Soviet press, too, has published a wealth of candid material on this traditionally sensitive subject. What emerges is that after years of rosy official assessments the national problem in the USSR is in fact complex, acute and potentially explosive.

So what is going on and what is at stake? Is it a case of 'nationalists' and 'extremists' taking advantage of Gorbachev's more liberal policies and causing all the trouble? Or is the issue a far more basic and serious one?

In the West, where the terms 'Russia' and 'Soviet Union' are frequently but erroneously used as synonyms, it is all too often forgotten that the USSR is the world's largest multinational state and the last of the great empires. The Russians themselves account for barely 50% of the USSR's 285 million inhabitants, but they remain very much the dominant nation.

The present troubles reflect the divergence between theory and

Vol. 18, no. 5, 1989

practice in Moscow's nationalities policy. Force alone, as Lenin realised, was not enough to weld together the fragmented tsarist Russian empire, or 'prison of nations', as he called it. So, after military conquest, the non-Russians were wooed with concessions designed to win their trust and loyalty.

The implicit 'national contract' promised the non-Russians sovereign statehood, equality, and full cultural rights within a Soviet federal structure. Moreover, the imperial Russian legacy was to be disowned and Russification prohibited. In practice, however, apart from a short period in the 1920s, only lip-service was paid to this tacit arrangement, referred to in shorthand by the non-Russians as the 'Leninist principles' of Soviet nationalities policy.

Until recently, discussion of the nationalities question was in effect prohibited, non-Russian activist imprisoned, and a policy of Russification was pursued, entailing the imposition of the Russian language at the expense of the native languages together with the extolling of all things Russian. Thus not only was all significant decision-making concentrated in Moscow, but the languages, cultures and histories of the non-Russian nations were subjected to strong assimilatory pressure camouflaged behind internationalist rhetoric.

The result was that while the existence of a nationalities problem was officially denied, resentment and disaffection among the USSR's non-Russian people mounted. Indeed, by the 1980s there were not only signs of unrest in some of the republics, but the national problem had come to affect the Kremlin's ability to deal with key problems in the economic, socio-political and military spheres.

Glasnost releases genie

Just as they did in the second half of the 1950s, when controls were relaxed following Khrushchev's partial denunciation of Stalin, the non-Russians under Gorbachev and glasnost have started airing grievances and calling on the Kremlin to honour the terms of the original national contract on which the Soviet Union is supposedly founded.

Yet when Gorbachev came to power in March 1985, his initial attitude seems to have been to avoid tinkering with the thorny national question unless economic exigencies demanded it. Inadvertently, however, he soon released the genie of non-Russian nationalisms from its container.

After embarking on his economic restructuring drive, the new Soviet leader realised that in order to mobilise the heterogeneous Soviet population behind him, he needed the support of the USSR's intelligentsia, particularly the opinion-makers – writers, artists and media workers. To win them over he began reducing censorship and loosening controls in cultural life. But glasnost gradually began to acquire a dynamic of its own and to spread from Moscow and Leningrad to the non-Russian republics.

From the outset, it was clear that the non-Russian intellectuals had different concerns and priorities from those of their Russian counterparts. At the first major forum at which the non-Russians spoke out – the Eighth Congress of Soviet Writers held in Moscow in June 1986 – they expressed anxiety about the displacement of their native languages by Russian and complained about Moscow's control over the national cultural life of their nationals generally. Some of them even used terms like 'great-power chauvinism' and 'denationalisation'. By contrast, the more outspoken of the Russian representatives pressed for the easing of censorship and for the publication of the proscribed works of Pasternak and Akhmatova.

At first the language question became the main battleground. The non-Russian spokesmen, many of them writers and poets, did not challenge the cogent and practical need to have a *lingua franca* in a multi-national state that covers a sixth of the world's land mass and in which about 100 different nationalities live. What they objected to was the insensitive way in which the Russian language has been not so much promoted as forced upon them, while the non-Russian languages were treated as secondary, provincial, and in the long term unnecessary. Party and official business, higher education, science and technology – all these spheres were made largely the preserve of the Russian language.

In December 1986, for example, 28 Byelorussian intellectuals appealed to Gorbachev to save their close to 10-million-strong nation from 'spiritual extinction'. Russification of their republic had gone so far that there was only one urban school left that provided some instruction in their mother tongue. Their neighbours, the Ukrainians, revealed that although they made up 73–76% of the republic's population of 50 million, the percentage of Ukrainian schools in the major cities had been reduced to 16, and approximately 50% of the children in the republic were being taught in Russian schools and kindergartens.

Kazakhstan is also a telling example. After the Alma-Ata riots in December 1986, *Pravda* accused Kazakh patriots of 'national egoism' because they wanted more Kazakh schools and kindergartens opened. Later, however, it was revealed in the Kazakh press that in 1987 only about 6% of the republic's one million or so children in pre-school facilities were being taught in their native language.

Together with the Balts, the Ukrainians and Byelorussians began demanding constitutional safeguards to bolster and protect the status of their national languages. This soon grew into a call for the native language to be made the state language of the given republic, as was already the case in Georgia, Armenia and Azerbaizhan. At first the response from both Moscow and the local Party authorities was negative. But the pressure grew, and by the beginning of 1989 the popular forces for national renewal in the Baltic republics had achieved success and paved the way for others. There are signs that in Ukraine and Moldavia, and perhaps in some of the other republics, the authorities will be forced to give way.

Linked to this is the problem of the many millions of non-Russians who live outside their republics in other parts of the USSR and who until now have been deprived of basic cultural facilities in their own language. For example, six million Ukrainians who have settled in the Soviet Far East, Kazakhstan, Russia and Moldavia have not had a single Ukrainian school, newspaper or radio programme since the Stalin era. Condemned to denationalisation themselves, they are potential agents of Russification.

On the other hand, the close to 25 million Russians who live outside the Russian Federation do not have these difficulties. Indeed, the problem from the non-Russians' viewpoint is that the overwhelming majority of these Russians have not bothered to learn the local language and often behave as if the national republics were simply extensions of their Russian homeland. Not surprisingly, the non-Russians, especially the small Baltic nations and Moldavians, have sought to limit the inflow of Russians into their republics and see this issue as a matter of national survival.

Recovering the histories

A major concern of the non-Russians has been to retrieve their national histories and to secure the rehabilitation of prominent cultural and political figures that were either killed, imprisoned or placed off limits during the previous decades of Soviet rule. Some idea of the seriousness of the injustice done to the non-Russians in the historiographical sphere was recently acknowledged by the Chairman of the USSR State Committee for Public Education, G.A. Yagodin. Speaking in December 1988 at the all-Union congress of Soviet educational workers, he admitted that 'the textbooks on the history of the USSR to a considerable extent still remain the history of the Russian people and the Russian state system'.

Quite early on it was announced that the works of the monarchist

Russian historians, Karamazin, Solovyev and Klyuchevsky - whom non-Russians regard as pillars of Russian *imperial* historiography - as well as of the anti-Soviet Russian authors Gumilev and Nabokov were to be published. Pointing to these concessions to the Russians, the non-Russians stepped up their efforts for the rehabilitation of their own banned historians and writers. Simultaneously, they began pressing for the removal of 'blank spots' in their history.

During the last 18 months or so, the non-Russians have made quite a bit of headway in setting the historical record straight. The Ukrainians and Kazakhs, for instance, have finally secured official recognition of the fact that, as part of his ruthless collectivisation drive, Stalin killed millions of their countrymen in the early 1930s through terror and famine. For their part, the Balts have forced the authorities to agree to the publication of the text of the Molotov-Ribbentrop Pact and to discuss the Nazi-Socialist collusion that sealed the fate of Estonia, Latvia and Lithuania.

Religion is another important aspect of the nationalities question. The more liberal approach of the Gorbachev leadership in this sphere had benefited some, but by no means all, of the USSR's religious groups. The main beneficiaries have been the Russian Orthodox Church, and to a lesser extent the Lithuanian Catholic Church and official Islam. However, like the Ukrainian Autocephalous Orthodox Church, the Ukrainian Catholic Church is still banned and appeals for its legalisation continue to fall on deaf ears. The pressure against unofficial Islam has also been kept up although calls for a change in the official attitude towards this religion have recently begun appearing in the Soviet press.

Whose millennium?

Last year, the limitations of the Kremlin's modified approach to religion were demonstrated in the way that the millennium of the Christianisation of the ancient state of Kievan Rus' was celebrated. Although the Russians, Ukrainians and Byelorussians are all said to trace their historical and cultural heritage from this medieval polity, the jubilee was depicted as a solely Russian affair and there was no recognition of any specifically Ukrainian or Byelorussian aspects. In fact, even Gorbachev and the then Soviet president, Andrei Gromyko, hailed the anniversary as a celebration of 1,000 years of 'Russian' culture and statehood. This approach elicited quite a few angry letters and protests from Ukrainians. In February 1989, a Ukrainian priest, Father Bohdan Mykhailechko, broke ranks, denounced the policies of the Russian Orthodox Church towards his nation, and after being removed from his parish, formed an Initiative Group for the Restoration of the Ukrainian Autocephalous Orthodox Church.

A number of Central Asian authors have also pointed out that while the state was sponsoring the lavish celebration of the millennium of 'Russian Orthodoxy' many mosques remained closed or ruined and attacks in the press against Islam were not abating. In February, the growing Muslim assertiveness was manifested in a demonstration in Tashkent against the head of official Islam in Soviet Central Asia, Chief Mufti Babkhanov, which resulted in his replacement.

The other major issue of great concern to the non-Russians is the protection of the environment. It overlaps with the nationalities question because it is Moscow that decides on where, say, nuclear reactors or chemical plants are to be located. The Chernobyl disaster, the catastrophic consequences of the desiccation of the Aral Sea, and the alarming level of pollution of one form of another, have not only sensitised people to ecological questions but also brought home the powerlessness of the republics before the 'diktat' of the central ministries. Some non-Russian spokesmen have openly compared the ministries in Moscow to trans-national corporations. Environmental and 'green' movements have sprung up throughout the Soviet Union. Central Asians, for instance, have begun protesting about the grave consequences of the cotton monoculture imposed on their republics, while Ukrainians have put up strong public opposition to the further expansion of nuclear energy in Ukraine.

Piecemeal solutions

Despite the growing pressure from the non-Russians on a broad range of issues, up until last summer Moscow refused to acknowledge the need to review and alter its nationalities policy. Instead, it sought to defuse the problem by making modest piecemeal concessions in some of the republics, such as setting up republican commissions on ethnic affairs, easing the pressure on some of the non-Russian languages, and by calling for more tact. By the summer of 1987, it became clear that this would not suffice and that matters were coming to a head.

The cultural elites in most of the republics had by now demonstrated that they were determined to take glasnost and 'democratisation' at face value and that they saw the injection of 'new thinking' into Soviet nationalities policy as a prerequisite for the success of these processes. Highly respected non-Russian cultural figures such as the Kirgiz author Chingiz Aitmatov, the Byelorussian writer Vasil Bykov, and the Armenian poet Silva Kaputikyan, were speaking out on behalf of the non-Russians in the central press.

Moreover, the unrest in the Baltic republics, and particularly the Armenian–Azerbaizhani conflict over the disputed enclave of Nagorno-Karabakh, had exposed the dangers for the Kremlin of simply muddling through.

The Nagorno-Karabakh issue had, after all, been festering away for decades. As far back as 1966, Silva Kaputikyan had warned that Moscow was displaying 'an indifference unbecoming to the country's leaders, towards some of the problems that deeply trouble our people'. She had also warned that 'history is replete with examples of multinational states disintegrating after failing to manage their nationality problems'. Appropriately enough, the celebrated Armenian poet was one of the two Armenian delegates who met with Gorbachev in February at the height of the unrest over Nagorno-Karabakh and who, two months later, after her hopes had been dashed, addressed a poignant samizdat letter to the Russian intelligentsia expressing her nation's deep disappointment with the way that Moscow was handling the crisis.

What really pushed matters forward, though, was the radical programme adopted by the Estonian cultural unions in April 1987 and the appearance of mass-based patriotic movements in the Baltic republics - the popular fronts in support of restructuring. The Estonians, followed by the Latvians and later the Lithuanians, shifted the focus away from purely cultural and environmental concerns to political and economic issues, and especially to the question of restoring the sovereignty of the non-Russian republics.

At last summer's 19th Party Conference, other non-Russian representatives followed the Balts' lead. A number of republican Party leaders openly called for the return to a more genuine form of federation and the restoration of the national contract. So forceful was the stand taken by the non-Russians at this important gathering that some of their demands were incorporated into the conference's resolutions. Thus a breakthrough was achieved: the Party leadership was forced to broaden the rights of the non-Russian republics.

Or so it seemed. Despite this victory for the non-Russians over a crucial principle, the tug-of-war contest between Moscow and the republics has, if anything, intensified. In October 1988, the Gorbachev leadership attempted to backtrack from the positions adopted by the 19th Party Conference by introducing amendments to the Soviet Constitution which, rather than enhancing the rights of the republics, would in fact have limited them further.

A major constitutional crisis ensued, with the Estonians leading the opposition to these regressive changes and defiantly affirming their republic's 'sovereignty'. In November, an uneasy compromise was arrived at but the entire experience has soured the atmosphere.

Gorbachev has announced that the Party will hold a special plenum of the Party Central Committee this summer to chart the future course of Soviet nationalities policy. In the meantime, the problems and forces described above continue to grow in scale and strength. Trouble of one form or another is brewing from Moldavia in the south-west of the USSR to Tadzhikistan in the eastern part of Soviet Central Asia. The seriousness of the situation and the realisation that the success or failure of perestroika may well depend on how the nationalities problem is handled seems to have produced a change at least in the Kremlin's tone.

On 6 January 1989, Gorbachev met with representatives of the Soviet cultural and scientific elites. In his address he seemed to go out of his way to reassure the non-Russians that he now recognises the need for a more accommodating attitude towards them. Declaring himself an opponent of the concept of 'merging' nations, he stated that the Party 'cannot permit even the smallest nation to disappear' or 'the language of even the smallest people to be lost'. Four days later, the Party Central Committee issued an appeal addressed to the Party and the Soviet people in which it pledged that the forthcoming plenum on the nationalities question will see 'a considerable expansion of the rights of the republics' and the strengthening of their sovereignty. Gorbachev has also promised a new language law designed to offer some protection to the non-Russian languages.

Nevertheless, much of what Gorbachev and the Party leadership have been saying about nationalities policy remains vague or ambiguous. The Central Committee's appeal, for example, put forward the slogan of 'a strong centre and strong republics' as the underlying principle for reform in the nationality sphere, though this would seem to be a contradiction in terms.

Meanwhile, the debate about the future direction of nationalities policy has been intensifying. A number of Russians have now publicly acknowledged that the still essentially imperial relationship between the Russians and the non-Russians has to be reviewed and the latter offered a new deal.

This 'psychological restructuring', however, does not seem to have reached the Kremlin. The draft programme for republican economic autonomy that was unveiled in March foresaw the republics receiving only limited control over their budgets and Moscow maintaining control over most heavy industry. Just as telling was the fact, announced on 8 April by Radio Moscow, that a special working commission of the USSR Supreme Soviet had rejected calls by the non-Russians for a new union treaty that would provide a new basis for relations between the republics and Moscow.

During the spring, two further developments highlighted the fact that while Moscow was continuing to procrastinate and to offer half-measures, the national problem was becoming even more complex and volatile. The election results in March confirmed yet again the strength of the national movements in the Baltic and the growing frustration and radicalisation in Ukraine, Moldavia and other republics. The following month, another major crisis erupted in the nationality sphere, this time in Georgia. On 9 April troops were sent in against protestors in Tbilisi and at least 19 people were killed.

The crucial question is whether Gorbachev and his team will see the present spring of Soviet-ruled, though far from wholly Sovietised, nations for what it is and face up to the new realities. The non-Russians have been galvanised and in some cases are going for broke. Either the national contract is restored in some form, or the strains in the restless Soviet empire may eventually become unmanageable. The preservation of empire and 'democratisation' are incompatible, and Moscow will not be able to have it both ways.

A Trip to Moscow

Andrei Sinyavsky

Translated from the Russian by Julian Graffy

If it had not been for the death of my friend Yuli Daniel I would not have gone to Moscow. And I would not have been let into Moscow. For a year and a half Moscow had been refusing to grant my wife Maria a visa. We had been informed by telephone of the last refusal (there had been several of them) from the Soviet consulate in Paris on the morning of 30 December. In the evening of 30 December Daniel died, and after two days of negotiations they were obliged to give us a visa. If they had not given us one, there would have been a threat of a scandal breaking out. After all for many years, from the time of our arrest, my name had always been linked with that of Daniel (Sinyavsky and Daniel, Daniel and Sinyavsky). We were not in time for the funeral. We flew in on the following day, and for the five days which we were allotted by Moscow we lived with Daniel's widow, Irina Uvarova.

Daniel's death probably coloured my impressions. Moscow seemed to me to be incredibly gloomy. I had not been there for 15 years. To these should be added my six years in camp, a period during which I also became relatively unaccustomed to the glorious city in which I had lived my entire life.

What strikes you is the darkness. At the beginning, when we were still in the airport, we even imagined that there had been an electricity breakdown and that the feeble light must be coming from a weak portable motor. This sense of neglect and abandonment is aggravated by the dirty blackened piles of snow along the sides of the dark streets. It wasn't like that before. Where are the streetlamps? What's happened to the majestic yard-keepers who once used to keep Moscow clean? At least it is a good thing that the papers are writing about it. It was not like that before either. 'Glasnost' saves you psychologically from destitution. But it is still a long way from physical signs of *perestroika*. The leftist young fellow who was driving us made a melancholy remark about the lousy state of the roads we were bounding along, cursing as we went: 'this is the way many great empires ended!', he said. I was amazed at the boldness and the aesthetic refinement of his words. In my time people didn't speak so freely . . .

As is always the case, certain amusing details imprinted themselves upon my memory. Buying a branch of laurel at the market outside the cemetery to put on Daniel's grave, Maria told the simple, resourceful old woman: 'We've got the same thing growing in our garden'. 'Where do you live?', the woman asked. 'In Paris.' 'I live in Sochi.' That was the whole conversation. But what is strange is that Paris aroused no surprise in the old woman and seemed just as ordinary as Sochi. Or maybe in her view Sochi is a place of greater distinction and beauty than Paris?

At the same market someone tried to photograph our group. The watchwoman intervened: 'You're not allowed to photograph the market! The director doesn't allow it!' Why? Could it not be because the market was catastrophically empty?

At the entrance to the Vagankovo cemetery, where Daniel is buried, there is a memorial on the grave of Vladimir Vysotsky. The upturned guitar behind his back looks like the halo of a saint. The folds of his clothes are like ropes tying up the singer's body. Multitudinous excursions make pilgrimages to the grave. Vysotsky is now fashionable. Several buses full of children drew up. It was the school holidays and the children were being entertained. Then suddenly there was a flash of bridal veil, and a newly-married couple led a procession up to him. Once the wedding ritual prescribed a far more heroic visit, to the tomb of the Unknown Soldier.

The cemetery church was packed and someone either pushed into someone or trod on someone's foot, which provoked the angry response 'What were you doing in 1937?'

In the street I found myself turning round from time to time when I heard my native language being spoken. I thought it was a close acquaintance. It is such a shock to hear Russian in the street!

If the town's air of neglect instilled a feeling of pity and bitterness, the calm dignity and mature reflections of its inhabitants were a source of joy. It seemed as if the electric light which was so feeble in the streets had migrated into hearts and souls and been lit by the illumination of faces. In the time we were allowed to spend in Moscow we met a mass of people we hadn't known before, not to mention our old friends. It was a stream of people, mainly those flowing through Daniel's flat from morning until late at night. As a result of all these encounters I can draw some conclusion about the striking changes that have affected the minds and mood of the people of Moscow. The main thing is that the sense of fear which for so many years was a feature of Soviet life has disappeared. And that is in spite of the obvious, though not always visible, presence of the KGB, which accompanied us. Sometimes it struck us as unseemly being tailed and shadowed over a newly dug grave. Or should the death of an old camp inmate and disgraced writer be arranged in accordance with his life?

As a symbol of the KGB's power one might point to the two enormous new temples constructed next to its ministerial cathedral on the Lubianka. Sometimes it seems that thanks to *glasnost* the KGB's apparatus is growing out of all proportion. After all, they now have so many suspicious people to shadow; they must eavesdrop on the voice of the crowd; and keep their hand on the throat of public opinion! I formed the impression that apart from the army and the bureaucracy the KGB is now the main enemy of *perestroika*. How can this armada be budged? *Perestroika* does not suit the KGB. The natural state of freedom which society is attempting to enter is inimical to it. Who will then foot the bill for all its colossally inflated staff of dependent specialists in the crushing of freedom?

When, before Daniel's death, I considered the possibility of making a trip to Moscow, I saw myself being absolutely unneeded and completely alone in that city, where everyone except for a few of my old friends had every right to be apprehensive of me: a political criminal, an émigré ... And to strike up new acquaintances or to seek encounters in Moscow with my brother writers who had got friendly with me on their trips to Paris during my emigration I considered to be tactless importunity. Say, for example, I arrive in Moscow and ring Bulat Okudzhava from a public call box. What shall I say to him? 'Would you like to meet?' In a word, I was afraid that my turning up would compromise them. It would be far better for them to come to Paris!

And suddenly it became clear that in Moscow – in particular circles, it goes without saying – I was a welcome guest.

This probably was not to the liking of the KGB, who tried to hamper and limit my contacts in every way and purposely created a show of shadowing me vigilantly, as if they were squeezing me out of my native town. There were always watchers walking up and down outside Daniel's house. 'Why are they standing around doing nothing?!', my wife Maria swore. 'Give them each a spade and at least they can clear the pavement round the house'. I felt gratitude to the foreign correspondents in Moscow who ensued our well-being by making any provocations the object of *glasnost*. For example, the police suddenly turned up at the *dacha* twenty kilometres from Moscow where Daniel spent the last years of his life and announced with embarrassment that as foreigners we had 'infringed a forbidden zone' by calling in there for an hour. The good-natured policemen made little attempt to hide the fact that they had been forced to file a report on KGB orders. Our reward for this 'infringement' was the snow falling silently on the forest nook outside the window and reminding us of the Russian winter.

It was a long time since I had experienced such a surge of love and warmth. After all I have been living for several years under constant fire from the leaders of the Russian emigration. Maybe only once in my life have I had a similar reception, and that was when I was brought to the camp. But that was from zeks, who like me were considered to be 'particularly dangerous state criminals'. They met me like a brother, and the more furiously the newspapers stigmatised Daniel and me and the authorities tried to crush us, the better they treated me. 'but the boss cannot be wise. Because he cannot', the in the words of Galich's camp song.

We knew there was a protracted ideological civil war going on in our native land. Not long before we set off we received a letter from a well-known Moscow poet, who wrote: 'Everything's gloomy and unstable now. Very many people dream of the rustle of bloodshed, of brutality and ferocity with all the "useful fossils": tyranny, the iron fist, a terrible boss, army discipline. There are already calls from here for cutting Korotich down to size. He irritates them most of all and now the host of "the loyal and the prudent" are marching against him ... Whatever songs the optimists of perestroika may be singing to you, the situation is very difficult and life is terrifying. An enormous amount of anger has piled up, there are oceans of worthless money, a fury that stems from penury, starvation and homelessness, national enmity and contempt; and all this is bursting out from the depths and being cleverly directed against the intelligentsia which has been ungrateful enough to forget that during the reign of the genius of all times and peoples, prices went down every year, there was order and every people knew its place.'

But it's one thing to read a letter from afar, and it's one thing to read a letter from afar, and it's a completely other thing to find yourself in the very thick of battle, in the editorial offices of *Ogonek*, with Vitaly Korotich, who is the rallying point for the democrats.

One of the acute questions today is attitudes to the emigration. And if the magazine *Novoe vremia* (New Time) includes an interview with Lev Kopelev, the famous Russian dissident, who now supports *perestroika* from Cologne, then the newspaper *Sovetskaia Rossiia* (Soviet Russia) immediately lays into Kopelev in the best tradition of Stalinist–Kochetovist phraseology, adding for information that Kopelev is a Jew and that is why he is so bad.

Involuntarily you find yourself remembering the old Russian round dance game, in which one group of dancers sings: 'And we sowed the millet, we sowed the millet ... ' And the other replies: 'And we'll trample the millet, we'll trample the millet, we'll trample the millet ... '

So where does the Russian intellectual who by his very nature is a liberal and a democrat go now? To *Ogonek*; to Korotich, Rassadin, Natalia Ivanova, Benedikt Sarnov. And the Russian nationalist? To *Nash Sovremennik* (Our Contemporary) to Vikulov, Rasputin, Proskurin, Bondarev, where everything that the democrats are attempting to sow today is carefully trampled.

We were invited to the magazine *Ogonek*, to the newspaper *Moskovskie novosti* (Moscow News), and to the new magazine *Nashe nasledie* (Our Heritage), which intends to publish me. Everywhere the conversations were every open and the tone was completely unconstrained. And moreover these conversations were not held privately but in the presence of a large number of the staff. I do not even remember Aleksandr Tvardovsky speaking so freely when *Novyi mir* was at its most liberal. Vitaly Korotich, the editor of *Ogonek*, who is so hated by the Russian nationalists, seemed more unfettered, and I felt closer to him.

But the most interesting thing is that the 'front' sometimes passes through areas you would not expect. It has also passed through the Russian emigration. Our trip was coloured by a most amusing coincidence: the day we flew in, on 3 January, *Moskovskie novosti* published an interview with Maria and me which they had taken by telephone way back around the end of September. After three months of struggle over it between various forces it was finally published. Let me say frankly that I was satisfied. The point is that we have set in motion a completely official re-examination of the Siniavsky–Daniel trial, we made contact with my lawyer, paid the necessary sum to the college of lawyers, and now we are awaiting the results with great interest. And I managed to say for the first time in my native land that art is not something under the jurisdiction of the law, that Daniel and I never considered ourselves guilty, that there were remarkable people with me in the Soviet camps, and that my article 'What is Socialist Realism?' contains nothing criminal. Everything I said in the interview

I had once said at my trial. You would think that my being able to say things for which I had once been tried would be a cause for rejoicing. But no sooner had we got back from Moscow than the emigration responded to my interview in *Moskovskie novosti* with abuse. The following sentences provoked particular censure: 'My acquaintance with the world of the camps provoked in me, especially in the first years, a sense of profound, bitter happiness. This time was probably the most arduous in the physical and psychological sense ... But at the same time aesthetically there was no happier time. In the camp I encountered my "reality", my "milieu", my "nature", something every artist dreams about.'

The émigrés were indignant. They said that I had dared to aestheticise the camp, to assert cynically that I was happy there, and by so doing to laugh at a funeral! But in this instance I was speaking of my own subjective feelings as a writer, without applying them to the reality around me. Let me hold on to my own 'happiness', my own style. And if we are all agreed that it is a sin to laugh at a funeral, I could represent this style by a phrase which I have long been saving for a novel, and which concerns only me, the writer, and nobody else: 'And when they began to sing "Eternal Memory", the deceased, lying in the coffin, joined in merrily.'

We are returning to Russia by the back entrance. Is it strange that there is an element of black humour in our writings? ...

We sensed for the last time the oblique fatal shadow of the KGB hanging over Moscow at the border and at the customs when we were flying back to Paris. I have never seen such a crowd of border-guards nor, for all this abundance of staff, seen them working so slowly and lengthily checking passports and belongings. What are they guarding? A ruined country? They would do better to clear the snow from the streets! They could clean and repair the roads!

They threw themselves upon manuscript papers, telephone numbers, addresses, bills from the Paris dry cleaners. My wife, who has been corrupted by Western ideas of the inviolability of the individual, just could not understand what business the Customs had with her intimate correspondence and her various bras and panties. She told the customs officers what she thought of them in some detail, while they, wheezing dolefully, carried on reading: 'Ring Zhenia – morning ... don't forget about Iura ... Sima ... Sonia ... Liusia ... Evening – 157-29-09 ... ' My wife did not give up. I found the whole thing tedious: why were they doing it? They had not confiscated anything ... To put us in a bad mood? To sniff something out and remember it for the future? Were they waiting for today's very limited freedom to come to an end and then everything they had sniffed out today would come in useful as operational material? But maybe there was a simpler and cruder explanation – they just did not want us to forget ourselves, to get into a state of euphoria: 'Look at them, they have been to *Ogonek*, met their friends, given an interview ... We the KGB are in charge here, we can do anything we like, we can look into any cranny from above or from below and there is no point your coming visiting. Just so as you know!'

But before the customs there were our friends. Old friends, friends of Daniel and me, but also people we had managed to make friends with during those five and a bit days, and even some young people, mere boys and girls, that we had never seen before. Someone carrying my books ... To complete our happiness, among the people seeing us off was a first-rate guitarist. First he sang some poems of Daniel's, then some other songs in my favourite camp genre. While we were waiting for the customs examination, we had formed into a circle around the guitarist. Inquisitive bystanders from all over the airport gathered around us, children ran about under our feet. And no one was afraid of listening to a seditious camp song, Aleksandr Galich's stunning ballad 'Queen of the Mainland', a surrealistic song that seems to have been written in delirium, about the White Louse that rules the country with its innumerable camps:

One day all those who come back,
And those who don't come back,
We'll arrange a parade in Her honour,
And what a parade it'll be!
And let them give us new sentences,
You give us eternal peace,
You, the zek's Sovereign,
Your Majesty The White Louse!
Our majesty The White Louse!
Queen of the Mainland!

I thought that this spectre of Death would cause people to scatter. But nobody left ...

At the passport control Maria asked a sternly inaccessible young border guard: 'Why are you so serious? Smile, please!' The border guard smacked a stamp into her passport and suddenly – smiled, 'Try to smile more often,' said my wife. 'You'll find life gets easier and more interesting ...' That is how we parted with Moscow.

***

Before we set off for Moscow my book *Soviet Civilisation* had been published by Albin Michel in Paris. In it I had tried to trace the basic parameters of my chosen subject: the revolution, the Leninist state, the Stalinist state and so on. Naturally, when I arrived in Moscow I was always comparing the picture before my eyes with what I had written. The last chapter of my book is called 'Can you restructure (*perestroit*) a Pyramid into a Parthenon?' The pyramid signifies the singularly heavy, conservative Soviet civilisation; the parthenon democracy of the Western European type. The book concludes that it is very difficult to remake a pyramid into a parthenon. The impressions that I garnered from my brief visit to Moscow are the same.

Uzbekistan: The Hostile Earth of the Friendly People

Shirin Akiner

The Uzbeks have a strongly ingrained tradition of hospitality. A guest must be treated better than one's parents, they say. This is the spirit in which they have welcomed outsiders who, over the years, have come to settle in their republic. On a personal level there may have been friction, but there has sometimes been no history of generalised inter-ethnic hostility in the region. The Uzbeks have taken a genuine pride in producing the millions of tons of cotton, the 'white gold' that they contribute annually to the Soviet economy. It coincided with their image of themselves as bountiful givers; it helped stifle any misgivings that might have arisen as to the scale or the methods of production.

Central Asia was a showpiece of Soviet achievement, a shining example of what the system could achieve in a Third World setting. Cheerful posters and newsreel pictures of radiant workers reinforced the impression of a prosperous, burgeoning society.

The reality was different. Away from the cameras, out of sight of the well-fed officials in the capital and inquisitive visitors, conditions were often appalling. In many regions the standard of living was far below that in other parts of the Soviet Union. In some it was on a par with that in the poorest developing countries.

Within the last couple of years the full extent of the problems in Central Asia have become widely known (although there were earlier indications of the gravity of the situation in specialist publications). In the pre-*glasnost* era there was a complacent assumption that conditions were much the same everywhere; where it was clear that something was particularly wrong, it was brushed aside as a localised misfortune. There was also fear, a legacy of the purges of the thirties, to discourage people from probing too deeply into unpalatable facts. The lack of information meant that there was ignorance as to the sheer size of the

Vol. 19, no. 1, 1990

problem. And by no means least, there were the inhibitions imposed by the social *mores* of the community itself – a reluctance to count the cost of a gift, to stint the hospitality.

These were some of the factors that helped to keep the Uzbeks quiescent while conditions about them steadily deteriorated. It took the combined efforts of progressive journalists in Moscow and Central Asian intellectuals in their own republics to alert people to the dangers of the situation. Today, as Uzbeks begin to ask questions and to demand answers, they are confronted by a state of crisis in virtually every sphere – the economy, ecology, health care, food supply, housing, employment and much else besides. Their response is one of shock and dismay, compounded by a profound sense of anger. Economists may dispute the causes of the calamity; some will hold that the republic has gained more than it has given to the Union; others will maintain the opposite. The popular perception takes no account of such nice arguments; its verdict is simpler, sharper, and couched in terms of the traditional culture: the code of hospitality has been violated; the 'guests' have despoiled the land and ridden roughshod over the sensibilities of the hosts. The word *hurmat*, 'respect' frequently recurs; 'We must be shown respect' they say. How the equilibrium is to be established no one knows. All that is certain is that matters can no longer be left as they are.

Central Asia, unlike some other parts of the Soviet Union, has no period of national independence to look back to. The region passed directly from the control of semi-feudal khans into the hands of Tsarist colonial administrators, who in turn were replaced by Soviet officials. The ethnically based republics that exist today are an entirely Soviet creation, brought into being in response to a strategy imposed from above (and outside), not a popular grassroots demand from below. There are many, including several Central Asians, who think the division of 'Turkestan' into separate republics was harmful to the social and cultural development of the region.

What is germane here is that Central Asian affairs have for so long been directed by others that there has been little opportunity for the indigenous population to develop a political culture in the modern, western sense. This, added to a large, local bureaucracy with strong vested interests in preserving the *status quo*; also the fact that the centre is a very long way away and people on the periphery know little of new developments there, and even less about how to interpret them correctly – all of this has made the democratisation of society a far slower and more problematic process in Central Asia than in other parts of the Soviet Union. There is much that can be said and done in Moscow that can as yet scarcely be dreamed of in Tashkent or Ashkhabad. Here *perestroika* and *glasnost* have barely begun to take root.

A political debate is emerging. It began among the intelligentsia but is slowly broadening out to include other walks of life. The writers have played a crucial role in raising the consciousness of the people. The largest and best-organised popular movement in Central Asia is based in Tashkent at the Uzbek Writers' Union. *Birlik* ('Unity', 'One-ness') was inspired to some extent by *Sajudis* and other such movements in the European USSR, but it has an identity and an agenda that are very much its own. It is just over a year old, but it has had a notional base since 1984, when a group of writers wrote an open letter to the authorities outlining their areas of concern.

On 11 November 1988, the movement was formally launched. However, it has still not been granted official registration.

The membership of *Birlik* is thought by some to have reached 500,000–800,000. The uncertainty over numbers arises from the fact that, as the movement is not registered, it is unable to have a bank account. Registration fees and membership dues cannot be collected, and the membership files have drifted into chaos. There is a severe crisis in the movement as funds are needed for many of its activities, including the printing of its newssheet. However, *Birlik*'s programme has just been printed in the official organs of the press, so it is hoped that the present setback is merely temporary, and that a formal working relationship will soon be established between the government and the movement's representatives.

Meanwhile, problems have sprung up within the movement itself. There had been an element of ambiguity in the organisational structure. In theory, the leader of *Birlik* was its chairman, Abdurahim Pulatov, a lecturer in mathematics at Tashkent State University. In practice, however, it was undoubtedly Muhammad Salih. This was not a position that Salih sought, but one that was thrust upon him. One of the most talented of the new wave of Soviet poets (he writes in Uzbek, but has been translated into other languages) he has campaigned openly and courageously on his own for some years, on issues such as the ecological situation and the social and medical needs of the rural population.

The *Birlik* leadership invited him to be their candidate for the March 1989 elections to the Congress of People's Deputies. Salih agreed to cooperate in this, but refused to become a member of the movement and indeed, publicly distanced himself from it. His following among the people, in particular among the students, is very strong; however, owing to a series of 'dirty tricks' by the authorities (changing the venues of meetings without warning, rigging the votes of the selection committees, spreading disinformation and disregarding the laws on election procedures) he was not elected. He later did join the movement and is now a member of its 'praesidium'. He still refuses to accept the post of chairman on the grounds that it is not compatible with his official position as Secretary of the Uzbek Writers' Union.

Tension has been growing between Abdurahim Pulatov and Muhammad Salih for some time. They are men of very different characters. It is not so much that they disagree about aims, but rather about the means needed to achieve them. Pulatov is the more flamboyant of the two. A good communicator, he is in his element at mass meetings. He feels they are necessary in order to disseminate information and to arouse the masses. That such meetings might lead to confrontations with the security forces, even to violence, in no way deters him. His detractors say that he welcomes such clashes as a way of intensifying the struggle. Salih, by contrast, is not a demagogue. More at ease with the written word, he prefers quiet, behind-the-scenes negotiations. As a young conscript he served in Hungary, then took part in the Soviet invasion of Czechoslovakia. The experience left an indelible mark on him and has shaped his determination to avoid conflict whenever possible. His primary goal at present is to achieve the official registration of *Birlik*. Unruly, illegal meetings, he feels, do nothing to further this end, but merely give the movement a bad name.

Matters came to a head this autumn. On 8 October Pulatov withdrew from the main body of *Birlik*, splitting the movement into two factions. The larger group remained with Salih, but a not insubstantial number of supporters, including some 1,000 students, followed Pulatov. Pulatov, still using the name *Birlik*, published his own newssheet and organised a mass rally for 18–19 October, the eve of the 11th Session of the Supreme Soviet of the Uzbek SSR. There were violent clashes between the two factions and the rally ended with 130 people arrested, Pulatov among them. The detainees were released within a few hours, but the incident was used as a pretext to deny *Birlik* formal recognition, and to launch a media attack on all informal groups. An uneasy truce has been established. A *Kurultai* ('meeting') has been called for 11 November, the first anniversary of the founding of the movement. A new organisational structure is to be created, and a new chairman elected. Neither Pulatov nor Salih are standing for this post, but the whole movement is so fragile and fluid that confidence in the other candidates ebbs and flows. Pulatov or Salih will continue to act as *de facto* leaders, and potential rivals.

The first issue to mobilise public opinion on a large scale was the fight to gain official acceptance of Uzbek as the state language of the republic. *Birlik* spearheaded the campaign, giving direction to hitherto uncoordinated demands. It was a matter of psychological importance, the first and most fundamental step towards re-establishing the Uzbeks' self-esteem; the first marker of their determination to redefine their identity, to reassert their right to be masters in their own home. Not only had it become standard practice for street signs, official forms and public announcements of every sort to be made exclusively in Russian, it had also become impossible to use the language of the republic, the native language of 70% of its population, for a whole range of functions, from sending a telegram to presenting a thesis at the state university. Much of this was rectified in the language law passed on 21 October 1989 which gave Uzbek the status of state language. In the bill, in which Uzbek is referred to, in parentheses, by its historical name, *Turki*, it is required that the old, i.e. Arabic script, abolished in 1930, be reintroduced into the school curriculum, albeit as a separate subject; classes and textbooks are also to be made available for adults wishing to learn this script. The non-Uzbek section of the population is now required to learn the state language, and free tuition is to be provided in order to facilitate this.

Earlier in the year, when the language campaign was still in its infancy, there was a simplistic but widely held view that once this issue was resolved, everything else would fall into place. Some even thought that the *raison d'être* for *Birlik* would disappear. It was only later that the realisation dawned that this was but the beginning of a very long and arduous road. Behind the language question towered the formidable ranges of the economic, ecological, and social problems of the region.

The monoculture of cotton lies at the heart of the matter, but ramifications reach out in every direction, creating complex clusters of problems that have since developed their own momentum. For years the production targets for cotton have been utterly unrealistic. In an attempt to satisfy them, more and more land has been given over to this culture, massive doses of chemicals have been used to boost yields, and water, such a precious commodity in this arid region, has been expended with culpable extravagance to irrigate the crop.

The ecological balance has been severely disrupted, and human, animal and plant life has suffered accordingly. The most dramatic consequence of the mismanagement of water resources has been the shrinking of the Aral Sea; unless drastic measures are taken soon, it is likely that it will dry up completely. The desiccation process is already seriously affecting the climate and causing widespread desertification of the surrounding country. The food supply has suffered as a result of the cotton mania, as much less land is available for growing fruit and vegetables and grazing livestock. The soil is contaminated by the toxic chemicals used on the cotton; this contamination is passed into the food cycle. Traces of pesticides have apparently been identified in mothers' breast milk.

The bazaars of Tashkent are still full of colourful mounds of produce, and the main thoroughfares are filled with the aromatic smells of grilling shashlyk. In the back streets, though, there are many who cannot afford such luxuries. Their diet consists of bread and tea, supplemented in summer by a few slices of melon. In the countryside, according to official statistics, the average consumption of meat per person per year is eight kilos, but doubts are openly expressed as to whether this estimate is not too high. Protein, vitamin and iodine deficiencies are rife, causing retarded physical and mental development, and a lowered resistance to disease. Water supplies are so contaminated that, specialists claim, there is not a glass of clean drinking water to be had in the whole region.

Cotton even affects education, as children and students are required to help bring in the harvest. A couple of months are lost out of every academic year, from school through to the last year of university (children are officially exempt from this work, but most people believe that away from the capital the practice still continues).

The enormity of these problems would be enough to defeat the most able and experienced of administrators. Given the quality of the present bureaucracy, and the inexperience of the activists, it is not surprising that no clear ideas have emerged as to how to proceed. The *Birlik* leadership has invited specialists to work with them to formulate policies, but this initiative is too new to judge whether or not it will produce good results. In the absence of carefully researched studies and rigorous analyses, it is inevitable that arguments about such complex questions as the optimum level for the production of cotton, a sustainable irrigation policy, or a strategy to save the Aral Sea, should be approached from a largely emotional standpoint.

The sincerity of the protagonists is not in doubt; the soundness of their proposed solutions is sometimes less convincing. Other informal groups have now begun to appear and independent political activists are also making their voices heard. In this atmosphere of heightened awareness and greater determination to seek responsible solutions it is possible that more realistic proposals might eventually be forthcoming.

No discussion of Central Asia can be complete if it does not take Islam into account. There have been great changes in the religious life of the community this year. In March a new mufti was elected, Muhammad Sadyk Mahammad Yusuf Hodzha-ogli. Born in 1952 in the Andizhan region, he studied first in the medresses of Bukhara and Tashkent, then in Libya. He became Rector of the Tashkent medresse when he was only 35 years old. Two years later, amid unprecedented scenes of religious fervour, he was called upon to replace Mufti Shamsuddinkhan Babakhanov as head of the Spiritual Board for Central Asia and Kazakhstan. Mufti Babakhanov was accused of leading too dissolute a life and of not being properly qualified for his high calling. There may be truth in the first charge, somewhat less in the latter. Clearly, the main reason for his overthrow was that he was too closely identified with the 'years of stagnation'.

A new face was needed by government and believers and Muhammad Sadyk could provide It. He has proved to be a fortunate choice. Widely respected for his integrity and piety, he has presided over an improvement in conditions for the Muslims. The first major event of his tenure was the return of the Othman Qur'an from the civil authorities to the religious. Believed by Central Asians to be a genuine seventh century copy of the Qu'ran, this is one of the most revered relics in the Muslim world. Its repossession bestows on the new mufti a religious legitimacy never granted to Mufti Babakhanov.

Permission for a new edition of the Qu'ran, based on this copy, with a print-run of 50,000, has been given. It will go some way to fulfilling Mufti Muhammad Sadyk's aim of providing every Muslim family in Central Asia with a copy of the Holy Book.

Other notable concessions have been the opening of several new mosques (at one point this was running at an average of two or three per week), and permission to take in more students to the medresses. New dormitory accommodation is under construction. Contacts with foreign Muslims have also become much easier. Only 31 believers from the 55 million-strong community of Soviet Muslims were allowed to go on the *haj* this year, but there are rumours that more will be allowed next year, and over 4,000 applications have been registered in Tashkent alone. There are requests for religious programmes to be broadcast by the state-controlled media.

The reaction of the Muslims is one of dazed delight. Mr Gorbachev, the architect of these new freedoms, enjoys enormous popularity and gratitude. It matters very much to the Central Asians that their mosques should be open for worship and that their beliefs should be treated with respect. To some extent these moves have defused the religious situation, by making it possible for religion to come into the open. If organised 'underground' movements ever did exist – which many Central Asians would deny – there is little pressure on them now to remain concealed.

The recent developments have been very heartening for Muslims yet they have presented Islam with something of a predicament: what is its role to be in contemporary Central Asian society? To what extent can Islam enter into the political debate, offer practical guidance in the solution of society's ills? Muslim scholars in Central Asia have been cut off from modernist trends elsewhere in the Islamic world for so many generations that they are out of touch with recent thinking in these areas. At present their chief concern is to consolidate the formal aspects of the religious life. Once that has been achieved there will be an urgent need to consider how best they are to fulfil their role as leaders, in the Islamic sense, of their community. The secular Party-Soviet authorities may not be averse to giving them a more active function if this will help to stabilise society. For the great danger now is a breakdown in law and order.

The pressures of high unemployment, economic deprivation, a lack of the most basic amenities, as well as a sense of having been humiliated and abused, have triggered a fierce wave of disaffection. Hooliganism, accompanied by serious acts of violence against property and persons, is widespread. Regional factionalism, never far from the surface, has taken on a harsher aspect and is being transmuted into a general tendency to xenophobia. Popular Islam, under a 'fundamentalist' banner, could certainly act as a rallying point for a particular group at a particular time. It is not in itself a cause of the present tension, but it is not inconceivable that it could be appropriated in this way. There is some evidence that this is what happened during the disturbances in Ferghana this June. Then, not the party officials, not the Mufti, not the *Birlik* leadership, were able to exert any control whatsoever over the mobs.

Given time, wise leadership and a colossal injection of financial aid, Central Asia could yet solve its difficulties. A new constitutional framework will be required. There is agreement that the republic must have sovereignty, to order its internal affairs as it sees fit. A minority do have separatist dreams; the majority, however, still see their future within the Soviet Union. The unpredictable element is the young, predominantly rural population. Disenchanted with everyone, out of patience, they could disrupt the region. The outlook at the end of 1989 is not promising.

Berlin–East: The Other Side of the City

Lutz Rathenow

Translated from the German by Agnes Stein

The excerpts below are from the third edition of Berlin-East: The Other Side of the City. *Originally published in West Germany in 1987 by S. Piper Verlag and reprinted in 1988 by Hartenberg, this edition, published by Basisdruck (a new publisher located in the East of Berlin) has added two chapters to bring the book up to date. These give an impressionistic account of the days just before and after unification.*

Berlin from above. Shabby, blooming-cloud factory.

Spray-can that will not be emptied.

A phono-disc with a crack.

Smells tattoo the city.

Houses expand in the morning, shrink at night.

The city will not be squeezed into a few lines. This city that slowly attempts to raise its head. For years I've been trying to see its face.

The Centre, East Berlin. I have always loved it at night when it has mostly been empty of people. The once glorious Unter den Linden and the Platz der Akademie, with the Schinkel Theatre, rest in their restored glory. All the buildings are bathed in a soft light, removed from their daytime function. 'Good old Europe', an American lady is heard to say. During the day, these memorials to times past allow some of their lustre to reflect on the rulers that have maintained them. Now that the Wall is down, there are more people around at night. The museum is filled with people. But there are still places in the city that lead into realms of unreality. I was in Treplow Park with a friend viewing the World War II memorial to the Soviet soldier. Complete darkness. We made our way with a flashlight. Stared at the copper relief, the chiselled history of war in stony images, glowing with Stalin's golden phrases. Alone in this vast area we felt like actors in a surreal production.

Architecture remains one of the most enduring residues of the old system. Delayed vengeance? While the post office building in Marzahn received wide architectural acclaim, not everything was as successful. There are the wooden doors on the facade of the Ministry for State Security, carefully fashioned at the beginning of the 1980s. These highly decorative doors cannot be opened, a source of much ironic comment. The clients had reached the top of the post-modern trend!

First the U-bahn and S-bahn stations are to be connected. Will the posters disappear from the Alexanderplatz the moment they no longer serve an ideological purpose? When future archaeologists, sifting through future layers of propaganda posters, hit upon these productions will they conclude a high-level culture disappeared here? Once again.

Karl, 27, moved from East to West Berlin before 1985. In the beginning he was wildly happy, really elated in his new environment. Depression followed, reinforced by disappointments in his girl and his job and the fact that he could not visit his old home. At the border crossing Friedrichstrasse, Karl, in 1986, asked for permission to return to the GDR. Three men in business suits drove him to a building in Pankow, East Berlin, the home of the Department for East German Immigrants. For days there were interviews, questionings, the lot. Was he as spy for the West Berlin information services? Would he like to do intelligence work for the GDR? Compensation, three marks pocket money and meals, together with a bottle of beer.

Karl is not allowed to leave the premises. He now realises why he left two years ago. He asks for an exit visa to West Berlin. The officials seek to keep him. They call his parents. If he remains he will be allowed to leave the camp immediately. But the more he is talked into staying, the greater his desire to leave. Three weeks pass and he is given permission to leave.

In 1989, Karl is joyful to see the opening of the Wall. In the meantime, he has made his adjustment to life in the West. His enthusiasm for the open border lessens as the East slowly seeps into the West. Karl's friends and he vote for the 'alternative list', suppressing anxiety about aliens.

Now he understands what disturbed him about the GDR – from the autos to the helpless gestures made in front of the array of goods. His friends crack jokes and he tries to laugh with them. These helpless *Ossies* (East-siders) remind him of his past. and now there are all the friends who come to visit and spend the night.

Karl wants to leave Berlin. But for that he needs money and a plan.

The other cities in the German West are too boring for him. By chance, he finds place to stay in East Berlin. He tells neither his friends in the East nor the West of the city. It just happens that he's rarely at home in the old living quarters. Meanwhile, Karl searches for the last cheap, undiscovered property capable of renovation in a not too ugly neighbourhood of what is still the GDR. His imagined life in the West, Karl says, can most easily be pursued in an East Berlin niche.

About one o'clock on a sweltering summer night, I am pumping myself full of liquid to preserve the film of sweat on my skin. Stinking protection against the oppressive sultriness. Others keep themselves fresh with other means. Two hours ago, I heard a street cry: 'Jews out of East Berlin!' In the afternoon, I had a visit from a friend who had just arrived by a train from Leipzig. Football fans were scandalised by the repeated anti-Semitic chants - one referred to the 'Jew East Berlin'. I have become part of the sickness by which others feel themselves threatened.

I think of the flies. For hours I was working at the open window without seeing one. After a short visit to the kitchen, the desk was suddenly covered with a swarm. As if this had always been their centre, 20 to 30 insects buzzed about the typewriter. Where had they been earlier? How did they collect? Only flies - a reassuring thought to drive away fear as I sit down at the typewriter. I almost thought it the property of the flies.

1 July, 1990. A state exits. Into another system. No-one can any longer make a personal migration.

It is not only the currency that is changing its looks after the exchange equalisation. The signs are changing with the times. The time of signs with unequivocal meanings is past. Tonight the dustbin men are carting off the rubbish after a strike that lasted about a fortnight. In the past, such a strike would have caused a sensation in the city. Today I'm not even sure how long they were on strike. I only know that with the GDR mark as a sign, nothing would have induced then to cart away the rubbish on a Saturday night going into Sunday.

The burial of a currency. A breath of anarchy in the interment; so completely can the authority of a state be relaxed. Melted down. We should have preserved the coin of an Ostsee island. As reserves for ex-service Stalinists. Not everybody had the right contacts to flee to Chile.

With enthusiasm, sorrow, fear, joy, intoxication, pride and irritation we said goodbye to the money that did not sound like money. Coins below one mark will at first remain valid. Actually, with its disappearance, the Eastern coin reaches par with the West. At first, coins of both currencies will ring in the same pocket. But his has its limits. The scarce Eastern coinage hastens the conversion. And automatic machines greedy for Western coins will accept only these. And people? Frenzied enthusiasm, gun salutes, midnight rockets. Some fire themselves with courage. At the New Year, one man is proud he invested some of his money in fireworks firms.

'We pensioners had a rough time before, now there's another kind of rough time,' an old lady says. She intends to drink up her East German money by midnight.

'East-shit of the West – you can't properly curse the East any longer now that it's become the West'.

'At least I can now play the Big Max in Hungary – as a Westerner'.

Naturally one celebrates. Whether from joy or sorrow only time will tell. Early days. One thing learned in the GDR: never dismiss any holiday no matter how idiotic the cause for celebration.

The German flag is flying. For the length of two stations, a kid sings in a surprisingly sad voice: '*Hoch solln Sie leben ... Dreimal hoch*'. (Raise them high ... Three cheers for ...) His mother gives him a whack and drags him out of the train.

A policeman explains to a journalist: 'I've always tried to remain a man. Today I rejoice I have become a German official'.

People rush through shops searching. Earlier they were pursuing Western products or rare goods on the shelves, today they are searching to profit from the low prices of domestic products.

Everything is changing, turning and winding. Some change slowly. The slowest are those in a mad rush.

I am not sure what disturbs me more: this Germanic D-mark satisfaction (everything has got to improve now) or the resigned whine for the good old, real old, socialist days.

'Who will march with a smart Prussian goose-step now that the East Guard Regiment with its relief are gone?' a West Berliner complains.

The Television Tower. I suddenly realise the Television Tower still stands. What can it signify now? What is the point of it now? Before, yes. The only place available to all comers for a view of West Berlin. The beams of light that nightly stroked the city have lost their glamour.

Yesterday at the cemetery which unites three. No picture in the *Berlin-East* book was reproduced as often as Hauswald's angels kneeling in front of the wall. The same place that a few days earlier had been closed to the public. At that time everything could be put into a prohibited zone. The peace of the cemetery preserves the silence of dictatorship which used to come streaming from the Wall.

The Thalmann head in the Thalmann park. Such blown-up

memorials, such glorious provocations for satire will no longer be with us. Now Thalmann no longer rouses us to anger. Now this *kitsch* can only serve to amuse. Perhaps as warning or subject for analysis worth preserving.

Recently a Munich film team filming *Zärtlich Kreist die Faust* (The Fist Rolls Tenderly) noticed that the sound reception near the bronze memorial was continuously disturbed. The bronze head confusing the recording system? Or the ghost of old Thalmann? What does he want to say?

I can't rid myself of the notion that there is somebody inside the hollow memorial.

I run through the city and see pictures I cannot snap. Which I could not assemble into one picture. My head stores what my eyes present. My head is untrustworthy.

More and more pictures collect and contradict each other. Only words will do to release the images, transpose them into sentences, deconstruct the barrage of the visible.

The photo-view takes the city as cinematic space, a first-class setting for a work in which everyone collaborates. Up to now, patience was the dominating theme. Replaced by movement with every kind of significant nuance.

What remains of 40 years of the GDR? A heritage of postage stamps that will set a collector's heart beating. And an equally rich collection of neuroses in its people.

Our influence on the West of the city. Suddenly there are queues in front of shops, the S-trains lose their punctuality and the shop clerk replies, 'Haven't a clue'. Telephones stop working, taxicab drivers grumble about the traffic blockages.

In 20 years' time will we notice in the erstwhile East Berlin that we are living in the former East of Berlin?

A show of confidence in the city to guarantee that history will not repeat itself.

Everything is past. Everything begins.

Every period demands the beginning of a new sentence. One plus one equals the unknown.

To continue gathering pieces for the Berlin puzzle. For a picture that more and more promises to evade completion.

The Rapid Demise of Sarajevo TV

Nenad Pejic

Interviewer: Ursula Rushton

Since your election in July 1989 as editor-in-chief, Sarajevo Television's independent stance attracted criticism from all sides in politics.

Sarajevo Television was accused of something at every press conference given by political leaders. Each time, we said 'Give us examples of what we did or did not broadcast, and tell us what was wrong'. But they were not able to do so. This was routine, from day to day and week to week, and not only at the press conferences, but during public political meetings. We always broadcast their complaints. When the Serbian Democratic Party (SDS) said that we hated Serbs, we broadcast it. The next day, when the Croatian Democratic Party (HDZ) said that we hated Croats we broadcast that, too. And after the November 1990 elections, politicians added threatening telephone calls to journalists to public pressure. They called me, for example, and some of my colleagues, and calls were also made to my children saying that someone will kill their father, things like that. And, later on, we started to get different kinds of menaces. More direct ones. They said, 'We will kill you if you don't broadcast this particular report.' We tried to ignore these problems, but something remains in the brain, a warning. Those were hard times for us. Then, towards the end of 1991, the political pressures became greater and greater.

Most of us had sent our families out of Sarajevo and, from April 1992 onwards, were living in the TV building itself, working 24 hours a day, sleeping when we could. This is the only reason television has continued to work in Sarajevo. Then, still in April, I heard that Serbian TV had broadcast a report saying that I was on a death list held by the

Croat forces; and Croatian TV broadcast a report saying that I was on a Serbian death list. Can you imagine! My son called me from Belgrade and said 'Daddy, just a few minutes ago, they broadcast a story about you'. Can you imagine what is going on in the minds of kids right now?

From 4 April, when the paramilitary groups came looking for me at the television station, I had to spend each night at a different friend's house, moving around Sarajevo. I know it was a paramilitary group, though I can't say which one, that rang my friends to say that a bomb would be thrown onto their balcony if it was found out that I had been staying there. Eventually, they called my office when I was there and half-an-hour later a bomb really was thrown onto the balcony! So I decided to leave. Psychologically, physically, I had reached the end. I was without any kind of motivation, without any kind of security, without money. I still have to deal with my feelings about leaving my friends. I feel guilty personally, in my heart, although in my mind I am sure that they will understand, because they know that my situation was dangerous.

Until September 1991, four out of five letters that arrived on my desk would accuse us of not being objective, but each came from a different national perspective. In other words, Muslims would say that we were not a good television station for Muslims, Croats for Croats, and Serbs for Serbs. After that date, four out of five letters would support us, and only one would criticise us from a nationalist perspective. My own feeling is that the reason for the change was that during those months of 1991 we tried to broadcast news from all political sources; and only facts, no speculation and no comment. For example, when the Serbian Democratic Party established a (secessionist autonomous) Serbian parliament in Bosnia in Autumn 1991, we broadcast the event live. The SDS was very surprised, viewers were surprised. I received 26 telephone calls from viewers saying that they were not satisfied with our coverage. Months later, the Muslim-led Democratic Party of Rights (SDA) held a congress. Again, we broadcast it live, and this time there were no complaints. So, what I want to say is that we tried to teach viewers that they have to listen to the other side. In Bosnia that is particularly important, because we have three national groups, with 44% Muslims, 31% Serbs, and 18% Croats. If we have managed to teach viewers something I would regard that as my greatest success.

Every evening, viewers in Sarajevo would see three different news reports. On the first channel there was news from Sarajevo; on the second channel news from Belgrade or from Croatian TV, alternating from day to day; and a third service from Yutel (the pan-Yugoslav satellite service set up by former Federal President Ante Markovic).

After Yutel was closed down by Belgrade, they started to use our studio for broadcasts from Sarajevo. But Belgrade jammed the signal after Serbian forces took control of the transmitter.

We would title our broadcasts with the place of origin of the report, whether from Sarajevo, Croatian or Serbian TV. And people liked that, because they could compare them. It was, in a way, a kind of television comedy, because to try to compare the three services was like a terrible game. If one person says that I am black, and another says that I am white, and other people see that I am grey, for example, it is comic. Almost. Well, tragicomic! But it was important, because people learned to see the facts for themselves.

In early April, thousands of people marched to the front of the Republican Assembly, past the television building, chanting, 'Sarajevo TV, Sarajevo TV'. I was really proud. Taxi drivers organised a demonstration in support of TV Sarajevo ...

There is another thing of which I am very proud. During the past couple of years, there have been a number of journalists who went over to the nationalist parties. Now there are fewer of them. Out of 11 journalists who were nationalist party supporters in mid-1991, there are certainly under 10 now, and the others are supporting our independent position. In Sarajevo now journalists of all nationalities are working together. And this is something to be proud of in such difficult conditions.

How was it possible to maintain your independent position for so long? Was it attributable to the power vacuum in the country?

That was one reason, but the main one was that support from the people was really big. Unfortunately, some of them did not pay their monthly fee for the service. This was because since January 1991 the main political parties appealed to them not to pay – to boycott the television station. At the end of 1989, 91% of our revenue was from the fee, and 9% was from advertising. By the end of 1991, 77% of our revenue was from the fee, with 23% from advertising. After that came the civil war, and now there is no revenue, no monthly fee, no advertising, no nothing. I cannot give you a figure for 1992! So, yes, the money comes directly from the people, and people in Bosnia are poor. For example, out of four million inhabitants, 1,200,000 have a TV set but only 700,000 declare that they own one. And of these, only 300,000 paid their fee. (This was before they stopped paying altogether.) A few months ago, we did get some money from the republican government.

That was two months ago, and it was only for salaries. Now I am not sure whether anyone is receiving a salary.

My colleagues at the TV station are trying to remain there, but it is very hard. There is nothing. During the last 20 days, 20 cars and two cameras were stolen from us. It could have been anyone, because this is a time for criminals, anyone may stop a person and demand money, their car, anything. Since August 1991, the Serbian Democratic Party has stolen seven of our nine regional transmitters and just two days ago (on 5 May) they destroyed the main one.

Between November 1991 and January 1992, the Serbian Democratic Party and the Croatian Democratic Party proposed the division of the television station into three national stations. This was a crazy suggestion. Political pressure from the Serbian party was the greatest. They first proposed the split in November 1991. I asked Mr Karadzic, President of the SDS, how he imagined this could be done. He answered that the Serbian assembly (in Bosnia) would choose the Serbian editor. You know what this means: exactly the same routine as under the Communists! The SDS wants the right to say who is a good Serb and who is not. It is the same elsewhere. The Croatian Democratic Party calls me a bad Croat, which is true in a sense, because my profession is not to be a Croat, it is to be a good journalist.

Over dinner once Mr Karadzic suggested that we divide only the News department, saying, 'Maybe we don't need to divide anything else in Bosnia'. So I said to him, 'Can you guarantee that if you divide only the News department you will stop the division of Bosnia? Because if you can give me that guarantee I will sign it'. He said that he could not, of course.

The Muslim party did not want the division of television. But although we and they were practically on the same side over this, there was an important difference, because they took the unity of television to symbolise a united Bosnia, while we wanted it in order to be a professional TV service, not a political symbol. To all three parties we said the same thing: 'OK, if you want to divide TV, we will accept it, but only if you can agree on the terms of the split.' Of course we knew that such agreement would be impossible. When we broadcast the 1992 demonstrations on the streets of Sarajevo live, they all said we had tried to implement a putsch. It was the first time in maybe a year that they were able to reach agreement with each other!

Privately, in conversation, members of all the political parties usually talk of their respect for television, and tell us that we are doing a good job. In public, though, they constantly criticise.

Was there ever any practical suggestion of how this idea of splitting the television station into three separate national stations might be accomplished?

The proposal of the Serbian Democratic Party was as follows: we already have three channels, two of them covering all the territory of Bosnia, and the third local to Sarajevo. The SDS suggested that one day they take the first channel and the Muslim party take the next channel and so on – that the political groups would rotate the service (in effect, ending up with a political propaganda service to rival no other!). It was absolutely crazy, and if not a technical impossibility, a logistical one. According to this system, a Serb editor would send his cameraman to record exactly what he wanted to see. Then another cameraman would go to the same event to record something else, and a third would go to find something different yet again.

So in practical terms it would mean that for each event we would need three cameramen. Nobody asks who will pay for this, nobody! They have no time for that. They want to produce conflict.

Under their suggestion for national division of television, there would be no competition, only mutually exclusive information systems. Is it a question of political power, nothing more?

Yes, of course. And people are frightened of these divisions. I tried to make a suggestion to the political parties: OK, if you want to keep peace here, if you want to make an agreement, if you want to create conditions for a long discussion about our future, then let us do it. Leave the first channel free and professionally controlled: one third by government; one third by professional experts, political scientists, etc; and one third by the employees. Then, divide the second channel as you like, and leave the third channel as a commercial channel. I failed. I guess that everyone knew that in that case no one would choose to watch the second channel.

I believe that the best journalists would have worked for the first channel, while the worst would go to the second channel. Colm Doyle, who remained the sole representative of the EC in Sarajevo, told the parties that they could divide the television into three or even 20 channels, but under two conditions: they should do it peacefully; and they should do it together. This they can never do. When they told Cyrus Vance that they wanted to divide up the television, he said, 'I find it very strange that you should want to divide the only institution now in Bosnia which is professional and which is a common institution'. When Mr Doyle said he did not understand the proposal,

I said that it was aimed at destroying Sarajevo TV precisely because it was professional and common to us all.

Support from foreign countries has been greater than you can imagine during recent months, from all kinds of institutions, like the European Institute for the Media here in Manchester, from the European Community, and from the United States, and so on. Yet it is interesting to note that while Sarajevo TV received so much support from so many countries, not a single one of our friends supported us with technical equipment. The reason is simple: we are a public television service. I understand this. Private media are not associated with the state, or with the old structures of Communism.

Nobody can help us, because the problem lies in Bosnia, not outside, at least not outside Yugoslavia. We have a big problem with [President of Serbia] Milosevic and [President of Croatia] Tudjman.

Speaking of moves influenced by Croatia and Serbia, there seems to be a political equivalent of the national division of Sarajevo Television in the suggested cantonisation of Bosnia. Do you think the latter is as much of a logistical nightmare as the former?

The reason for the cantonisation proposal is that each camp wants to bring all kinds of life in their camp under their own political control. For example, would it be possible, after cantonisation in Bosnia, to establish elections in the republic? If not, then it means that in the next 10 to 15 years, or for the foreseeable future, it will only be possible to establish national parties. It will be practically impossible to establish local democratic parties. There is no way that anyone will be able to connect the different parts of Bosnia. In my view it is one of the main reasons for the stealing of our transmitters, by which they deprived not only viewers in Bosnia but also those in Vojvodina and Belgrade, who also watched us. Serbian people in Slavonia and Kniiska Krajina were also watching Sarajevo TV. Our transmitters were stolen so as not to let people see the other side.

Is it true to say that people in Yugoslavia, possibly the majority, who want to see another side, are silenced because they are too afraid to speak out?

Yes. I guess that Sarajevo TV is now only able to broadcast to about 15% of its former territory. The transmitters which were taken are now used to broadcast Belgrade Television.

To give an idea of the difference between us and the other

Yugoslavian TV stations, I usually mention two examples: during the civil war in Croatia, Croatian TV would give news about a Catholic priest who had been beaten by the Serbian forces, and the same day, absolutely the same story would be reported by Serbian TV, but about an Orthodox priest who had been beaten by the Croatian forces. The point is that both stories are true, but the important thing is that Serbian TV did not broadcast the story about the Catholic priest and Croatian TV did not broadcast the story about the Orthodox priest. We broadcast both stories. That gives you our position. We tried to be successful as professionals. But if you try to be professional during a war you will not have success with either side. You are a traitor to both. There is no precedent for a television station which was founded by both sides trying during wartime to be professional and to broadcast the story from both sides. Maybe this has been our greatest misfortune.

The real problem in Belgrade and Zagreb is that, on both sides, the first line of journalists has been sacked from the media. Then came the second line. Now third or fourth grade professionals are working for the television stations. The governments achieved this simply enough, with massive changes in editorial staff. If a journalist didn't do as the government wanted, they were sacked and someone else brought in. It is crazy! If you give a typist a chance to become a journalist, he or she will accept any kind of order. That is normal. It is not realistic to expect typists to carry on the fight for the freedom of the press. This happened in Croatia, after Tudjman came to power. One interesting story (though not confirmed), has it that a letter was sent to 800 employees of Croatian TV telling them to stay at home because there was no room for them in the air raid shelters. After five days, they received another letter saying they were fired because they had not turned up for work! What a game! Someone is playing chess with them.

What has become of the first line of journalists in all this?

Some of the best went to Yutel; some went to the printed press, to *Vreme* for example; some of them are still employed. They try to file real stories but the authorities won't broadcast them. None of them came to Sarajevo TV, because our salaries are very small compared with Belgrade where the salaries are excellent, or in Croatia, especially. It is better in such circumstances to shut your mouth and to earn a living ... all of them have families to think about.

Can you imagine a situation in the near future where there will be an information vacuum to replace the political power vacuum?

Not a vacuum exactly, because half of Bosnia can receive Belgrade TV. But there will be a real propaganda barrage. But I think that the most dangerous situation will come after the war.

What about the press in Sarajevo? Has that already divided into nationalist camps?

No, it is free. Of course, you have a political party press, but that is normal. Those papers do not dominate the scene. The dailies are financially independent, but I don't know what will happen to them now. I believe that their situation is very bad because it isn't possible to sell copies throughout the republic. Because travel is so difficult. I think that they are almost without income. In this, the papers are like television - who will pay them now?

All these stories are examples of attempts by the political parties to establish censorship. It is worse than under Communism. Of course I remember a better time of Communism, though only during the last few years.

Is this because the type of censorship which has been applied to Sarajevo TV has been an attempt to put the media to war?

I am absolutely sure that each man killed during the civil war in Yugoslavia was in a sense already killed by the news department of Belgrade and Zagreb TV. Before the war each was dead in mind if not in body.

You are talking about the way in which people were programmed by the national propaganda which was fed to them by the major TV stations?

Exactly. I heard a speaker on Croatian TV who named the pilots who were bombarding Croatian towns. He not only gave their names, but also their home addresses, their car numbers, details of where their womenfolk were working, in which school their children were studying. It was terrible - practically a call for a lynching!

So, something worse than censorship has occurred. The media instead of being a victim of oppression has taken an active role in silencing the enemies of governments.

It is the worst possible situation. Here, at the European Institute for the Media, I will try to research the role of the media in the disputes and wars which result from political and ethnic tensions. I am sure that without a media war, wars in the world would spill less blood.

All this started in Yugoslavia many years ago under Communism. The position of viewers and readers in Croatia is worse than that of those in Serbia because, practically speaking, they have only one newspaper, the weekly *Danas*. They have no *Vreme* or *Borba* [independent papers in Belgrade], nor do they have a strong political opposition. During all the years under Communism, Belgrade was the centre of liberation, of freedom. During those times, I remember going to Belgrade to find a book that was banned as anti-Communist propaganda, and you could always find it there. It was much more difficult to find these things in Sarajevo, because the Communist regime was especially hardline in Bosnia.

How are relations with other journalists in Yugoslavia?

Officially, our relations are really very bad, although Serbian and Croatian TV have said nothing publicly either way, either for or against us. Privately, in restaurants, their journalists passed on information, supported us and warned us of dangers. They wanted us to stay on the stage, although as I see it now, without a free television in Belgrade, for example, it is impossible to support a free television in Bosnia. Because Belgrade is the capital, and it has the most intellectual energy in the region, I am absolutely sure that when Belgrade begins to be free, freedom will follow in all the former Yugoslav republics.

The Last Albanian Waiter

Robert Elsie

As an Albania specialist, I always enjoy returning to Prishtina in the southern Yugoslav province of Kosovo. It is not the exciting culture shock of Tirana, and possesses none of the beauty and refinement of a European capital, but it does have an atmosphere and charm of its own, in a run-down sort of way.

The Grand Hotel of Prishtina has seen better days. The economic collapse of Kosovo is visible in every corner of the building, which was once the architectural pride of a new Yugoslavia. Five neon stars still shine from the rooftop, although at least four of them should have been removed many years ago. But no matter. I have always felt at home here, and in the venerable Hotel Bozhur.

The Grand Hotel was strangely quiet on my arrival after a six-hour bus ride from ugly Belgrade. My delight, at long last, at being able to speak Albanian was dampened at the reception desk by a polite but quite definitely Serbian '*molim*?' [Can I help you?] We settled on English.

After a few hours in Prishtina, it all became painfully evident. What I had heard at home in Germany was true. Virtually all the Albanian staff at the hotel had indeed been fired and replaced by Serbs. And not only at the hotel: 115,000 Albanians were out on the street in less than a year after the Serbian government seized power in what had been the Autonomous Region of Kosovo. Should I ask why at the reception desk? Would the question be considered provocative or simply naïve? Should I stay at the Grand at all or look for another hotel? The Bozhur would no doubt be the same and I could not envisage a smoky Albanian *han* [inn] in private ownership in downtown Prishtina. 'You are a foreigner,' I reminded myself. 'Do not meddle in Balkan politics on your first day in Yugoslavia.'

The hotel lobby was serene: black leather sofas, plastic plants, a few people drinking at the bar and a businessman reading a newspaper in

Vol. 21, no. 9, 1992

Cyrillic characters. Much like the lobby of any big hotel. 'Do they all know?' I wondered. 'And if they do, what do they think?' Everything looked so normal. I felt uneasy and decided to go out for a walk to gather my thoughts.

In contrast to the external appearance of the building and its surroundings, the restaurant of the Grand has managed to retain something of its original dignity. Almost romantic lighting, table flowers, even a pianist playing 'Strangers in the Night'. Individuals, couples and small groups of well-dressed patrons wining and dining. I could have been out for dinner in Germany or the USA.

I insisted on using Albanian to order my meal and a glass of red Kosovo wine, and managed to make myself understood. As I sat listening to the lull of the music and studying the faces of the guests, it suddenly dawned on me that everyone in the room was speaking Serbian. There was not a single Albanian patron in the restaurant, or anywhere else in the hotel. Were the Albanians, who make up 92% of the population of Kosovo, no longer allowed into their own hotel? Were they perhaps boycotting it? I did not know. My immediate reaction was frustration, fury and helplessness. I would not have patronised a restaurant which refused to cater to Blacks or Jews. By this time, I was so upset that I could not eat the meal placed in front of me. This was, after all, 1992, not 1935.

The spectre of Nazi Germany arose before me as I watched the guests laughing, joking and enjoying their meals, seemingly oblivious to the injustice. I pictured myself in the 1930s in an elegant restaurant in Berlin. Music, fashionable patrons dining by candlelight without a care in the world in a hotel recently made *judenfrei* [free of Jews].

The next evening I was served by an Albanian-speaking waiter, the last one. Fatmir was in his mid-twenties and had worked at the restaurant of the Grand Hotel for several years. While the other waiters were busy in the kitchen for a moment I asked him how it had all taken place and why. 'Almost all the Albanians have been thrown out,' he whispered. 'What can we do? They are hiring Serbs with no qualifications at all. Now they have introduced new uniforms with the Serbian cross on them.' 'And what will you do?' I asked. 'We are Muslims,' he shrugged, giving an embarrassed smile. 'We have a crescent and a star, you know, but not a cross. The Orthodox, the Serbs, have the cross. But perhaps they won't do it after all. They seem to change the regulations daily.' It was at this point, when I was filled with a mixture of indignation and confusion, that my eyes fixed upon the crosses which had been discreetly embroidered into the waiters' jackets; I had noticed the cross for the first time on nationalist posters in Belgrade and later seen it sprayed black on walls and in the hotel elevator.

Since the Serbian government seized power in mid-1990, the population of Kosovo has been cast into limbo to starve in what is already the poorhouse of the European continent. Only those families who have a relative abroad, in Germany or Switzerland, can survive. A few of the 115,000 victims of power politics had the consolation of a polite lie that they were redundant; but most of them were told the truth, 'You are Albanian'.

One afternoon I talked to Professor Zenel Kelmendi, a leading Kosovo surgeon. After 27 years' teaching at the Faculty of Medicine, he was dragged out of the university building one morning in August 1990 in handcuffs. What did his Serbian colleagues, with whom he had worked for so many years in the same operating theatre, say? 'You don't know Kosovo,' he replied. 'They were the ones who called the militia.'

Virtually all the Albanian hospital staff have now been replaced by Serbs, exceptions being made only in cases where no qualified replacement could be found. In the maternity ward in Prishtina, where 40–50 children used to be born every day, only three to five women have dared give birth this year.

I also learned that in the first six months of 1991, Albanian schoolteachers had received no salaries. Their Serbian colleagues, who often teach in the same school buildings, have had their salaries doubled and trebled during this period. The excuse is 'parity with Serbian teachers in Belgrade', where wages are higher. Why do the Albanian teachers continue working? 'If we don't, they will close down the school. That's what they're aiming at', a high school teacher from Prizren told me.

Serbs and Albanians have been living together on the 'Plain of the Blackbirds' for centuries, and history has made them enemies as it has of the Jews and Arabs in Israel, and the Protestants and Catholics in Northern Ireland. After the final collapse of the Ottoman Empire in World War I, Serbia was awarded Kosovo, which it had coveted for centuries as the cradle of Serbian civilisation. The inclusion of the province in the Kingdom of the Serbs, Croats and Slovenes left almost half the Albanian population outside their Albanian homeland.

The Kosovo Albanians, who now make up the second largest language community in Yugoslavia (after Serbo-Croatian), did not fare much better under their Serbian rulers than they had under the Sultans. Hundreds of thousands of Albanians were forcibly expelled to Turkey up to 1960 under the pretext that they were Turks; Serbian colonists settled the newly vacated farmlands. The memorandum of the 'Expulsion of the Albanians' and the colonisation of Kosovo, prepared by noted Serbian historian Vasa Čubrilović (1897–1990) and presented to the Belgrade government on 7 March 1937, reads like a watered-down version of the minutes of the Wannsee Conference [in Germany] of 1942.

The systematic persecution of the Albanians in early post-war Yugoslavia was finally ended by the overthrow of Tito's Vice-President, Aleksandar Ranković (1909–1983), in July 1966. Yugoslav–Albanian relations improved in the wake of the Soviet invasion of Czechoslovakia in 1968 and full diplomatic ties between the two countries were established in February 1971. This brought about a political thaw for the Kosovo Albanians. In 1968, they had won the right to fly their national flag, and in November 1969 the University of Prishtina, the only Albanian-language institution of higher education in Yugoslavia, was opened. Full cultural autonomy was first achieved after much delay under the 1974 Yugoslav Constitution.

The semblance of autonomy and freedom which the Albanians enjoyed in the 1970s was brought to an abrupt end in 1981. The popular demand for republic status and equality with the other peoples of the Yugoslav federation, a demand supported by over 90% of the population of Kosovo, was met with tanks and automatic rifles.

Throughout the 1980s, the political and economic situation in the province deteriorated and inter-communal relations took a drastic turn for the worse. It was a harbinger of what was to come for all of Yugoslavia in the 1990s. The Serbian military invasion of Kosovo in the summer of 1990 brought the province to the verge of civil war. The elected parliament and government of Kosovo were deposed, the only Albanian-language daily newspaper, *Rilindja*, banned, and all Albanian-language radio and television broadcasting shut down. Since them, 'emergency legislation' has facilitated the direct takeover of all Kosovo's industry and the firing not only of Albanian management but of all employees of the 'inferior race'. Nowhere since the fall of Nicolae Ceausescu in Romania have human rights in Europe been so flagrantly and so systematically violated as in Kosovo.

Fatmir, the last Albanian waiter at the Grand Hotel, disappeared, no doubt to join the swelling ranks of hungry and angry young Albanians. On my last day in Prishtina I ventured to ask the other waiters what had become of him. 'He is on his holidays,' one of them answered with a smile.

Former Yugoslavia: Embargo on People

Svetlana Slapšak

Serbia and Montenegro are under UN boycott. The new states like Croatia and Slovenia, not to mention the dying Bosnia-Hercegovina, are still under different forms of arms embargo, but this is a field in which everybody seems to manage beautifully. It is the breaking of the cultural embargo that agitates the state intellectual *nomenklatura* in Croatia and Slovenia.

There are no Serbian periodicals to be found in Croatia, and few in Slovenia: Serbian books are silently disappearing from the shelves in libraries and bookshops; the Croatian Minister of Culture proclaimed that non-Croats should not teach Croatian in schools. Most of the boycott imposed on culture between these countries that used to form an area of intense cultural communication, is simply a personal matter of competition, cheap vengeance, triumphalism and the settling of old accounts. There is no need to compete any more, 'ours' is the best, the rest are justly punished. Yet there are voices in Slovenia which boast of a free press, despite this new trend.

Nationalists from different parts agree on many points: the pacifists, Yugoslav communications, and new networks among intellectuals should be stopped. Instead of attracting émigré academics and artists, the finest and most productive élite from the rest of Yugoslavia, after an initial period of openness liberal Slovenia imposed a growing set of rules and conditions against settling in Slovenia.

I have been married to a Slovenian for 17 years; I used to commute between the main cities in former Yugoslavia – teaching in Zagreb and Ljubljana, publishing in Beograd and Novi Sad, working on joint projects in Sarajevo and Dubrovnik. During the socialist regime, this was one of the ways of escaping local censorship and control. Under no conditions am I now allowed to enter Croatia, to see my friends, my

Vol. 22, no. 4, 1993

editor and my colleagues for example, or to spend time in my mother's summer house on the Adriatic coast. My teaching of Serbian literature was no longer required and my contract at the Department of Slavonic Languages and Literature in Ljubljana was not renewed after a series of political attacks and denunciations in a leading daily in Slovenia, by, among others, my colleague from the department. No one seems to be moved by the fact that Serbian literature is now hardly heard of from the Chair that has 'Serbian' in its official title.

All the new states of former Yugoslavia systematically break the boycott when it comes to weapons, oil and other goods; but they observe it to the letter when it comes to human rights (the right to communicate, for example) and culture.

Being a Serb, I do my best to denounce Serbian responsibility for starting the war and causing most of the destruction; to blame Serbian policy and to demand public repentance for crimes against other nations, like Albanians, Croats and Muslims, and for the destruction and dispersal of their own nation. I demand practical measures including prosecution of war criminals. And I acknowledge the difficulty of being a Serb in a time like this, and the limitations the international measures impose upon me. The crucial question for every intellectual and every citizen - Serbian, Slovenian, European or other - will be whether, and to what degree, the citizen should obey state-imposed restrictive measures. Merchants will break measures secretly; intellectuals, by definition, openly.

An embargo encourages racism and restrictions on human rights; it prevents certain forms of cultural exchange.

But there is one aspect of the embargo which is the responsibility of the nations that imposed it: it is the embargo on people.

It will take years before the new states become sympathetic to the multicultural type of education and living which was the characteristic of former Yugoslavia. It will be a decade, at least, before educational systems capable of forming new, multicultural and tolerant young academics, free of destructive ideology, nationalism and stereotypical thinking develop in the new states. More young people will try to get out of the former Yugoslavia and live a different kind of life.

There are no quick and easy solutions. The war will go on; eventually it will become less widespread, maybe less bloody; maybe some stability will return; maybe life will be possible in some corners of the former Yugoslavia. But the question now is how to enable young people from Yugoslavia to survive abroad. This is the only way of fighting the embargo and its stupidity.

Keep these children here. They are well educated; they are impregnated with Western culture and consumerism, sometimes in an exaggerated way. The schooling system of the former Yugoslavia was overbearing and ideological, but ideology is the first thing they forget; and they should be helped to forget the nationalist rage which they witnessed. They represent the future of the region, the only possibility for tolerance and peaceful development. Young people who do not want to be involved in war or nationalist clashes stand no chance within most of the new states of former Yugoslavia. But those who are here can be helped. Be tolerant and generous toward Yugoslavs of all nations; treat them equally with other foreigners and migrants; do not deny them the right of education and information, of culture and communication; do not impose an internal embargo on them.

Some may stay forever; with help, others could build a new, tolerant society in any one of the countries of former Yugoslavia.

Goodnight, Croatian Writers

Dubravka Ugrešić

Translated by Celia Hawkesworth

'Goodnight, Croatian fighters, wherever you may be' is repeated at the end of all evening news broadcasts on Croatian television. This message to the defenders of Croatia came into use in peak viewing time more than a year ago and is still in use today.

The life of a Croatian writer in these difficult times is not easy. When the fundamental coordinates of everyday reality have become staying alive and surviving, the Croatian writer's situation is somewhat more complex. He would also like to write - and writing, to put it as its simplest, means thinking. Why is this so hard for some Croatian writers, in particular for the one who concerns us here?

Our Croatian writer is sitting today over a piece of blank white paper as though it were a minefield. Many of his colleagues are on the other side of the field, they are waving to him, calling kindly to him: 'Come over,' they say, 'it isn't difficult.' Our writer shakes his head doubtfully; some of his colleagues did not make it, others barely did. Some are standing on the edge, not daring to cross. Others again cross, and have the decency to leave markers after them: BEWARE OF THE MINES! The unwritten pages of white paper lie before our writer and it seems as though everything were teeming with warnings: there are little red 'stop' signs everywhere; narrow green crossings; amber lights urging caution; black death's heads ...

Our Croatian writer finds himself in a completely new world of communications brought about by the new and terrible reality of war. Sometimes it seems to him that the task of sending artistic messages has been reduced to the mere process of distinguishing noises, removing barriers, to a painful endeavour to explain what he has, in any case, already said. It seems that a small text of a few pages demands twice as many explanatory footnotes. His text is no longer understood as it was before: something gets in the way, the words no longer mean what they used to, each one rebounds in his face.

It seems to our writer that this is because things can no longer be implied, and they cannot be implied because there is no longer a common code, or that such a code has been established and become common to others, but not to him.

Further, it seems to him that this is because the world *he* knew, for better or worse, has fallen apart leaving everything in pieces. That is why his, the writer's, perspective has been called into question; it too is a victim of the chaos of war. That is why it seems to the writer that he no longer recognises the orientation of those he is addressing. They have changed, but he has not; or he has and they have not. In any case, in the very nature of things, his message is certainly read differently by those in the trenches, those on one side and those on the other, those without a roof and those with a roof over their heads, those who are hungry and those who have enough to eat, those who have experienced the new-style concentration camps and those who have only seen pictures of war on television.

In this new communications order our writer is called upon to build into his text the clear signals which his readers expect: they too want to find their way through the text, read it from the 'right' angle.

The starting signal - which in the present situation determines the text - is the writer's origin. If he is a Croat he will be condemned but forgiven for a critical stance towards the new-style reality. He is 'one of us' after all, thinks the reading public contentedly. If he is a Serb, a Croatian Serb, of course he will never be forgiven - for a long time he will simply not be forgiven for being a Serb - but at least it will be perfectly clear which way the wind is blowing. If no one knows who he is, he will be publicly labelled: someone will know, or think he knows - no distinction is made between 'thinking' and 'knowing'.

In the map of the world according to blood group, the fundamental marker for every public act, for an ordinary 'Good morning' to a neighbour, is the Holy Blood Group. In a system of generally induced paranoia, one's national origin is the essential fact, the measure of all things. It determines perspective, it is the most fundamental assumption in the relation between sender and recipient. The first demand made of the writer and his text is the clear and public expression of that primary assumption. For fear of not being understood, in the desire to be understood no matter what, the writer makes his first signal. The message now slips differently along the channel of communication. We understand one another, we belong, even when we don't understand one another; or we don't belong, even when we do understand one another.

Another exceptionally important signal in understanding the text – or even that ordinary 'Good morning' to a neighbour – is the social origin of the writer, or at least his implicit or explicit adherence to various political options.

Yugo-nostalgia is one of the most loaded signals of political qualification in a paranoid communications system. It is more loaded than many other labels in use today, such as *chetnik*, nationally colour-blind person, Commie, Great Serb and the like. This little term conceals many dangerous things. It conceals a perfidious doubt in the new system; the old one, the Commie one, was better. Doubt in the new system is a hostile act against the new state, questioning its values, implying condemnation of the war, accepting the option that our enemies are also people. It also implies subscribing to Communism and the whole ideological package it carried with it. But, most of all, nostalgia is dangerous because it encourages remembering. In the newly-established reality, everything starts again from scratch. And to start from scratch, everything that came before must be forgotten.

That is why the writer more or less joyfully builds additional signals into his text. They are clear or cryptic, depending on his background and style, but essential if the text is to reach its audience in clear. Hence, I am not a 'Yugo-nostalgic', I am not in favour of 'the prison of nations'; I was not a 'Communist', or I was, but only for a short time; or I was, but I always had a low opinion of them. And so on.

Just as ordinary people wear badges which will smooth communication with others and put things in their proper place – crosses round necks, stickers with the Croatian coat-of-arms on the windows of flats, on cars – a similar system of signals, simple and comprehensible to all, is also expected of the writer. He is the sender of messages and his message must reach the recipient without hindrance.

But the recipient today no longer seems to be the reading public but the people. And our writer, like it or not, suddenly finds himself in the completely new situation of sending messages to the people! He becomes, by chance or intention, like it or not, a writer of the people. And what exactly that is our writer doesn't know, just as he doesn't know exactly what 'the people' is. His literary memories search and strain, connecting that whole vague complex with 'popular' novels, with the nineteenth-century, with the theory of 'commission', with patriotism, with 'the role of the intellectual' in difficult times. And why is 'the people' suddenly doing the commissioning, grumbles the writer, when there are so few books in any case, and when 'the people' are not too concerned that there are so few, when culture in these unhappy times is in any case reduced to the level of communication of hearsay!

Our writer knows that the war has changed everything: no one is the same any more; even his own reality, his own norms, have vanished. In their place a new reality is coming into being before his eyes: new values are being established, a new world is being built into which life will be breathed once it is named.

The business of building begins with naming. This is a house; this is the homeland; this is black; this is white. Our writer is confused. He humbly recalls that naming is the work of God. He is surprised by this passion for naming; it appears to be intended to convince oneself and others of the actual existence of the new reality. It is only in firm coordinates, in a clear and named world, that we shall not be lost, not threatened by the chaos of madness, ambiguity, multiple truths. Because we are at the beginning, we need ONE truth.

An alarm bell rings in our writer's head: his work, that of a writer, is not, and cannot be, adherence to one truth. But in the new relationship between him and his audience, there is room for only ONE truth - or what has been proclaimed the truth. Everything else is a lie.

Our writer finds himself in a new communicative situation akin to that of the photographic, in which, like a double exposure, things overlap even within himself: he no longer knows where the private person ends and the writer begins, where the boundaries between his heart and his mind lie. In this fragmented state, he is being asked to provide something he does not understand and that is beyond his strength: he is being asked to be the spokesman of his people, the loudspeaker and conveyor of 'correct' political truths, a soothsayer and a leader, a popular singer and healer, examiner of the 'national being' and its spiritual renovator.

Our writer is disconcerted, inner alarm bells ring wildly in him, the memory of his 'genetic' password, the password of *his* 'people', the writer's people. He remembers decades, centuries, times filled with the sweet appeal of national community and bitter rejection. He recalls the consequences of agreeing to roles; remembers the history of careers, the words, those before and those after, spoken by the same lips, written by the same pens; recalls both the shameful and the glorious moments from the general history of the writer's craft.

Our writer is a Croatian citizen: he has a heart connected to the mega-bloodstream of general suffering. His world is split in two, reality unfolds before his eyes like a grotesque nightmare. One half of him, the writer in our writer, resists the proposed strategies: naming terrorism by forgetting; the new utopia projected on the ruins of the old; unambiguous language; mental florets which come to life in the consciousness like new blades of grass. All this has been done already, not so long ago; he has learned about it from the history of the link between culture and politics. The other half, the citizen in our writer, is torn apart by the numerous miseries of his countrymen, his present and that former country. How can he separate them, and how connect them? How go on?

In his search for answers, our writer turns to his colleagues: writers, journalists, intellectuals. Of those who still make their voices heard these days, his colleagues, the majority of them, have adapted. They have accepted the codes of behaviour of a changed communications order and a newly-established reality: they have preserved the old mechanisms of their guild life. With little artistic or moral difficulty they reproduce the same language, the same mental and linguistic formulae, the same articulation of the unhappy reality which has affected everyone equally. From the outside, they appear to be innocently and contentedly submerged in the warm, smoke-filled, sweet collectivity. It is as though they have no inkling that what is in store for them is the destiny they have already lived through – as though a benevolent amnesia had wiped out all their memory.

Our writer sees his colleagues arguing, with a zeal that sometimes surprises themselves, over what needs to be done: should the greatest classic writer of Croatian literature be published in full, or should his political essays be omitted, particularly the ones dealing with Yugoslavism (is it the right political moment?); should such a writer be published at all? He watches his colleagues zealously discussing whether another colleague (who has in any case been getting up their collective nose for some time) should be destroyed. He sees them forget that they used to be guided by one set of principles and now subscribe to another, that this is what used to be done to them. His colleagues discuss things in corridors, hatch plots in almost non-existent editorial boards, accuse one another, the true believers accusing the heretical.

In the newly-established and paranoid communications order, in their everyday life, his colleagues are suddenly waging invisible wars for the right way, the right idea. They are suddenly surrounded by a self-styled army of little patriot-informers who slip them reports about the antipatriotic behaviour of this or that colleague. What is at stake is what is right, what is at stake are sincere patriotic feelings and all methods are permissible. Forget methods: this is being done in the name of the homeland, which is in danger. Without noticing it, his colleagues are slowly becoming policemen, courtiers who take the collective patriotic pulse. With the serious, grey mask of true believers, unconsciously copied from their predecessors, on their faces, his colleagues are turning themselves into executives. In collective systems which confirm their vitality simply by hunting down individuals, by collective lynching, it is a logical assumption that one day the executioners will become the victims. And *vice versa*. Because they, the vital ones, leap up more swiftly than maize from popcorn machines. And while his colleagues raise their spear-pens with holy, dedicated concentration and aim them at their enemies, while they click their carefully sharpened censor's scissors (temporary only: it is not the right moment), convinced that they are doing it for the first time (it's our lives, our freedom, our future that are at stake), behind their backs rises the supple shadow of a younger and more skilful hunter.

I, too, the author of this text, am a Croatian writer. I have no alternative, it was not my decision. But as I write on these white sheets of paper, I have at least decided not to take note of labels. I am prepared for the explosive consequences; I am not complaining. Everyone chooses his path. Of course, I allow that in these unhappy times everyone, from the ordinary citizen to the State President, from the arms smuggler to the fighter, believes that he has the right to expect the writer to fulfil his duty to the homeland, to be the spokesman of the people, to be a loyal son (where are the daughters?) of his Croatian homeland, that he declare his love for it, out loud, clearly and publicly. But I shall allow myself to refuse such demands.

From the history of my people, this writer's people, I have learned what misfortunes result from confusing roles: for the writers themselves, for their people, for freedom of speech, for literature itself. Therefore, as a writer I shall not defend the barricades of my homeland. I prefer to stroll along the barricade of literature or sit awhile on the barricade of freedom of speech.

I am still not sure whether I should quite believe Osip Mandelstam, who considered that the writer was 'a parrot in the deepest sense of the word'. 'A parrot does not belong to any time,' says Mandelstam, 'it does not distinguish day from night. If it bores its owner, the latter will cover it up with a black cloth, and that becomes a surrogate of night for literature.' I am equally not sure whether it has become completely dark here yet. But, just in case, goodnight, Croatian writers, wherever we may be.

Former Yugoslavia: Close-up of Death

Slavenka Drakulić

They say that a little girl, AM, was killed while eating a Ramadan-pie. It seems that it happened like this: it was morning at the end of February, bright and chilly. You ask yourself how that woman, her mother, made the pie in Sarajevo, ten months after the beginning of the war? What flour did she use, what oil, what did she fill it with? She must have baked it the night before – but then again, how? There is no electricity, or there is, but only sometimes. Or did she do it on an open fire? But there is no wood: all the trees in the city have been cut long ago ... In any case, still half-asleep, the two-and-a-half-year-old girl had been sitting at the table, eating breakfast. At that moment, she heard the sound of shelling. Maybe she was frightened by it, so she ran to her mother – but maybe not. The sound of shelling is normal around here. No, she couldn't have heard that sound, they say that those who get hit have no time to hear anything, they have no time to get frightened at all. A shell went through the roof of their house and landed in the kitchen. The girl fell to the floor. It all happened with lightning speed and she was dead before her parents or her grandfather had time to understand what was happening. By the time her father took her in his hands and looked for help, it was all over.

Then – then a TV camera arrives on the scene. Judging by certain details this happened perhaps only one or two hours after the shelling. We see the small kitchen already without the little girl, the floor is covered with brick and plaster debris, scattered shoes, her little boots. The TV camera zooms in on the roof, on the hole left by a shell, as sky and cold descend into the kitchen through it. The father is sitting with his arms on the table, crying. The camera shoots a close-up of his blue eyes and his tears – in fact it looks as if he is crying on camera – so that

Vol. 22, no. 7, 1993

we, the television spectators, can be sure that his tears are real, that he really cried, the little one's father. He has on a white pullover made of a rough peasant's wool. You do not usually sit in your kitchen dressed warmly like that, but what do we know about the kind of cold that he is suffering from at this moment? From his eyes, the camera moves to that pullover so that we can see a red stain on it, left where he held his girl when he picked her up from the floor - when it was already too late. The blood is not dry yet, the stain is bright red, it looks fresh. I know that raw, handspun wool that his pullover was made with. I can feel it under my fingers. It takes forever to dry, soaked blood stays wet a long time ... Looking at this blood is nauseating. Still the camera returns to it several times. This is unnecessary, but you have no defence from those kinds of pictures - and there is no one to tell how useless it is.

Now we are in the hospital, this is the first time we see the mother, too. The reporter's voice explains that she has been wounded in her stomach. Then he (or was it she?) says something absolutely too much, too much in the moment of despair of the woman whose child has just died. The voice says that the young woman probably will not be able to have any more children. She lies on a kind of stretcher, covering her face with her hands. She sobs, her voice comes out as if broken in pieces. The father comes in, in his white pullover with the red stain, and embraces her. It is clear that they meet there for the first time after the little one's death, in a hospital room. On camera - for the first time. The mother lets out something, in some other setting you could probably call it a cry, a howl. But now it is only a sound of emptiness; with that sound the woman tells her husband she has just lost everything. This is the end, this has to be the end. The camera can't go any further than the inhuman suffering of the mother who has lost her child. Neither we, the television spectators, nor the people that we do not see who are standing behind camera - a reporter, a cameraman, a soundman - can stand all this any longer. This has to stop, I repeat to myself while the camera rolls on. I don't believe my eyes, but that's how it is: now we are looking at a white sheet with red spots. We have already forbidden this, we recognise that same sign. Red on white, that's the sign of her death. My God, how very bright her blood is, I think, while my whole being cries: enough, enough, enough. I don't want the camera to enter under that cover hiding her small body. But someone's hand surpasses my thoughts and lifts the white sheet. Her face, we see her face. Her small deformed face, no longer human, framed by untidy tufts of her black hair. Her half-closed eyes. We see a close-up of death. Then cut. The funeral. People talking, an off-screen voice, the father, the grandfather, a little coffin in the shallow, frozen ground. The report is finished. It has lasted a total of three minutes ...

A moment later, we become aware that the TV broadcast that we have just seen is the tragedy of one family filmed only a couple of hours after they have lost their child, and that *the hole tragedy has happened on camera*. The only thing we have not witnessed is the moment of death of the two-and-a-half-year-old AM. (A take from outside, when the shell hits the roof. Then, from inside, a scene where the girl falls from her chair, in slow motion, as if she's flying. A piece of pie drops from her hand and rolls on the ground. That's it! The reporter is pleased.) Well, why not? By now, we too, the public, are mature enough to stand it, all in the name of documentation, which we obviously believe in. That is the only thing we have not seen on our TV screens so far.

We have already seen beheaded corpses being eaten by pigs and dogs. Eyes gouged out, scattered bodily parts that do not belong to anyone, anything. Skeletons and half-rotten skulls, children without legs, babies killed by sniper fire. A 12-year-old rape victim talking about it on camera.

Day after day. Death in Bosnia has been more and more well-documented. In 10 months, Sarajevo has been hit by 800,000 shells. In the city, 80,000 kids are imprisoned - that makes it the biggest children's prison in the world. Five thousand of them were killed or simply died. The rest await hunger and long death, slow death. Fifty years ago this is how Jews suffered. Now it's the Muslims' turn. Do you remember Auschwitz? Really, does anyone remember Anne Frank? Oh yes, we do remember it all and, because of that memory, we have the idea that everything has to be carefully documented, so that shameful history can never be repeated. And yet, here they are. Generations have learned about concentration camps at school, about factories of death; generations whose parents swear that it could never happen again - at least not in Europe - precisely because of the living memory of the recent past. *They* are fighting this war. What, then, has all that documentation changed? And what is being changed now, by the conscious, precise bookkeeping of death that is happening in our lives, in our living rooms, while we watch transmissions of the dying in Sarajevo? The little girl's death is only one horror out of many, each of which prepares us for something even worse.

The biggest change has happened within ourselves, the audience, spectators, public. We have started to believe in our role in this casting: that it is possible to play the public. As if the war is theatre. Slowly, and without our noticing it, something has crept into us, a kind of hardness, an inability to see the truth – the signs of our own dying, the close-up of the girl's dead face was one scene too much. Because it was senseless. The feeling that for the first time it is possible to watch war from so near in its most macabre details, makes sense only if, because of that, something can change for the better. But nothing changes. Therefore, this kind of documentation is turning into a perversion, into a pornography of dying.

Bosnia on My Mind

Salman Rushdie

It is, in spite of some signs that things may be improving, still impossibly hard to make any sort of statement at all about the situation in Bosnia-Hercegovina. It is possible to read that it was the threat of air strikes that persuaded the Serbs to withdraw their heavy artillery from positions above and around Sarajevo, that it was the Russians who persuaded them, that in fact the Serbs relocated their tanks in civilian areas where air strikes against them would not be possible and from which they could attack Sarajevo just as easily as before, that the Russians and Greeks are backing Nato, that the Russians and Greeks, in defiance of Nato are ganging up with their Orthodox allies the Serbs to ensure the success of Serbian strategy, that now that the Bosnian Croats under Tudjman are willing to form a federation with the 'Muslims' this may provide the basis for a deal with the Bosnian Serbs to preserve some sort of unified state of Bosnia-Hercegovina, that the partition of Bosnia into three mini-states is inevitable and the 'Muslims' must be forced to accept it, that black is white and yes is no and down is up and stop is go and it remains only to join the demented old codgers in James Fenton's *Ballad of the Shrieking Man* and sing:

Tramps are mad
And truth is mad
And so are trees and trunks and tracks.
The horror maps have played us true.
The horror moon that slits the clouds
The gun
The goon
The burly sacks
The purple waistcoats of the natterjacks
Have done their bit as you can see
To prise the madness from our sanity.

Vol. 23, nos. 1/2, 1994

It will not do, however, this codger-fashion despair. It will not do to decide, in the saloon bars of our hearts, that they have hated each other for millennia over there, they have been wanting to slaughter each other for centuries, and now the goblins are out of the bottle, the warlords are standing at their roadblocks, let them get on with it. Equally unsatisfactory is the cleaned-up, Newspeak version of the above, which says the Situation Is Complex and there are No Easy Answers and do we really want Our Boys to be embroiled forever in What Is, After All, A Civil War?

It will not do because there is still such a thing as truth, however much the war and the world's politicians may have shredded it. And that truth, for me, lies in the nature and meaning of the city of Sarajevo, where, as Susan Sontag has said, the twentieth century began, and where, with terrible symmetry, it is ending.

I have never been to Sarajevo, but I feel that I belong to it, in a way. I am proud to be an honorary member of the PEN club of ex-Yugoslavian writers, and I hope they will not think me presumptuous if I say that as a result of this newly-forged connection I, too, can claim to be, in some sense, an exile from Sarajevo, even though it is a city I do not know.

There is a Sarajevo of the mind, an imagined Sarajevo whose ruination and torment exiles us all. That Sarajevo represents something like an ideal; a city in which the values of pluralism, tolerance and coexistence have created a unique and resilient culture. In that Sarajevo there actually exists that secularist Islam for which so many people are fighting elsewhere in the world. The people of that Sarajevo do not define themselves by faith or tribe, but simply, and honourably, as citizens.

If that city is lost, then we are all its refugees. If the culture of Sarajevo dies, then we are all its orphans.

Sarajevo's truth (as opposed to the saloon-bar version) is that the different communities have not been hating each other since the dawn of time, but have been good neighbours, schoolfriends, work-mates and lovers; that in this city miscegenation and intermarriage have been not the exception, but the norm. (And if they were bad neighbours, enemies at school, and rivals at work, and if their marriages failed, it was for the ordinary human reasons of personality and affinity, rather than the 'cleansing' evils of nationalism.)

Sarajevo's truth (as opposed to the Newspeak version) is that the city has been the scene not of a civil war but of a war of aggression by the Serbs; that if the Serbs do once and for all cease their bombardments, it will be because they have already seized 'their' quarter of the city, forcing a *de facto* partition on what should have remained united; and that the outside world seems bent on imposing on this hybrid city the 'logic', the 'reality', of ethnicity, and on giving the aggressor the spoils of war.

Sarajevo's truth is that its citizens, who reject definition by religion or confession, who wish to be simply Bosnians, have for their pains been labelled by the outside world as 'Muslims'. It is instructive to imagine how things might have gone in former Yugoslavia if the Bosnians had been Christians and the Serbs had been Muslims, even Muslims 'in name only'. Would Europe have supported a 'Serbian Muslim' carve-up of the defunct state? It's only a guess, but I guess that it would not. Which being true, it must also be true that the 'Muslim' tag is part of the reason for Europe's indifference to Sarajevo's fate.

I have not been to Sarajevo – I have wanted to, but it has thus far proved impossible to arrange – but I have in recent months met three of its many extraordinary citizens: Zdravko Grebo, of the radio station that is the city's voice and conscience, Radio Zid; Haris Pasovic, a man bursting with projects, the man who brought about last year's Sarajevo Film Festival – and what an achievement, to stage a festival of over a hundred movies in the midst of such a war!; and Kemal Kurspahic, editor of Sarajevo's battling newspaper *Oslobodjenje*. They taught me a further, simple truth: that to define the people of besieged Sarajevo simply as entities in need of basic supplies would be to visit upon them a second privation: by reducing them to mere statistical victimhood, it would deny them their personalities, their individuality, their idiosyncrasies – in short, their humanity. When UNPROFOR officers limit the number of personal letters that can be carried in or out of the city; when permission for artists to visit the city is refused, as Pasovic can attest it has been; and when Western government spokesmen avow that culture is a luxury in wartime, this denial of Sarajevo's humanity is precisely the crime they are committing.

Grebo, limping from a wound, overwhelmingly impressive in his gentle dignity, seems to embody Sarajevo's spirit; Pasovic, its determination to keep its culture alive. Kurspahic is more melancholy, and a recent essay by his *Oslobodjenje* colleague Zlatko Disdarevic expresses the city's present mood. 'Sarajevo no longer believes anyone ... Sarajevo has seen everything there is to see till now, and it has felt the worst there is to feel upon its own skin. The results are obvious. Until six or seven months ago, every true Sarajevan needed at least an hour to walk from the Holiday Inn to the cathedral. You had to stop and say hello to so many people, to ask after everyone. Now that same distance takes just 15 minutes because no one stops. No one has anything left to ask anyone.' He tells of a boy whose father was killed, and who now says, 'Last night I dreamt about my father. I dreamt about him on purpose'. 'Somebody will one day have to watch out,' Dizdarevic warns, 'for boys from Sarajevo who dream about their murdered fathers on purpose.'

A city, a people, does not have an unlimited supply of spirit, not even this city, this people. Will the secular 'Muslims' of today become vengeful fundamentalists of tomorrow, dreaming on purpose of the dead? So far, by all accounts, hard-line Islamism has made amazingly small strides in the city, but that's just so far. Will Sarajevo be saved? Sarajevo scarcely believes it will. But the fact remains: that the fight for the survival of the unique culture of Sarajevo is a fight for what matters most to us about our own.

I have just seen a strange short film in which a man driving down the sniper-infested streets of Sarajevo repeats, over and over, like a mantra, my name. *Salman Rushdie, Salman Rushdie, Salman Rushdie; Salman Rushdie; Salman Rushdie, Salman Rushdie; Salman Rushdie, Salman Rushdie, Salman Rushdie.* Is he chanting it to remind him of his danger, or as a kind of spell to keep him safe? I hope it is the latter, and it is in that spirit of sympathetic magic that I have begun to murmur, under my breath, the name of this unknown city of which I declare myself to be an imaginary citizen:

Sarjevo, Sarajevo, Sarajevo,
Sarajevo,
Sarajevo, Sarajevo,
Sarajevo, Sarajevo, Sarajevo,
Sarajevo, Sarajevo,
Sarajevo

Post-German, Post-Jewish

Leszek Szaruga

Translated by Irena Maryniak

Borders are lines we see on maps, or checkpoints we cross when we travel by land. Our ancestors travelled by land, but borders meant less and national distinctions did not always provoke war.

'Post-German' was the term we used for everything the Germans had left behind: furniture, books, houses, streets. My childhood was full of it. I lived in a small village called Glebokie near Szczecin. A walk to the woods could yield a whole range of fascinating objects: mines, guns, pistols, grenades. They were my childhood toys. And it's extraordinary that in all the time we used them in our games, we incurred the loss of only a single arm.

My parents collected post-German artefacts: a 40-volume collection of the complete works of Goethe rescued from a peasant household just as it was about to be used for fuel; a Steinway grand serving as a bar-counter which the barman used to slide beer mugs to his guests; some nice modernist furniture which had somehow survived the war. It was all post-German.

My parents were 'pioneers'; this was what the official press called the inhabitants of the new western territories assigned to Poland. In official parlance they were the 'recovered lands', but the settlers called them the 'western wilds'. Most of the pioneers travelled or were deported here from *Kresy*, the lost territories of eastern Poland, lands east of the river Bug, reaching as far as the river Neman to the north and the river Dniester to the south. People of many different nationalities lived here: Ukrainians, Lithuanians, Belorussians, Russians, Poles, Jews, Germans, Hungarians, Romanian, Czechs and French. In Polish literature the region had been dubbed *Miedzymorze* or 'The Land between the Seas': the Baltic and the Black Sea. After World War II it ceased to exist.

Vol. 23, no. 3, 1994

Jerzy Stempowski once wrote: 'All these shades of nationality and language were in a semi-fluid state. Frequently, the sons of Poles were called Ukrainians, the sons of Germans and Frenchmen - Poles. In Odessa Greeks became Russians; Poles joined the 'Union of the Russian People'. Mixed marriages led to even greater ethnic complexities ... Nationality was not a racial issue, there was no inevitability about it. It was largely a matter of choice. And the choice was not limited to language. In the Dniester valley, which bore the vestiges of so many great civilisations, every language carried different historical, religious and social traditions, each had a specific ethical system, developed by centuries of triumph and disaster, aspiration and debate.'

Reading this, I understood why my own father, who was born in Odessa, felt that it was equally important that his lineage was Lithuanian and that his mother was Greek. At home they spoke Russian, though the language was neither my grandfather's nor my grandmother's. After leaving the Soviet Union, the family settled in Gdynia. My father was of mixed parentage, which made him a Pole. After almost five years imprisonment in a German POW camp, he came to Szczecin with his new Kaszub bride from Gdansk. They both spoke excellent German and later translated German literature, including Thomas Mann's *Doctor Faustus*. They were cast ashore in Szczecin by political circumstance. Nor were they alone. It was here that people with 'inconvenient' pasts found refuge, those who were seeking to cover their tracks. But above all, this was the place designated for the people who had lost their homelands beyond the Bug. Where were they to go?

Official propaganda did everything to confirm their sense of mission to settle these 'eternally Polish lands'. They, however, knew perfectly well that here even the stones cried out in German. They could see the gravestones, the Church inscriptions ...

Years on I would reach for a historical atlas, leaf through its pages, and look upon the ever-changing borders of the Polish state. Once it had lain on the river Oder, then it moved away, now it was back. I saw in this not a restoration, but a reparation. I thought about it in terms of the cost of the war Germany had lost. If she had won, Poland would doubtless not exist, and the German border would be in the Kamchatka. But she had lost. Historical arguments were unimportant. This is what they deserved, I thought. Post-German life left me indifferent. But this was not true of my friends and colleagues. To them, post-German meant alien, unwanted. Their homes were nourished by a different sense of space and other landscapes. When

I visited them I would see mementos of Wilno or Lwow. They, and their parents, spoke a strange, melodious kind of tongue. It wasn't the Polish we spoke at home.

Gradually, I came to understand that for these people, and especially for their parents, settling in Szczecin was a punishment for crimes they didn't understand and had never committed. They had been uprooted and sent into an alien, hostile environment. There was nothing of the victor or pioneer about them. On the contrary, they were longing for a home they had lost. The more so since they could neither speak nor write about it. 'Their eyes spoke of the fear and confusion of people herded out into the unknown', Katarzyna Sucholska writes in her story 'A meeting in Wolkenberg'. Attempts were made to rob them, to destroy the memory of generations. They spent decades sitting on suitcases, waiting for a miracle to happen. In their flats, beside other mementos of their lost home, they kept little bags of earth.

****

In 1968 a brutal anti-Semitic campaign was unleashed in Poland and many people were forced to leave the country. Frequently their only connection with Judaism lay in a dim and distant past. Friends told me with a mixture of surprise and fear that they had only just learned of their Jewish background. Many were categorised as Jews because they were 'outlanders'. Though the police generally checked, I too was exposed to arrest and insult, but received an official apology in prison a few days later. That was how I discovered that the police held dossiers relating to the background and nationality of Polish citizens. Perhaps it is true that someone, somewhere, always collects documents of this kind.

The anti-Semitic campaign launched by the Communists took place in an atmosphere of social acquiescence, much like the German extermination of the Jews in Poland in the 1940s. The two events bear no comparison, of course. Just as one cannot conclude from them that Poles are anti-Semites by nature. They are as anti-Semitic as the French or the Germans: they display xenophobia when the conditions are right. Clearly, not everyone is actively involved. Not even the majority. But a minority can dominate the rest, and the majority be helpless in the face of rampant evil.

I remember my own helplessness and despair, and the guilt which remains with me even now. I remember a long walk around the streets of Warsaw with the distinguished Polish poet Arnold Slucki. He had been born into a Jewish family in the early 1920s and joined the Communist Party as a boy. He came from a small village, in what is now Ukraine. Slucki knew no Polish then, only Ukrainian and Yiddish. Later, he learned other languages. He spent the war in the Soviet Union, and then chose to live in Poland. He learned the language, began to write and became a distinguished lyric poet. He told me all this because he had to tell someone who was staying and whom he could trust. He was leaving the following day. He went via Vienna to Israel, but longed to return. He moved back to Europe and as close to Warsaw as he could, settling in West Berlin. More than 20 years ago he was buried in the Ruhleben cemetery. He was barely 50. That is how exiles and those who have been hounded out of their homes come to die: silent, unnoticeable deaths.

I remember seeing my friends off on that train to Vienna. And those repeated farewells when the exiles distributed possessions they would not or could not take with them: books, furniture, paintings, household utensils. Nor will I ever forget learning a new word that day. It was the adjective 'post-Jewish', and meant everything the Jews had left behind ...

****

We live in this nightmare daily. At times its manifestations are more intense, at times less so. To resist it we must first give it a name. We have called it racism, nationalism, xenophobia, enmity towards strangers, but today words like this mean little. In recent decades the phenomenon has undergone changes which are hard to express. And although we frequently make analogies between this new wave of hostility to outsiders and the inter-war years, I feel that this tends to obscure rather than clarify the real state of things.

The explosion of nationalisms before World War II came when the idea of the 'nation state' was at the height of its popularity. The present debacle is an expression of the same idea in crisis. One of its causes is undoubtedly the lack of any alternative political concept that is widely accepted or understood. Perhaps it is a question of finding a new educational approach. The model which has nurtured us and which recounts the history of nations has proved deceptive. Can we find a substitute? Not so long ago national distinctions did not, of necessity, provoke tensions. Wars were fought to settle conflicts of a different kind. Rulers changed, but this did not mean that the inhabitants of their lands were driven out.

One answer might lie in the return to a cultural perspective lost in recent decades. In the eighteenth century, it gave every educated European a sense of belonging to a community which shared an idiom descended from a common Greek and Roman antiquity, a familiarity with the classic texts, and a sense of European cultural identity alive in

Athens, Sofia, Constantinople, Rome, Paris, Lisbon, Oslo, Stockholm, London or Vienna. Borders are lines we see on maps, or check-points we cross when we travel by land. Our ancestors travelled by land more than we do, but borders meant less to them ...

Outsiders in Russia

Irena Maryniak

Glas issue 6: Jews and Strangers, *edited by Natasha Perova, Glas Publishers, 1994, Moscow 119517, PO Box 47, Russia or c/o Dept of Russian Literature, University of Birmingham, B15 2TT, UK*

In Russian the word *sobornost'* conveys the perfectly integrated community, unanimously bound by cultural and religious values, through which personal wilfulness is reoriented towards the Greater Good. It was an ideal espoused, particularly, by the Slavophiles, the purist patriots of nineteenth century Russia. They held that the country had a unique historical destiny and moral status in the world.

Today, the Slavophile vision, tinged with messianic hopes, still retains an attraction for many Russians as they look for cohesion and identity in a fragile and fragmented political environment. And it is tainted, as ever, with a tendency to categorise everyone by nationality: French means frivolous and superficial; German - schematic and unimaginative; Polish - infantile and vain; Jewish - cunning and mercenary. Clichés which have lost their piquancy in the West remain, in much of Eastern Europe, the bench marks by which people make sense of the world.

The literary journal *Glas*, one of the few carriers of new Russian writing in translation, recently devoted its sixth issue to the theme of outsiders, exclusion and inner exile. It is entitled 'Jews and Strangers'. Unusually for *Glas*, it spans over a century of prose and poetry, from the 1880s to the present, proving how little some things have changed. And it attempts to address one of the chief preoccupations of fallen empires: who are 'we'? Where do 'we' end and 'others' begin: psychologically, geographically, politically? This is another of those dilemmas which fill the pages of Tolstoy and Dostoevsky and continue to be the subject of impassioned arguments in contemporary politics. For it is precisely in Russia, the land 'beyond all rules and limits' where words, feelings and promises are fluid as the rouble that, as Lev Anninsky writes in *Glas*, 'the most desperate attempts are made to retain one's identity, to withstand this overpowering fusion of colours ... The call of the ancestral homeland is one of the last life-saving footholds'.

In 1988, after decades of being refused the right to emigrate, Russian Jews began to leave for Israel in droves. The desire to go was heightened by the loss of the protection the Soviet state had offered, mitigating the sporadic cultural, educational and professional restrictions it had also imposed. In the Soviet Union, a Jewish background was a shaming liability best ignored or forgotten, as Liudmilla Ulitskaya's nicely shaped and keenly observed story '1953' illustrates. The humiliation of exposure to racist taunts was augmented by the awareness that one was denying and repressing a barely known heritage.

Under *glasnost'*, rumours of impending pogroms grew rife. In this, 'the era of belated confessions, accusations, self flagellations and words ... words ... words ... unimaginably candid, repentant, terrible and superficial', the ideological concern with class was transformed into a passion for tracing national pedigree. There is a tradition among Russian nationalists that gives an almost metaphysical character to the revolutionary incursion into Russian history, and that identifies it with a conspiracy of Jews and Zionists aided and abetted by anonymous 'cosmopolitans'. In the 1960s, for instance, there circulated in *samizdat* a document compiled by one A. Fetisov that offered an interpretation of world history as a struggle between the forces of order and chaos. Jews personified chaos. They had created disorder in Europe for 2,000 years, the story ran, and the regimes of Hitler and Stalin represented a positive Teutonic-Slavic intervention which put an end to all that. Fetisov and his collaborators were bundled off to psychiatric wards in 1968, but their views found considerable support among people looking for an accessible vindication of the failures of Soviet Communism.

In fairness, though, *perestroika*'s predicted pogroms failed to take place and these days the incentive for Jews to get away seems economic rather than political. Perhaps Anninsky is right to invoke the common legacy of 200 years of Russian-Jewish cohabitation and the characteristics which these 'two nations in mirror reflection' share. Medieval Muscovy referred to itself as 'Jerusalem' and 'the new Israel'. What is Russia's relationship with the Jewish tradition if not that of a newly proclaimed chosen people towards an older rival? One senses in the pages of *Glas* some of the bitterness of a failed historical mission.

'Jews and Strangers' offers a window on the lost years on the lost years of Russian and Soviet Jewry, at times giving the Jews an exotic, photogenic image which highlights the distinctiveness of Jewish culture and experience. As an attempt to give a voice to a community so long denied one, this is courageous and salutary. But in that it emphasises the 'otherness' of what is sometimes viewed as a quaint cultural type, it could continue to nourish traditional stereotype and prejudice, despite the best intentions. The inclusion of Osip Mandelstam's eulogy of Jewishness in the visual arts, 'Mikhoels' (unfortunately with no indication of date or context), and Nikolai Leskov's 1882 pamphlet in defence of the Jewish contribution to cultural and economic life, is timely given the moods in contemporary Russia. But the two documents also underlined the extent to which the Jewish tradition is still viewed as a remote oddity.

Much of the content makes excellent reading. Vassili Grossman's 1934 story 'The Commissar' tells of the reluctant departure of a female Soviet commissar from the Red Army to a Jewish household to give birth to an unwanted child during the Civil War. Grossman depicts the Jewish environment as a preserver of warmth and domesticity – the only humane constant in a displaced world where experiences of childhood and gender have been neutralised or erased.

More ambivalent and puzzling is Leonid Latynin's portrayal of a timeless sequence of attraction and repulsion between Russian and Jew in the excerpt from the second volume of his novel *Sleeper at Harvest Time.*

There is an excellent, sharply drawn vignette by Nina Sadur depicting an episode in the life of the Rosenfelds – a big, sprawling family, nervous, gesticulating, swamped by 'streams of feeling'. They plan to leave for Israel and, to 'outwit the USSR', buy four diamonds to smuggle out of the country. Subsequently, they are robbed and systematically tortured in their own apartment.

To be an outsider is to know oneself to be morally reprehensible. It is to be deprived of the protective shield of self-esteem, to have no rights other than survival and procreation and, perhaps, shy aspirations to self-improvement which will remain unrecognised. In a society and a tradition where the communal experience is all important, it is the greatest transgression of all.

A Season of Hell

Zoran Filipovic

Translated by Vanessa Vasic

Hell is, by definition, a general place of *evil* where God sends the souls of those who have during their lives sinned so terribly and incorrigibly that there is for their sins neither forgiveness nor remedy. In that place their souls 'live' in eternal pain, making hard and unforgiving amends for the hard and unforgivable sins committed during the short life of man upon the earth. Sins that during their commission were limited and definitive in time, even if, sometimes, they lasted the whole of someone's life, are expiated in a time that is limitless, endless, definitive only in the knowledge of its existence in eternity. This place lies *somewhere* in the reign of eternal fire and where the souls of the condemned cry for *death* because it is so dreadful, so dreadful that it cannot be imagined, let alone described, and death seems to be the only escape from this hell, and yet there is neither death nor any other way out, because you only die once, and this hell is for *eternity*.

Sarajevo is a place of general evil. In Sarajevo there is no time. In Sarajevo there is no yesterday, in Sarajevo there is no tomorrow. In Sarajevo there is only now, a dreadful and remorseless now. To eat now, now to warm oneself, now to find and fetch water ... Until when?

It is hard to get to Sarajevo. The preparations for departure are filigree painstaking and lengthy, or the decision is made in an instant, come what may. One doesn't go there without a deal of trouble, without a dreadful and enormous need to be just there. Sarajevo is where you leave. Sarajevo is what you escape from. Departure or flight, the preparations are long and painstaking, anxious. Departure is discussed, openly or secretly, it is gone into, whether legally or conspiratorially, it is what is fantasised, dreamed of. Everyone wants to get out of Sarajevo. And those who say they would not want to, that they would rather stay, and they would too. These most of all. Leave. Disappear. For ever.

Sarajevo is a trap. Completely surrounded by chetniks, exposed to the mercy of the double, triple, quadruple enemy encirclement, of his infantry and his still more deadly and unpredictable artillery that fires indiscriminately, from time to time, and always scores a direct hit, because whatever they hit is a direct hit. Every shell fired from above, from the hills, means at least one life less below, in the city, and one place more in a shallow grave hurriedly scraped out of the stadium, a park or a car park, where people are now being buried because there has long, long since been not enough room in the cemeteries. They are buried in a hurry, with little groups that follow the killed (natural death has long since been a rarity) with no large gestures, without tears or mourning. The dry grey faces, a couple of them, the closest relatives, a shallow grave and the clay that sticks to the soles of your shoes, everyone throws a few clods of earth, a bunch of dried or perhaps even plastic flowers, and the simple marking that is knocked in above the heads: name, surname, year of birth and year of death, the grave-diggers with their shovels wipe the sweat from their foreheads while they throw in the soil, wipe it with their sleeves, there is little time, they don't talk, they don't rest. When they have finished that, they step aside, and say: 'Next.' They say it curtly and the spade is already throwing earth into some other, new grave, and some new, other group of people are saying farewell to their loved ones. Sarajevo is a trap. In Sarajevo there is nowhere to hide or take cover. Whichever part of the town you are in, or whatever street you are walking down, along whichever side, it is always the same. The probability that a shell will fall just here and that you will be the next victim is always the same. There is no rule. No good advice. There is no time of day when you can say: 'They have never shot at this time before!' They are always shooting. By night. During the day. In the morning. The streets are always full. During the day. People, looking for food and firewood. Waiting in queues for bread, and water. When a shell falls in such a place, it creates utter carnage, as it did then in Vasa Miskin Street, or not long ago at the brewery, where people were standing in line for water. This makes everyone in the city the same, equal. At night, when dark covers the city and everything vanishes in the blackness, people desert the streets, the city empties. Only a few people, who needs must be bold, dare to walk at night. The night swallows things up. People disappear. Then the city is covered by the headlights of crazily hurrying cars. They drive murderously. Suicidally. On every one of them you can see some sign: Police, Military Police, Special Police. They are all some kind of police. Everyone who has money for fuel (7 marks a litre) or has some power or authority, drives auto-police.

Sometimes the fog comes down, and it's thick and heavy, and it lasts for days. The visibility is bad during the day, but hopeless at night. Torch-light, switched on in brief bursts, is almost no help. But just in case. The fog is so thick it pinches and saws at your throat. Then you have to go haphazardly, by memory. It happens that sometimes you get your legs caught in the downed cables of the tram-lines. One night I could feel blood on my shoes. Don't ask how and why I knew, I just knew, I could feel I was walking in blood. When I switched on the lamp, there was a great frozen puddle. The streets were still covered in snow, which was firm and frozen in other parts. In this place the snow was red and tacky. There were a couple of such puddles along this part of the pavement. It was in front of the Presidency building. That day a shell had fallen here and killed six people. Two sentries guarding the building had had their legs taken off with shell fragments.

On Sundays there is mass. Mass at 11 in the chapel of Catholic Theology. The chapel is full. People in uniform. HVO. Special police. Civilians. All believers. The clergy say it's like that at all masses, in the Cathedral and at the Franciscans. One Friday I went to a mosque, in Vase Miskin, not far from the Cathedral. At noon, prayers. At the entrance, the Imam asks me where I am from, he can see I am a stranger. I say, from Zagreb. One of us, he says, welcome. And the mosque is full, and there are uniforms there too. The army of B and H. Civilians. It is unbelievers who are shooting at us, we say later. If those up there on the hills were believers, they would not do that, they wouldn't shoot at us. No. A believer would not do it. They are pagans. Sarajevo is a trap. In Sarajevo, there are still living some hungry, frozen, dirty missed people, those whom shells and snipers have somehow missed or passed by. Counted according to our peacetime calendar, it has already lasted ten months. In their time, it is a question of years. With one blast everything has gone, your family, possessions and memories. Yesterday, they had everything. Today, everything has gone. Even time has gone. Only the now is left. A dreadful, anxious, everyday now. The birds that left the town in the autumn won't know their way back in the spring. They won't recognise it, and will continue straight on in some other direction. Those that get here all the same won't have anywhere to come to. The roofs they would have alighted on will not exist any more, the trees they would have lived in will have gone. There are only people and ruins and their terrible fate, with their now. Until when?

Sarajevo-Zagreb, February 1993

* * *

It is four weeks now since I went to Sarajevo, God-knows-for-the-nth-time, and a full three weeks since I left Sarajevo God-knows-for-the-nth-time. Only this time the reason for my departure from the 'darkness' was different. I went to give back to Sarajevo whatever I had taken from it during my previous stays in 1992 and 1993. After more than six months of attempts and preparations, I managed to transport and prepare my exhibition, 'A Season of Hell', at the Art Gallery BiH. A moving meeting at the exhibition with the subjects of my photographic essay. Unusually crowded opening. Monsignor Vinko Puljic - the Archbishop Bosanski, and Mrs Azra Begic open the exhibition. Moving speech, beautiful words. While they speak, I wonder whether I have deserved them. It is difficult to bear these beautiful words with so many eyes watching, knowing that every one in the audience deserves respect at least twice as large as this.

It is difficult to bear this Sarajevo, different from all the previous times. Like a Satyr's mask, from the windows of shops previously ravaged, rows of bananas, pineapples and kiwis leer at me ... The shelves are filled with delicatessen from France, England ... beer from Austria, Holland, Denmark ... wine from Spain ... fashion accessories from Italy, shoes and clothing for all sizes and genders ... The prices are lower than anywhere on this planet. Like a fairy tale. Like a dream, a nightmare, Sarajevo is living through its phase between war and - war?! Friends take me round town, saying: look at this, look at that ... I moonwalk behind them thinking, heretically; the war was better ... The war was more truthful. What happens when the magic passes, when it stops and people wake up, or even worse, when those up on the hills wake up and everything starts again: the same hunger, the same cold, the same poverty and misery. What will happen? And even now, all this abundance, on the stalls and in the shops, who can afford it? Who has the money to buy anything? It was different before, the same for everybody: bad. And they all dreamt about the same things. These dreams are further than ever now, because they are at arm's length. It's impossible even to dream about it any more, because it just passes by in front of your eyes: like a guilty conscience. It is difficult when a person loses the capacity to dream as well, the last escape from brutal reality. This abundance is the abundance of the privileged.

My friends are taking me further, still showing me things. Look, they say, the tram is running! Yes, a moving target, I think, I do not want to spoil their joy, I know it will not last. Yes, I say aloud, nice. You see how it's all good now, how everything is better, they say – happy. Yes, I say, softly, hardly managing to open my mouth, while inside I am screaming . . . Enough! Enough! Nothing is good! Nothing is better! It's worse! Everything is worse – because it looks better!

Sarajevo is a trap. Sarajevo is a cage. Sarajevans cannot leave Sarajevo, nor enter it. Sarajevo is a golden cage. Now. Other people come to be photographed in Sarajevo. Anyone who cares about his image comes to have his photograph taken in Sarajevo. Statesmen, writers, philosophers, singers, jongleurs, circus people . . . Afterwards, they go home, to their friends, their governments and states. They hold press conferences, give interviews and say: 'You know, I was in Sarajevo', handing out their photographs: the people are impressed. Overnight they have become heroes of the media, who still haven't managed to get to those mythical places, but watch them, with envy, thinking: 'I will have my picture taken in Sarajevo, one day'.

Sarajevo, August 1994

Freedom and Garbage

Ivan Klíma

Translated by Paul Wilson

It may seem paradoxical to speak of 'culture' in connection with a totalitarian regime. One would have thought, after all, that the intellectual sterility, the dogmatism, the censorship, the central control of education and the arts as well as in the life of the church, would leave no room for culture. In reality, however, the situation was not quite so straightforward. Books came out; television programmes were broadcast, and not all of them were contemptible, even in the worst of times. Prague television broadcast marvellous productions of classical plays, nature films, wonderful animated films for children, and so on. Exhibitions were held, and theatres were full. The book market was a narrow one, with few titles available, and the same was true of the repertoire of theatres and cinemas, or even of tours offered by state travel agencies. On the other hand, books and tickets to cultural events were cheap, since everything permitted in culture was heavily subsidised. What was written in the papers or broadcast on radio or television news was, of course, deliberately mendacious and, in fact, mendacity reached into many spheres of life, from what was taught to children to the very act of elections.

Censorship was practised on the broadest possible basis: it not only shielded people from everything that was ideologically suspect, from everything new and potentially disturbing; it also protected them from the worst trash. The pornography or perverse and bloodthirsty thrillers that inundated free countries could be smuggled across the borders on videotapes, but were denied access to the mass media. An exhibition in which an artist kills a sheep before the eyes of his audience and then creates a work from its blood and innards would have been unthinkable.

When thinking about the culture of the so-called socialist era, we

Vol. 23, no. 6, 1994

should also remember that most people were not longing for things of real value, for change, or even for novelty. In fact, the rapid rate of change in modern life tends to encourage conservatism and supports the notion that art should entertain rather than disturb and provoke. From this point of view, the cultural policies of the totalitarian system corresponded, to some degree at least, to the taste and opinions of the average person, and if there was something wrong with it, it was in not going far enough to meet that average taste, in being too didactic, in not surrendering its basic requirement that art should first of all educate, that is, serve the political system.

The totalitarian system created its own way of life, its own hierarchy of values, by which I mean not the values it declared but its actual values. The way of life under totalitarianism at first glance had much in common with the way of life in Western societies: it was aimed at a limited consumerism, it had its own sports heroes, popular singers or favourite hockey teams. Among the values it inculcated were loyalty, obedience, measured optimism, discipline, a positive attitude towards work, egalitarianism. Officially it rejected racism, nationalism, colonialism; officially it declared solidarity with the poor, the oppressed, the non-white. The system cultivated an antagonism towards enterprise, excessive wealth, criticism, towards any kind of deeper thinking; which means it was antagonistic towards the creative intelligentsia, particularly those in the humanities. At the same time, it guaranteed work and wages (even for effort which was more simulated than real), free education (which, however much the system tried to control it, was sometimes a real education) and free health care, the level of which may have been constantly dropping, but which nevertheless was part of the total social security system.

The police state controlled the movements of every citizen, and secured the borders of the country with barbed wire. While this frequently kept decent citizens locked inside, it also kept the worst aspects of international crime out. The knowledge that the state was looking after him, that it was its duty even, became a profound part of people's consciousness and the average loyal citizen could even feel somewhat safer than he feels today in a democratic society. Regardless of how people rebelled against the system and its culture, they unconsciously accepted many of its features and, I would even say, with a certain simplification, that they deliberately developed qualities in themselves that were different from qualities in people who had grown up in free circumstances.

People who refused to accept this way of life, who saw through the mendacity and the falsehood of the system, were usually persecuted.

They suffered materially, but perhaps even more they suffered intellectually and spiritually: from a lack of freedom, a lack of information, from a wide variety of restrictions that touched almost every level of their lives. The realisation that they were cut off from the free world - which from a distance appeared in exaggeratedly attractive colours as a world of unlimited possibilities, plenty, affluence, and total freedom - infuriated them and made them feel that their lives had no future, chiefly because the entire social system in which they lived had no future.

This state of mind led to more than just a contempt for the totalitarian system; it led to the perception that a free society (despite the regime's propaganda attempting to persuade them otherwise) was capable of solving all human problems, that it was a model for a perfect arrangement of affairs both social and personal. The USA, as a symbol of such an arrangement, became as well a symbol of that perfection. Everything made in the USA seemed admirable. Alertness to the pseudo-values of the consumer life, resistance to the invasion of mass culture that was typical of cultural life in the free part of Europe - these, to say the least, were not aspects of the cultural climate in the unfree part of Europe. Most people east of the former Iron Curtain entered the new, freer conditions after 1989 culturally unprepared, with none of the antibodies against the chronic infections the value system of the market society and its mass culture concealed within itself (as indeed any human effort does).

In the first few months after the revolution, it seemed that the greatest boom would be enjoyed by things the former regime had forbidden. In literature, for instance, both the work of the dissidents and of Western bestselling authors like J M Simmel or Stephen King, or utter trash that simply reproduced westerns or action stories, became immediately popular. In theatre, it was the work of Beckett or Ionesco as much as plays like the musical version of *Les Misérables*. The public was simply curious. There was a queue a kilometre long for Václav Havel's first book. The work of dissident writers came out in print runs of 100,000 in a country with 15 million inhabitants. But Beckett soon disappeared from the repertoire of half-empty theatres and the work of even the most famous domestic authors sank to print runs in the thousands. Trash, on the other hand, began its victorious march through all spheres of culture. Curiosity had been satisfied, and mediocre viewer taste, no longer prompted or guided by anything, came to the fore.

These revolutionary changes touched all spheres of culture, including the value system. Nothing of what used to hold true yesterday held true today. Things considered a sin yesterday are considered meritorious today and vice versa. Even though most people accept this transformation, not everyone is capable of adapting and a form of culture shock affects all levels of society.

People accustomed to the simple schemata and precepts of the former regime (and in any case people always have a tendency to listen to slogans and simplified solutions) often subconsciously search for substitute ideologies, new superstitions to cut through the confusions of the current situation. One such popular superstition is the repeated declaration that the market will solve all essential problems by itself. I am not an economist and cannot judge how far that claim will get you in the economic field, but I know that it will not get you very far in the field of culture.

The changes in our country were, to a considerable degree, the work of intellectuals, but artists themselves played an important role in these changes as well. They now have what can be considered the most important things in any creative work, that is, complete freedom. Nevertheless many of them, along with a part of the cultured public, feel uneasy with the recent changes, if not disappointed.

Many non-conformist artists had become used to exceptional respect from the educated public, despite the fact that they were persecuted by the regime. They were considered spokesmen for the people, often the only ones who would express what others thought but were afraid to say. That rather privileged position vanished after the revolution. Exceptional courage was no longer necessary to express truths about society, and the former spokesmen for the people became what artists are everywhere in the free world: simply artists.

Most artists – even the conformists – during the former regime used to dream about the things they would accomplish if they ever lived to experience freedom. Actors, directors, writers, potential publishers, film-makers and television workers all had this dream. It was one aspect of the vaguely articulated notion of a 'third way': after the fall of the regime, the state would continue to be a patron of the arts, but at the same time it would grant complete freedom to creators and invent ways to limit the spread of the worst forms of trash. Few realised that, if complete freedom came to them, it would come for everyone else as well. Very few reckoned with competition, or realised that decisions about what would be bought, and thus produced and sold, would be made with the tastes and interests of the average reader or viewer in mind.

Suddenly, almost overnight, society found itself in the free conditions of a market economy and everything was quite unlike what the dreamers had imagined. Instead of the dreaded but familiar enemy

– the censor – came the marketplace. The marketplace has no use for dreams, it requires capital, experience, courage, enormous effort, good judgement, talent. Most of those who dreamed about freedom had none, or almost none, of those assets. They looked on in shock as they watched their grand dreams of art, of freely created and eagerly awaited work elbowed aside by trash (trash, moreover, of foreign provenance), as the audience on whom they had pinned illusory hopes turned its back on their authentic creative work, preferring the most banal consumer items.

The present developments have undoubtedly meant some cultural losses. Czech animated and puppet films that were once among the best in the world have been forced out by Disney megakitsch. The same may be said for Czech children's literature, including the tradition of children's illustrations, created over the decades by the best Czech artists. Czech cinema, one of the best in Europe during the 1960s, is vegetating and mostly just producing a hybrid of silly comedies, pornography, and action films. The theatre is trying to survive on a diet of shallow, trashy comedies, and musicals. Cultural magazines are dying, deserted by their readers. Many publishers of the 2,000 or so that came into existence after the revolution, specialise in publishing trash and are enjoying huge market success.

A public unprepared for the sudden explosion of choice appears not to know its own mind, and is a fickle market. Academics in the humanities, who might have bought serious works, are so badly paid they have no money left for culture.

The situation has its positive side: illusions about the third way are fading and those who are creating culture can, for the first time, determine their true standing in the contemporary world. On the other hand, it is unfortunate that we have been able to learn so few lessons in the cultural sphere from the experiences of free societies: that television screens are dominated by violence, that village shops which only recently offered, along with the rest of its merchandise, editions of a classic book or work of children's literature now offer only Harlequin Romances and comic books, and thus are not only depriving the customer of choice, but degrading his tastes as well.

Society will, one day, recover from its culture shock. Even today, many publishers and booksellers are focusing on the production and sale of serious literature, just as one of the two channels of public television is concentrating on programming for sophisticated viewers. Funding organisations are also being set up, both state and private, who have set as their goals support for the development of serious works of art.

Unlike censorship, the marketplace offers free choice. This does not mean that those who give thought to the future of art, who are persuaded that the main meaning of human life does not lie in mindless, time-killing entertainment, do not have the right – the duty even – to do everything to win over as many supporters to their side as they can.

Small War, Big Deal

Judith Vidal-Hall

3 a.m. Sunday 9 October 1994

We bucketed in on the tail of a storm. Long before we could see land, or even the perpetual fires that burned on shore, the white horses whipped up by the storm had turned into a grey spume, like spent chewing-gum. It broke off the top of the waves and rolled across the darkening surface of the sea. As we made our sluggish way towards the dawn and the distant mountains, our wake burned red and green on the darkening water. And when we woke at anchor in the morning - around 3 a.m. - the fetid stench turned the stomach.

So this was Baku, object of our journey, 'land of fire' and birthplace of the Zoroastrian god Ahura-Mazda himself. Now, I had read some days before, with oil deposits 'to rival those of Kuwait', and where the holy fires had spurted up from the rocks since the beginning of time a new temple was planned. There had been a time when boomtown Baku produced more oil than the whole of the USA. Great fortunes were made in the nineteenth-century oil rush: Norway's Nobel brothers made their first pile here before going on to bigger booms back home.

We had crossed six seas and gone through three captains in a month to bring food to refugees from Azerbaijan's war with Armenia.

At nights we had battened down the hatches against river pirates on the Volga who circled us in the dark and left our rusting hulk and its dubious cargo intact.

The streets, when we finally walked out of the port into the 'revolution' we had watched on the ship's flickering television, were quiet. There were tanks guarding key government offices, the army was much in evidence but the curfew was more threatened than real, simply another way of extorting money from those who could be forced to pay.

Beyond the guns at the hotel door, a motley crown of local mafia, senior US and UK oil bosses, equally senior and heavily armed Afghans in close conversation with men in Mercedes, Turkish 'businessmen', Iranian 'students' and Pakistani import-export men gave the lobby a semblance of life and normality. Coup or revolution, no-one was leaving while there was money to made. But the food was good.

Monday

The sea sparkling in the early morning sun beyond the waterfront and broad, tree-lined boulevards of a pleasant Russian colonial seaside resort. On closer inspection it was covered by a thick layer of black crude oil studded with debris from many lands. Pollution seems irrecoverable. Further out of town, forests of antiquated derricks and clapped-out pumps abandoned to an oily wasteland, stretched for miles.

The promenade was a shallow facade of a town - or towns, there are several quite different and distinct - down on its luck. Independence and new-found nationalism doesn't translate into civic pride. The grand neo-classical Moorish of the Russian colonial town was neglected and crumbling; the narrow lanes of the old town, the commercial heart of the city before it lost its Armenians, were a shadow of themselves. Only up on the citadel behind its massy wall with elegant Persian inscriptions was there solace for the eyes in the glorious architecture of its early Muslim rulers. But even here, the heart had gone out of it: a place done up for the tourists who did not come - and to foster the Islamic identity that alone could make a nation out of seven million people more loyal to village or clan than to state they did not know and that did less and less for them. Self-appointed guides and scavengers drag the idle stranger down into the cellars of ancient houses. Among mediocre Caucasian rugs and chipped bric-a-brac, there are exquisite icons set in silver, one no larger than a large postage stamp on a broken chain. Only US$20. Too cheap for an Armenian life or death.

Cheap electrical goods, bolts of gaudy cloth and plenty of food for those who could buy it, all from Turkey, fill the shops and spill out onto the streets where stalls with nothing more than two or three packets of cigarettes jostle for space with old women from the villages selling their produce. It all seems oddly transitory: no-one is here for longer than it takes to get out again, gather a stake or do the deal in hand.

The only bookshop in evidence had been taken over by the Turkish Islamists and the best paper in town, sold out everyday, was the Azerbaijan edition of the Islamist paper *Zaman*, printed and edited in Ankara, flown in daily. The shop was packed and bearded young Turks were doing a brisk trade in small practical manuals on *The Meaning of Islam*, how-to-do-it books on prayer, duties, observances and rituals.

I ask how many mosques there are in the city for a population of near two million. Iftikar, the beaky young teacher of English looked puzzled. 'To the best of my knowledge and if I am not mistaken, I believe there are three.' From where we stood, high above the city, he could spot only one ugly modern minaret but pointed out the older and far more numerous Armenian churches dotted around below.

Tuesday

When a crowd of hundreds of thousands demonstrated in the centre of Yerevan in February 1988 demanding the immediate annexation of Nagorno-Karabakh - a majority Armenian enclave inside Azerbaijan - by Armenia, retaliatory pogroms against Armenians broke out in Sumgait, an unlovely satellite town 30 kilometres north of Baku. Hostilities were suspended for a year as Armenia dealt with its earthquake casualties. But almost a year to the day later, in December 1989, the Armenian Supreme Soviet voted to unite with the territory. Within days, Azeri mobs turned on Armenians in Baku. Soviet troops intervened in protests by the main opposition grouping, the Popular Front, and Azeris were killed. Armenians inside Nagorno-Karabakh hunted down Azeri communities and the exodus followed: a near-total exchange of Armenians and Azeris: 500,000, a million?

Thus began the war, the refugee disaster, the rise of the Popular Front and the vicious clan feuding within the political elite that has resulted in three presidents and several attempted coups in an many years. The successful Armenian offensive in Azerbaijan proper in the summer of 1993 pushed the total of refugee and internally displaced Azeris to - officially - 1.2 million. With nationalist temper running high, talk of peace has brought down successive governments in the same way as reputed oil deals of which Moscow is not a beneficiary. There is a lot of oil mixed with all this blood and misery.

Unofficially, but on the best authority, there are probably around 500,000 refugees. Not in conventional camps, only the Turks, Iranians and Saudis run these. In the main they were absorbed into the general level of misery, further increasing the burden on a society already near breaking point. Sixty per cent of the population live below the breadline and the social safety net is disappearing fast. The IMF arrived in town the day we docked. It demands that the books be balanced, social security cut and bread subsidies removed. Otherwise, it is said, Baku will not get the US$2.4 billion it needs for its stake in the latest oil deal with the West.

The average monthly wage is 14,000 manat - a bus driver earns 6-7,000M - many state employees have not seen a wage packet for months and the minimum cost of a month's basic food is around 20,000M. Easy to see why the arrival of extra mouths to feed has put the mass of the population in a precarious position. Winter is coming and the dying will begin.

Wednesday

Still looking for refugees and out with a European charity delivering flour to state institutions the government has abandoned. An orphanage, a school for abandoned homeless children, a home for handicapped adults, another school-cum-orphanage, a home for old people. But they don't want flour - bread is the last remaining cheap item. They want clothes for the children, medicines, paper, pencils books, blankets.

'We keep making lists,' says the headmaster of a children's home. The children are bright and noisy; the classrooms busy and decorated with pictures of martyrs of the national war. The headmaster plays the accordion and the children sing patriotic songs about the war, the army, freedom and the beloved fatherland. We dance. There are as many blond, obviously Russians as dark little Azeris. 'Many Russians left after independence and the war. They did not always take the children. Grandmothers cannot cope any more, families cannot feed and look after their old folk any more, the state does not look after us anymore.'

The government has said it will repay aid later. When the oil comes in, I suppose. But what are we doing feeding a population its government has subjected to a policy of social triage while it fights a war it cannot win, feuds among itself and cuts deals with the IMF on the back of a population already half starving. And sits on a fortune it cannot turn to account until its ends the war and resolves its internal battles. The human misery is all too evident; as is the lure of oil and gas reserves in excess of the whole of the Gulf, a potentially lucrative market and a strategic position that holds the Muslim states of Central Asia at bay. This town excites the interests of the USA, Turkey, Iran and the EU just as it continues to figure in the larger designs of Moscow that wants its troops back in Azerbaijan as well as Georgia and Armenia.

Conclude there is a lot of oil and politicking mixed up with this aid.

Thursday

'Contract of the century' read the headline in *Moscow News* on 29 September, three days before the coup. 'Azerbaijan and an international consortium of eight major oil companies have agreed to develop three large oil fields on the Caspian Sea shelf ... Moscow views the news negatively.'

Four days later, the Russian ambassador in Baku denies that Russia had either instigated the coup or felt any concern over the oil deal.

Now the new rush is on. Walking home in the dark, I was accosted by a man lurking round the long distance bus depot. In broad Lancashire English, he asked me if I knew how the buses worked and if there was one that would get him out of town and into Georgia from whence he could get a flight back to Odessa. A freebooter from Oldham in the hotel business, he saw a bright future: foreign oil men would always need hotel beds and 'I never worry about a bit of a war'.

The government, too, is pinning its hopes and survival on the oil. Meanwhile the economy's a mess, inflation is galloping away, much of the foreign investment that did venture to Baku has packed up and gone home. Meanwhile, the government prints billions of currency notes in Germany to keep going. Unfortunately, I'm told, it never reaches the banks and the whole exercise is repeated more and more frequently.

Friday

The Good, the Bad and the Ugly is showing on AZTV at breakfast time. The news has gone back to its normal, Soviet-style tedium of presidential doings and loyal demonstrations. The only private TV station, financed by local businessmen, was quickly taken over by the government who filled it with a diet of US Westerns and Soviet war films. Suitable fare for a wild frontier seeking to create heroes for its war.

With the exception of a single radio station broadcasting news in Azeri, Russian and English the broadcast media is entirely in the hands of the state. Radio is dull and amateur; TV, says an informant, 'does nothing to meet the national sensibility or the broader needs of the people'. The opposition, naturally, doesn't get a look in.

It turns out that the bulk of the 'press' is local in the extreme. Paper prices and the return of old-style censorship ensure that the 'national' press appears sporadically and is economical with its pages.

The most interesting publication is probably *Azadliq,* close to the opposition Popular Front. It had just re-emerged after three weeks off the market 'because of paper shortages' but there were blank spaces on the front page where copy had been cut, and savage cartoons on censorship.

The media in no way reflects the complex strands that make up the political web of the country. At a distance, Azeri politics looks labyrinthine; closer up it's amazingly simple. It goes something like this. The opposition, mostly grouped under the umbrella of convenience formed in 1989 by the Popular Front, has cornered the market in the high sounding buzz-words: democracy, free expression, ecology, human rights. Unfortunately it didn't perform well during its brief tenure of power under its leader President Abulfaz Elchibey, a former dissident of impeccable personal reputation though with some odd views on pan-Turkic solidarity and the prospect of a 'national war of reunification' in which Azerbaijan would invade Iran to liberate the 'other half' of the Azeri nation trapped in the land of the mullahs.

He was, however, no match for his wily ex-Politburo rival and present incumbent, President Haidar Aliev. He was manoeuvred out of power within the year, not before he too had stooped to some of the more repressive measures of his successors. The Committee for the Defence of Human Rights and the Committee for Free Speech and the Rights of Journalists are both in the hands of a splinter opposition party. There are now 42 opposition parties. None of them has a popular base and all, like the government itself, are based on clan and regional interests rather than solid policy or principle. Since the loss of its leader and its mauling by Aliev when he came to power in 1993, the PF has kept its head down.

But there is a second, more active opposition front: within the ruling elite represented by Aliev's New Azerbaijan Party. It is they who make the coups, raise their private armies against the government and put regional and clan interests high above those of the state. Prime Minister Suret Husseinov, accused by the president of organising the coup and sacked a few days ago, had already held Elchibey's government to ransom from his base in Gyandzha, 190 miles west of Baku last year, and now defies Aliev by remaining in the city in full view. About the same time in 1993, a former PF leader declared the 'Independent Republic of Lenkoran' on the coast south of Baku. Should Aliev fall, he and his Nakichevan clan could do much the same in their western stronghold.

And all have their foreign masters ready to help them to power and secure their own interests in the process.

It is a fissiparous place, closer to civil war than democracy. Democrats are just as likely as former Communists to carve it up between them. My journalist informant, a professor of history in the university as well as a correspondent for *Moscow Times* and the editor of a local paper, was not sanguine. He was closely linked with one of the newer democratic parties but came out with the familiar platitudes of 'new democrats' everywhere. 'The people are not ready for democracy: like a child with a new computer, they will break it. We only understand dictatorship and we shall have no democracy without dictatorship first.' He ended with a history lesson: 'History gave us two chances at democracy, 1918–1920 and 1992–1993. We made a mess of what little independence we had. All we can do now is put down the roots for the third shot, say in 2010.'

Who Goes Home?

W. L. Webb

Somewhere in *Black Lamb and Grey Falcon*, her epic panorama of Balkan landscape, myth and prejudice, Rebecca West says that she had come to Yugoslavia 'to see what history meant in flesh and blood'. One flinches, reading that 60 years later, following in her footsteps in what must seem to the South Slavs just another such 'low, dishonest decade' as the 1930s.

For the moment, their flesh and blood is mostly still safe in its skin, and not, thank God and His improbable agents lately in Dayton, Ohio, splashed around a market-place in Sarajevo, or the little square in Tuzla where boys and girls used to crowd of an evening to drink coffee and hope they were falling in love. Bosnia is still the sovereign place to go for such history lessons. It's also the place in which to contemplate the uses and abuses of cartography. What went on chiefly in the Bob Hope Hotel in Dayton, Ohio, was the endless drawing and tearing up of maps (even the final documents included an annexe of 102 of them), culminating in a session in 'the Nintendo room', the base's map-room, where fancy electronics reproduced the detail of obsessionally fought-over territories down to the last goat path - using, as the Serbs would have been well aware, the very programmes used by the Nato planes that had bombed them back to the conference table. so, as one reporter put it, while the warlords were returning to their strongholds, the resort to virtual reality produced a virtual peace.

Actual reality produces its own gloss on all that. Travellers in the convoy carrying the Helsinki Citizens' Assembly's assorted idealists and observers to its annual conference in Tuzla got an insight into the nature of this Balkan war as soon as they reached Pocitelj, the first strategically placed small town on the Neretva river which was fiercely fought over by all three sides. All its bridges were blown for miles along, including the lovely, springing arch of the sixteenth century bridge of Mostar, a treasure lost for all Europe.

The pattern Pocitelj showed was to be repeated endlessly in towns and villages between Mostar, Tuzla and Sarajevo in the next fortnight. Yes, look, they *had* once all lived together side by side: here, three intact, ordinary village houses, with chickens and children playing in the yard, were followed immediately by two blackened ruins; another patch of normality - an old man snoozing by a doorstep - then more darkness, half a row this time, and so on; after which village life resumed, men in allotments straightening up to stare at the line of buses and white UNPROFOR jeeps. Further on, the devastation was more comprehensive - whole hamlets wiped out - until, in the Muslim part of Mostar, the coach was silenced by the extent of the wreckage and the improvised cemeteries of lately-dug graves in parks and roadside verges. For the scale of damage, only Sarajevo, at the end of my journey, seemed worse, probably because there it was the *modern* buildings of its wide, central boulevard - the familiar shapes of tower blocks and shopping centres - that were so broken and ravaged.

The harder part of this history lesson was about the specific character of the destruction. The village houses, especially, were not just ordinary, shell-damaged casualties of war; no, they had been dynamited, bulldozed, systematically razed. It was as though giant goblins had been on the rampage, stamping them flat. What added to the sense of falling into some terrible Balkan *Märchen* was that among these places were alpine villages scarcely touched by the twentieth century, high above the deep wooded valleys of central Bosnia: these archaic pastoral idylls, too were blackened with the fierce scorch marks of history. (The nineteenth century dealt with them no less savagely, of course. In despatches for the *Manchester Guardian*, Arthur Evans described the fires of destroyed villages burning just as fiercely in the Balkan Wars of the 1870s; but then, of course, the valiant fighters for Free Bosnia were the Christian Serb peasants of the Krajina, struggling against the yoke of the Muslim landlord class, superior in strength and firepower ...)

It started almost at the beginning of the war, and continued even beyond the end. A week after the ceasefire, Tim Garton Ash and Konstanty Gebert, the Polish journalist and aide to Tadeusz Mazowiecki, who had driven down from Zagreb through the Krajina, arrived in Tuzla half-dazed at the succession of empty, gutted Serb villages, still smouldering, which specially detailed Croatian loot-and-burn detachments had left in the wake of Operation Storm, whose name Franjo Tudjman so loves to pronounce. But weeks after the initialling of the agreement in Dayton, more than a month after the ceasefire, the fires were burning still near the Posavina corridor, where the Croats seem determined to hand back nothing but scorched earth.

These images compose eventually into a comprehensive diagram of the pathology of war, the fact that this is an unusual species of civil war being significant only because civil war is the extreme case, in which the Others who you must drive out, slaughter, eradicate are people known and seen in desperate close-up: your neighbours, even kin by marriage, made alien and fearful by the exciting madness you have been infected with. Not only must you get rid of them, you must make it impossible for them or theirs ever to return and resume what used to be normal life, for then your madness would be seen for what it is. So while it would have been easier if the goblins could have made the Muslims or the Serbs and their houses simply disappear, one does the best one can with dynamite and bulldozers. Obliterating the memory of a place - making lives and communities as though they had never been - must be one of the ultimate forms of censorship.

There is an actual map which explains better than any narrative the complexity out of which all this came. This ethnographic map of Bosnia from the 1991 census must be one of the most extraordinary exhibits in the history of cartography, just as Bosnia's melting-pot was one of Europe's most curious pieces of nation-making. It shows at a glance the dense and complicated distribution of the Serb, Croat and Muslim mix across all the country's corrugation of mountains and valleys. Compare it with the maps of the ceasefire and what is known of the Dayton maps, and you see almost as quickly how few people are now at home in Bosnia. First, the Muslims of the eastern towns and villages above the Drina, whose centuries-old culture is recreated in the novels of Ivo Andric, were driven west. Then, late in the war, the Krajina (border) Serbs, descendants of those planted by the Habsburgs three centuries ago to stiffen the Croatian frontier against the Turk, were herded east by the US-backed Croat and Bosnian offensives of last May and August in the war's biggest ethnic cleansing - 200,000 or more driven into bulging Banja Luka and its hinterland - or replanted in unwelcoming Kosovo. And everywhere the skilled and educated from the towns had fled abroad, these economically viable ones much less likely to come back, of course, than the several hundred thousand whose permission to say in makeshift asylum in Germany runs out, with Chancellor Kohl's patience, in March.

It will be some time before it becomes clear whether many displaced Bosnians will be able to go home, or whether the whole notion of restoring Bosnia's communities to their multicultural status quo ante, in which so much liberal hope has been invested, really is the naive illusion some US power brokers were always sure it was. In Sarajevo someone described Richard Holbrooke's explosive reaction to talk about the importance of refugees returning to restore the uniquely mixed character of Bosnian communities: For Chrissake! They've got the whole map just about 90 per cent ethnically cleared. Don't start moving people around now and spoil it all: ie, don't upset this tidy new territorial balance which might get us some sort of settlement of these bloody Balkan quarrels.

Though no-one expects Muslims to return to Serb-held areas for years to come, the Bosniaks are otherwise committed to the return of refugees to their homes, and President Izetbegovic proposes his old city's tradition of tolerance and openness as the very pattern for democracy in Bosnia-Hercegovina: 'We do not see this as difficult. We are used to living like this ... We were attending classes together with people who had different names, a different religion or nationality. None of this is strange to us.'

But other voices will tell you that old Sarajevo is gone. Much of the old middle class, I was told, had evacuated itself smartly at the beginning of the war, leaving behind 'a militant mediocrity'. And Kris Janowski, the UNHCR's thoughtful spokesman, calculates that while it was true that 27 per cent of marriages in Bosnia before the war were ethnically mixed, there now remained only about 30 per cent of this original population, the rest being mostly refugees from the villages.

In Tuzla, that other celebrated example of the tradition Izetbegovic invoked, the ethnographic balance has been even more radically disturbed. Before the war, the 1991 census gave the proportion of Muslims to Serbs and Croats as roughly three to one; by 1995, UNHCR estimates showed, the tides of war had altered that proportion to twenty to one. The departure of many Serbs and Croats (though we saw some still in the surrounding villages, their churches undamaged), and the immense influx of Muslim refugees, leaving no billets for the hapless US troops whose headquarters the town has become, had made Tuzla statistically into a Muslim stronghold. In northern and eastern Bosnia-Hercegovina, the position is brutally reversed, the Muslim populations being reduced from 355,956 to 30,000 and 261,000 to 4,000 respectively.

Certainly the city's social democrat-dominated administration remains committed to Tuzla's tradition of tolerant multi-ethnicity. During Hitler's war, this miners' town's militant solidarity prevented the Nazis and their Croat *Ustashe* allies from taking its Jews to the death camps; and in October it played host for the second time to the hCa, drawing groups from all over Europe, not least a large contingent of opposition liberals from Servia, who had taken three and a half days, via Hungary and Croatia, to complete a journey that used to take three hours from Belgrade. But survivors of the old Tuzla are well aware of what the changes may bring. Multi-ethnicity was organic to this place, says Sinan Alic, editor of one of the town's two independent newspapers, not some ideology imposed by the authorities; but what the new arrivals from the Muslim villages say to such old Tuzlaners when they question a narrowing of attitudes is: if you don't like the new situation, you can leave.

It's important to remember how much Bosnia was and is a peasant country; only a third of its population lived in the few towns of any size before the war. Revealingly, Karadzic, himself a village boy made good, if that's the word, blames the desire for a strong, multi-ethnic Bosnia he so deplores on 'certain pro-civic circles'. Displaced townsfolk, says a refugee administrator in one of the hCa's workshops, are generally much more confident about trying to return to their former homes, villagers far more scared.

Unsurprisingly the census map was much cited as everyone counted their gains and their losses after Dayton. The Croats used it in arguments especially painful to them over the division (to give the Serbs a viable corridor) of Bosnian Posavina, along the valley of the Sava, and the future allocation of Brcko, postponed for a year when the agreement nearly came unstuck over it. This is one of the most dangerous minefields. Another, of course, is the reintegration of Sarajevo into Bosnia-Hercegovina, a question so vexed that President Chirac (Sarajevo is a French area of responsibility under the UN) has written to President Clinton saying that additional guarantees were needed for the 120,000 Serbs involved if the agreement was to be workable. 'The international community has become excessively involved in Sarajevo,' says Karadzic. 'It will have to pay the price, it will have to protect every single Serb house ... for at least five years.'

Hardly less dangerous is the question of whether President Tudjman can – or cares to – make his Hercegovinian Croats work constructively with the Bosniaks in the Federation, and give up the brutal apartheid they enforced in places like Mostar. There the Muslims who live on the east bank, where 60 per cent of the buildings are damaged, were simply stopped by the Croat police from crossing to the city's administrative offices, installed in a hotel on the western, Croatian bank. In an attempt to make this bitterly divided place into a functioning city again, the European Union installed Hans Koschnick, the tough old ex-Oberbürgermeister of Bremen, as administrator, with a posse of policemen collected from several European countries. But the series of agreements he arduously negotiated, aimed at getting the Croats 'to stop stopping people', were repudiated almost as soon as they were initialled. If the new post-Dayton agreement is still working this month that will be a small miracle, and as good an augury for the Federation's future as anyone can hope for at present.

At least now there are no bodies in the rivers, no more mass graves being dug. For the long uneasy moment, there is peace. 'Cruel but realistic', as Muhamed Sacirbey described it; 'the only possible peace', in the words of his rather more satisfied Croatian opposite number, Mate Granic. Is what has been done a betrayal of Bosnia, as Denis Healey among others has suggested? At Tuzla, Timothy Garton Ash put it to Peter Galbraith, the US ambassador to Zagreb whom unkind persons call 'the tenth member of the Croatian cabinet', that what was in the making in the impending dealings was 'a Yalta for Bosnia'. But it will only be that if 'the international community' - which is to say Nato, which is to say the USA - lacks the will to do what the actual international community failed to do through its common international institution, the United Nations: that is, whatever may be necessary to stop Croatia and Serbia taking Bosnia apart. (All the Balkan leaders, incidentally, and particularly Radovan Karadzic, address 'the international community' *ad hominem*, as if it were a surly bank manager, or a dodgy landlord who can't be trusted to keep the property in repair; or in the case of Franjo Tudjman, an indulgent rich uncle of whom he still has great expectations.)

If . . . The road ahead, as far as one can see through the snows of a Bosnian winter, is littered with 'ifs'. If implementation proceeds as quickly and firmly as President Izetbegovic insists it must, if it includes enough aid for reconstruction to make people think about the future rather than the past, if the US stays the course, and if no actual or metaphorical landmines blow the peace sky-high, then Bosnia may even manage something a little better than replacing unbearable misery with ordinary, everyday unhappiness, the therapist's traditional goal. But it will be some time yet before we can believe we have really got much further than the moment anticipated in the poem Laura Silber and Allan Little used as envoi to *The Death of Yugoslavia*:

On that day we'll say to Hell: 'Have you had enough?'
And Hell will answer: 'Is there more?'

Unwanted occupation . . .

On 28 June 1989, at the site of the Field of Kosovo seen by Serbs as the cradle of their history, on its six-hundredth anniversary, Serbian President Slobodan Milosevic launched his nationalist *jihad* which led to the death of Yugoslavia and of so many of its citizens. He told a million Serbian pilgrims, inflamed with *slivovice* and corked-up patriotic ardour, to be prepared for battle. Since then, Kosovo has been the last old-style Eastern European police statelet, bristling with police and informers, its Albanian schools closed and political leaders imprisoned. The Albanians see it as an occupation. More than 300,000 of them have emigrated.

Apart from having its supporters demonstrate loudly outside the Dayton talks, the ethnic majority's response to the autumn planting in Kosovo of 9,000 unenthusiastic Krajina Serb refugees was to leak in their press the basic principles of the European Contact Group's 'Plan K' for Kosovo, said to include the restoration of the province's autonomy and an internationally supervised one-year transitional period during which discriminatory laws would be annulled, and democratic local elections prepared. The reports said that the plan would be discussed at the first conference on former Yugoslavia to be held after Dayton, but the stony US resistance to linkage between Kosovo's situation and the negotiation of Bosnia's ethnic dilemmas doesn't augur well for the plan's prospects. (Peter Galbraith, the US ambassador to Zagreb, known unkindly in some UN circles as 'the tenth member of the Croatian cabinet', bluntly told the Helsinki Citizens' Association's conference in Tuzla ten days before the Dayton talks began that the question of civil rights in Kosovo and Sanjak were 'internal matters of Serbia and Montenegro'.) The day before the leak appeared, Astrit Saliu, a leading Kosovo Albanian journalist, was reported to have been arrested, beaten, and interrogated by the Serbian state security police.

1991 and All That

Vera Rich

The Republic of Belarus, an ex-Soviet state of some 10.2 million inhabitants, did not so much win independence as have it thrust upon it. In August 1991, its hardline Communist leaders openly gave their backing to the anti-Gorbachev Moscow coup. When the coup collapsed, the Belarusian hardliners in the Supreme Soviet, fearing the wrath of Gorbachev, made common cause with the small group of pro-democracy People's Deputies and, on 25 August 1991, proclaimed independence.

Belarus had, on paper, been 'independent' for more than 40 years; like Ukraine, it was a founder member of the United Nations and a member of UN agencies, including UNESCO and the International Atomic Energy Agency (IAEA). But this ploy by Stalin to get two extra votes in the UN, in spite of Soviet lip-service to the cultural and linguistic rights of the non-Russian nationalities that comprised almost half the population of the USSR, provided no defence against the long-term aim of *sliyanie* – the 'alloying' of more than 100 ethnic identities into a single, Russophone, Soviet 'nation'. And, though the decision was not at the time made public, Belarus was chosen by the Soviet ideologues as the test-bed of this policy.

It was, in many ways, an appropriate guinea-pig. Belarus had already been subjected to intensive Russification during the nineteenth century, its language forbidden and its mainstream religion, the Eastern-rite Catholic Church (which might otherwise have served, as it did in western Ukraine, as a guardian of national culture) forcibly merged with the Russian Orthodox Church. Following the national revival after 1905, and the window of 'Belarusianisation' in the 1920s, the intellectual elite of Belarus was virtually wiped out (either shot, or terrorised into silence) during the 1930s. World War II meant the loss of one in four of the population – including the destruction of the centuries-old Jewish community which, as its own members eloquently attested, had lived in amicable symbiosis with its Christian, Slav co-habitants for centuries. Furthermore, Belarus in the Cold War era was the most highly militarised area of the Soviet Union, being viewed as the advance post against the NATO powers. And, since Soviet military policy virtually never allowed its soldiers to serve in their home republics, and Russian was the language of the army, the military presence was inevitably a powerful tool of Russification.

Sliyanie worked well. By the early 1980s, there was not a single Belarusian-language school in the capital, Minsk. And since all teacher training was Russophone, even schools in remote rural areas where the language survived were, by force of circumstance, gradually Russified as elderly Belarusian-speaking teachers retired.

Since there was no other obvious unifying shibboleth and symbol of identity – as, for example, the Catholic Church was in neighbouring Lithuania – the language issue took on a special importance to those who wished to preserve national identity. The handful of *samizdat* and expressions of dissent in Belarus during the Brezhnev era concentrated on saving the language. The first manifestation of *glasnost* in Belarus, in December 1986, was a 'Letter to Gorbachev' signed by 28 prominent intellectuals, demanding the linguistic and cultural rights enshrined in the Soviet constitution.

But language alone could not kick-start an opposition movement. That was accomplished by two major revelations of the late 1980s: the excavations carried out at the Kurapaty (Windflower Hill) picnic ground in 1988 by a then-unknown archaeologist named Zianon Pazniak, which disinterred the remains of Stalin's victims (some of whose personal effects could still be identified by surviving relatives) thought to be as many as 200,000); and the even more traumatic disclosure, in February 1989, of the true extent of the fallout from the nuclear power station diaster at Chernobyl, in Ukraine, in April 1986. The hitherto-secret maps and data, made public by the efforts of a nuclear physics professor, Dr Stanislau Shushkievich, revealed that more than 20 per cent of the territory of Belarus had been seriously contaminated. Yet, for almost three years, in much of the affected area, agricultural production had continued and no special safety provisions made for the population. Furthermore, two 'hot spots' were revealed far from the main contaminated area, where rain had chanced to fall just as the radioactive plume was blowing back towards Moscow. Chanced? Or, as the rumours now began, deliberately 'seeded' to bring down the cloud and save the Soviet capital? The Soviet authorities denied the allegations, but many scientists studying the fallout patterns remain open-minded.

The shock of these revelations triggered various citizens' movements under the umbrella of what was originally called the Belarusian Popular Front for Perestroika-Renaissance (BNF). In the first-ever multi-party elections to the Supreme Soviet of Belarus in March 1990, several of these movements sponsored pro-democracy and pro-independence candidates of whom 38 were elected to the 360-seat assembly. As a sop to the democrats, Shushkievich was appointed deputy speaker - the one moderate in an otherwise hardline establishment.

A few token pieces of pro-Belarusian legislation were passed: Belarusian was made the state language, and on 27 July 1990, the sovereignty of Belarus was proclaimed. A few days later, on 6 August (the anniversary of the publication of Skaryna's *Psalter*, a group of young people, under the formal auspices of the Belarusian Language Society, proclaimed the re-establishment of the long-outlawed Belarusian Eastern-rite Catholic Church - an act that challenged not only the hardline rulers of Belarus, but also the Vatican bureaucracy who feared this initiative would rock the carefully trimmed boat of papal *Ostpolitik*.

With independence, the Soviet emblems were replaced by the white-red-white flag and *Pahonia* (Pursuing Knight), symbols dating back to the Grand Duchy of Lithuania-Rus. Schools and universities hastily introduced courses in Belarusian history. The hardline speaker of Parliament resigned, and Shushkievich took his place, becoming, in the absence of a president, simultaneously the head of state. Hitherto semi-official newsletters became fully-fledged, legally registered journals. Minority religions - including the Eastern-rite Catholics - were granted legal status. The restitution of Church property confiscated by the Soviets began. And a whole sheaf of nation-building initiatives came into being, including a search launched by Foreign Minister Piotr Krauchanka, for a twelfth-century treasure of deep symbolic importance - the Cross of St Euphrosyne of Polatsak with its double-barred form, as in the symbol of the pagan god, Yaryla - that had gone missing during World War II. Failing the recovery of the original cross, Krauchanka said, Belarus would use some of its tiny gold reserves, mainly recycled scrap from military electronics, to create a replica of the Euphrosyne cross as a national treasure for the future.

Economically, however, all was not well with the new state. The aftermath of Chernobyl ate up 15 per cent of GDP; Russia's oil and gas producers began to demand what they claimed to be 'world prices' for supplying Belarus's energy needs; 70 per cent of Belarusian industry had, in Soviet times, been military-related - and now the arms race was over. Ex-hardliners in government and Parliament blocked moves towards privatisation of industry and agriculture and, by their obstructive attitudes, deflected would-be foreign investors to more receptive business climates, usually to neighbouring Baltic states with a similar industrial base.

The first major blow to democracy came in December 1993. Public opinion, which had little understanding of economics, attributed the ever-rising prices and falling standards of living to corruption in high places. Alaksandr Lukashenka, an ex-hardline Communist member of Parliament, levelled charges of corruption against Shushkievich. Although the allegations were unfounded, Shushkievich (who had collapsed in the Parliament chamber with a heart attack) resigned. A few weeks later, when the presidential election campaign began, Lukashenka declared his candidacy, campaigning on a populist programme of an economic upturn and end to corruption - though with no policy proposals for achieving this. But with no expertise in assessing the claims of rival candidates and thinking anything better than the stagnation of the last three years, the Belarusian electorate chose Lukashenka.

In the 18 months of his presidency, Lukashenka, a former state farm boss, has failed to deliver the promised economic improvements. The most disadvantaged strata of society are worse off: he has cancelled even such concessions as the rights of pensioners to travel free on municipal transport; there has been no real movement on privatisation of either industry or agriculture; and major foreign companies who were considering joint ventures with Belarus are now pulling out. Lukashenka puts his hope for economic improvements in close ties with Russia, but the much-lauded customs union with Russia has brought no real benefits to Belarus and the Russian democratic politicians and pro-market economists have little use for Lukashenka's proposals. Lukashenka bolstered his pro-Russian policy with a referendum in May 1995 proposing closer economic ties. No media coverage was allowed to any viewpoint but his own. Though he won approval on the Russian front, the same referendum failed to endorse his wish to change the state flag and coat of arms back to those of Soviet times (minus the hammer and sickle) but the president simply announced to the world that the vote on the *symbolica* had gone his way.

The failure of the long-overdue parliamentary elections in May 1995 (there was insufficient turnout in 141 constituencies) allowed him six months of rule by decree. The country was peppered with directives which included a list of cadres not allowed to leave the country without his written consent (among others, university administrators and the editors of major newspapers) and a blanket ban on all textbooks in the humanities published since 1992. Many of his fiats have been ruled illegal by the Constitutional Court; but Lukashenka does not recognise its competence. He operates by a simple syllogism: the Constitution says Belarus is a presidential republic, he is the president, therefore any decision he takes is constitutional and anyone who opposes him is in breach of the Constitution.

In the past 18 months he has ordered the disconnection of the live broadcasting equipment from the Parliament chamber, sent riot police to arrest democratic members of Parliament, ordered the replacement of outspoken editors and tried to put the few newspapers which dared criticise him out of business. He has banned the newly formed unofficial union, arrested the leaders of the metro strike in August 1995 and sent its supporters to pick the potato harvest. While most of his decrees have been published in the official press, there is increasing evidence of a parallel system of unpublished diktats, delivered as telephoned 'hints' from the presidential aides.

Not surprisingly, the prevailing mood in Belarus is dark. The more politically aware intellectuals and young people are trying to keep alive the message of democracy; Belarusian PEN strives to foster at least the notion of freedom of speech and the printed word. And one positive spin-off from Lukashenka's one-man rule has been the drawing together of Russophone and Belarusian-speaking intellectuals. The notorious May 1995 referendum gave the Russian language equal status with Belarusian, effectively ending the post-independence programmes of positive discrimination. But if Lukashenka hoped this would split the country on language lines and marginalise the 'linguistic patriots', he was mistaken. Resentment of Lukashenka's methods is no less among Russophone democrats than among the most ardent advocates of the Belarusian language. And the most 'patriotic' Belarusian-language newspaper, the bi-weekly *Svaboda* (Freedom) now publishes a regular page of political commentary in Russian.

According to a political joke of the area, when the tanks are approaching, the Poles charge them with cavalry, the Russians attack them bare-handed and the Belarusians dig fox-holes and let the tanks roll safely over their heads. But even the greatest optimist must foresee a long, hard haul for Belarus towards democracy. On 10 December 1995, at the fourth attempt, the Belarusian electorate returned a quorate Parliament, 191 out of a possible 260 seats, but the pro-independence BNF was wiped out. A few pro-democracy candidates, including former parliament speaker and head of state Stanilaus

Shushkievich have got through and could form the nucleus of a possible opposition to Lukashenka. But the conduct of the elections underlines the bizarre nature of Belarusian 'democracy'. When Parliament's speaker, Miackyslau Hryb, wanted to address the nation, stressing the importance of a turnout adequate for a quorate Parliament, he was not given access to national television. Russian TV agreed to give him a slot, but President Lukashenka suspended the relay of Russian TV to Belarus 'on technical grounds.' Eventually, Hryb was able to address the electorate - but only via Radio Liberty from Prague.

In the meantime, one may recall the words of *Svaboda* after the trade union association of Papua New Guinea sent a telegram protesting against the suppression of the independent Belarusian trade unions: 'If only we Belarusians knew as much about what is going on in Belarus as the citizens of Papua New Guinea do.'

Surviving Communism

Geoffrey Hosking

The power structure of the Soviet Union is best understood as an interacting network of clans, sometimes internally bound by genuine kinship ties, but more often by shared political experience or loyalty to a common leader. Each authority figure, say the first secretary of a regional party committee, would gather round himself a coterie of clients and protégés, who would defend his interests, service his needs and generally advance his cause, while in return, if he was successful and climbed the ladder of promotion, he would raise them along with him, rather like a party of mountaineers. When Brezhnev became First Secretary of the Soviet Communist Party, he gathered round himself secretaries and advisers who had been associated with him earlier in his career, 'the Dnepropetrovsk mafia', as they were often called. All the way down the ladder the same practice was replicated at each level, and the ties of both obedience and loyalty thus generated constituted the sinews of the structure. This was the nomenklatura system, formalised and monitored in the file indexes (no doubt computerised in later years) in the Central Committee of the Soviet Communist Party.

The post-Soviet system has retained many of these features. Nearly all the political parties that have emerged since 1990 are centred around a small clique headed by a single leader. What divides them from one another is not ideology, but personal rivalry, and when they split and reform the reason is almost always personal conflicts. The president of Russia himself conforms to this stereotype: at all stages in his career Yeltsin, rather than create a political party – at which he has been very unsuccessful – has sought to surround himself with people he could trust. Immediately after the Soviet collapse, it was a circle of old regime nonconformists (if you like, liberals) from Sverdlovsk and Moscow. Nowadays, it is a medley of advisers from the 'power ministries', headed by his trusted personal bodyguard, Alexander Korzhakov.

The privatisation of trade and industry, though it is perhaps the most radical of the recent social transformations, has proceeded largely according to the same nomenklatura rules. Most of the newly privatised firms are either managed by ex-members of the nomenklatura elite, or are owned by consortia put together in the apparatus old boy network, usually using money stashed away in the final years of the old regime. This 'party gold' is such a sensitive subject that all attempts by the media to investigate it have met with a firm rebuff. In August 1991, immediately after the failed coup, Nikolai Kruchina, a senior CP official responsible for finances, died mysteriously after falling from his balcony. The KGB declared it a suicide, but the suspicion has remained that Kruchina was eliminated because he knew too much about the fate of the 'party gold'.

The other survivors from the old regime are its underground entrepreneurs, the activists of the 'black' or illegal economy. In the planned economy, enterprise directors had to do business with them in order to overcome the rigidities of the system: to obtain urgently needed spare parts, materials or fuel they offered bribes, backhanders or reciprocal 'services' in payment. Now that the black economy has been largely legalised, the personal relations struck up then have continued and flourished. Hence the hectic atmosphere of corruption and criminality which surrounds much Russian business.

Since the forces of law and order are also enmeshed in this system, each business needs its own protection, unless it can claim security through personal connections in the police. That is why most enterprise directors keep a personal bodyguard and hire armed guards to protect their premises. Sometimes clashes between them take place at the highest level: thus in December 1994, a squad from the entourage of Alexander Korzhakov, stormed a building belonging to the banking group. Most, in order to demonstrate to its boss, Vladimir Gusinsky, that his protection – his 'roof' as it is often called – was not strong enough.

Some observers believe that some such interaction of criminal and official structures precipitated the Chechen war. It is curious, for example, that for three years after Dudayev's declaration of independence, there was little serious attempt to negotiate with him. Perhaps this is because highly-placed figures in Yeltsin's administration were actually doing nicely out of clandestine deals which involved the Chechen mafia, with its access to oil, drugs and other valuable assets. When these cosy arrangements broke down, Yeltsin's entourage advised him to go to war.

In the case of agriculture, the connection with the past is much more straightforward. Although it has been legal for some years now for collective farmers to lease plots of *kolkhoz* land for life, and to sell the produce they cultivate on the open market, very few have in fact done so, and even fewer have made a success of it. Collective farms have proved unwilling to release their members in this way, and even more reluctant to hand over good land to them. Those farmers who have set up on their own have found it difficult to raise credit to buy machinery, fertilisers and the other essentials of small-scale agribusiness.

The Duma has consistently refused to allow full-scale private ownership of land, and it is only recently that Yeltsin introduced it by decree. But leased land is less valuable as collateral for a loan, and so restricts the farmer's ability to raise credit. The result of all this is that the output of food remains miserably low. Most food shops are full of imported tins and packets; local food is scarce, expensive and poor quality.

The cliquish arrangements in politics and economics are cosy, personal and easy to understand. They resemble those of feudal Europe, when the salvation of the individual lay in attaching himself to a powerful baron. The problem is that in today's Russia the majority of the population is excluded from the mutual back-scratching (or feuding) and regards the 'barons' with cynicism and embitterment. Back in 1991–92 they were told that the new Russia would bring them freedom, property and a stake in a prosperous economy. It hasn't turned out like that at all for most of them.

If internal politics depends on which is the strongest clique, then Russians are inclined to treat international relations in a similar light. Security depends on attaching oneself to the most powerful alliance of barons. That is why most Russians believe that if NATO expands eastwards, that can only mean that the alliance belonging to the USA has demonstrated its superiority over that belonging to Russia. There are, of course, people, especially in the Foreign Ministry, who seek security on less primitive lines, through co-operation with international organisations, but their voices get drowned by the dominant perception of a zero-sum game.

Russia cannot decide whether it is now a nation-state which recognises the rights of other nation-states, or whether it is still an empire, the residual trustee of the Soviet Union, with an abiding right and duty to intervene in the affairs of its other former members. In some respects, it has behaved like a nation-state, for example in withdrawing its troops peacefully from central Europe and the Baltic republics. But in other cases it has tended to assert itself in the old imperial manner, by leaning heavily on Moldavia, on Georgia (in Abkhazia) and on Tajikistan (in the name of the common fight against 'Islamic fundamentalism'). It seems now to be on the point of reincorporating Belarus, a step which many Russian politicians hope will be the first stage towards restoring the Soviet Union.

Ironically the Communists, whose candidate Gennady Zyuganov may be elected president in June, no longer represent the nomenklatura elite - not the successful ones anyway, for they have all found comfortable niches either in the private economy or in Yeltsin's power network. Today's Communists represent the unsuccessful apparatchiks, plus the old, the poor, the disadvantaged, army officers (many of them now poverty-stricken and demoralised), and those dependent on the public budget.

It is almost true to say that the Communists have learnt nothing and forgotten nothing. But in fact they have learnt one thing: that at heart they are imperial Russian nationalists. That was true in Soviet days too, but was masked behind an internationalist rhetoric. Nowadays it is out in the open: they say they wold restore the Soviet Union, and also revive the collectivist values of old Russia, with its heart in the *obshchina*, the village commune. Lenin must be spinning in the Mausoleum at the un-Marxist things his supporters now proclaim, but they have tapped the feelings of many Russians as they seldom did when they ruled the country.

One of the great gains of post-Soviet Russia has been the relative liberty of the media. Yeltsin's regime has not been blameless, but compared with any predecessor, its record on freedom of speech is estimable. But this is not just a result of greater state tolerance. Journalists, writers and editors have displayed great courage in widening freedom of expression and then defending the newly won frontiers. Lacking traditional means of censoring newspapers and television, those anxious to conceal compromising news have resorted to threatening, attacking and even murdering journalists, as a perusal of *Index*'s recent coverage demonstrates. The army, in particular, has done its best to keep them out of sensitive spots in Chechnya, and some journalists have displayed immense resourcefulness and courage to keep reliable information flowing.

If they come to power, the Communists cannot restore the old command economy. They would cause economic collapse and perhaps civil war if they tried. They would certainly face determined and highly placed opponents, able to summon up armed force. What they probably can do is renationalise some firms as part of a new corporate economy, protected from the harsh winds of global trade by tariffs and restrictions on the exchange of the rouble. If they do that, however, they will have to face the threat of mass starvation, since Russia depends on imports for so much of its food. At least there would be a return to queues and rationing.

There was never going to be any way of escaping from the Communist system painlessly. The unrewarded distress - shock without the therapy some call it - which most of the population has suffered during the transition was bound to restore some of the Communists' popularity. But no more than anyone else - less so, in fact - can the Communists now solve Russia's problems.

The great question now is not who wins the elections, which will really be a contest between successful Communists and unsuccessful Communists, but whether they take place at all in a tolerably credible form. If they do, then whoever wins, a big step will have been taken away from the post-Soviet politics of command and cliquishness, and towards a more open civic style, in which people believe they can vote for meaningful parties that have a hope of coming to power. In that sense, paradoxically, even a Communist victory might mean further progress away from Communism.

Old Griefs Revisited

Sergei Kovalev

Translated by Irena Maryniak

Human rights violations remain the most painful problem in Russia today. Human rights are protected by the constitution; their observation is guaranteed by international agreements to which Russia is a signatory; and everywhere they are abused - overtly and crudely.

All Russian politicians talk 'human rights', its slogans feature in the pre-election posters of many political parties, but no-one is prepared to defend them and when a choice arises between political interests and legal principles, political interests invariably prevail. Legal arguments are used by the authorities and the opposition as a political lever, but neither the law nor human rights present a serious obstacle to political expediency. They remain pure rhetoric, often shrouding blatantly arbitrary rule.

Sending its troops into Chechnya, the present administration spoke of the need to restore constitutional order in the region and protect the constitutional rights of its citizens. Since then, we have seen tens of thousands killed, hundreds of thousands of refugees, torture, summary execution, looting, disinformation or lies from the military and civil authorities, restricted freedom of movement, attacks on press freedom, the collapse of the rule of law, the falsification of electoral results, ethnic discrimination ... the sorry list could go on. Chechnya has become not only the ground for large-scale arms dealing and colossal extortion, but the testing zone for a new totalitarianism.

And a pretty successful one at that. Social apathy and xenophobia are rife. Disappointment with democracy and humanitarianism has diverted public attention towards new priorities. 'State', Communism, fascism are more than abstractions in Russia today. They are supported by powerful political groups, with set programmes and organisational structures, electoral constituencies and a readiness to fight for power. We witnessed their success in the December 1995 parliamentary elections. The run-up to the presidential elections in June 1996 has so far confirmed that the battle for power, for the hearts and minds of Russia's citizens, is not being fought between democratic forces on the one hand and totalitarian forces on the other, but between varying forms of the new totalitarianism.

The struggle is taking place in an arena where there is no room for authentic democratic values. What our state institutions, Communists and nationalists call 'human rights' bears no relation to the rights of the individual. It merely indicates the political, economic and social interests of select groups or individuals. In official parlance, the protection of these interests is the defence of the 'collective rights' of different segments of the population.

For our ruling party, the interests of the state represent the highest value. In fact these are no more than the interests of the ruling 'corporation': the caste of high-level civil and military officials in the ruling apparatus, central and regional. The development of the grouping was screened by democratic rhetoric. Its original function was to redistribute state property and re-establish spheres of economic and political influence; to squeeze out the old Communist nomenklatura from key posts. Having achieved its principal aim, the corporation is seeking to keep its spoils. The rule of law is not always to its advantage. Its aims are better served by the time-honoured principle of *derzhavnost*: the principle of the state, over and above the individual and society. The concomitant dangers are already apparent. Political reforms have been reversed; authoritarian rule is preferred; policy-making is unpredictable and covert; a nationalist ideology has been formulated. Increasingly, individual rights will be subsumed to 'the interests of the people' for which read the interests of the authorities.

On the opposing side stand forces unified by Communist rhetoric. On the basis of evident economic and social miscalculations, this grouping is attracting a significant contingent of electors nostalgic for times when there was no need to answer for anything, when the authorities guaranteed a life that was impoverished but relatively free of anxiety. Democratic-sounding slogans notwithstanding, a Communist victory is bound to prompt a wave of revanchism, aggressive isolationism, and the destruction of those weak shoots of democracy that have appeared in Russia over the past decade. State Communism will be even more disastrous for human rights than the policy of the present authorities: for the debasement of individuality is intrinsic to the Communist programme.

The third organised force in Russian politics is nationalism. This plays a supportive role: on the one hand it tacitly feeds state and Communism with a complementary dose of fascism and xenophobia; on the other, it provides an outlet for social anxiety. It is a context in which human rights simply do not apply. Strangely enough, the best example of the way in which ethnic supremacy transforms human rights can be seen in the way the authorities of national republics within the Russian Federation often pay scant attention to civil and political rights while fiercely defending their national or state rights. In regions such as Tatarstan, Bashkiria, Tuva or Chechnya, the level of human rights abuses is notably higher than in Russia as a whole. Clearly, the 'nationalisation' of Russian policy will make no difference to regional abuse, but rather increase its level in the country as a whole.

Any one of these political forces could triumph in Russia; their victory will mean defeat for political reform, and the negation of the priority (or at least the parity) of human rights over the principle of political expediency. The tough talking will begin soon enough, not just with Russian citizens, but with the West - doubtless provoking an equally tough response. Yet the notion of human rights in Russian democratic circles is not so very different from the western one. Depressingly, though, many democrats see human rights not as the foundation of democracy, but as something secondary, emerging from economic or political reform - which is one reason for Russia's failure to achieve democratic change.

Much could be said, and fairly, about the fact that the Russian tradition and mentality is not the most fertile ground for human rights. But any efforts by democrats to surmount this tradition, and change the mentality of their fellow citizens, have been outrageously paltry. The defence of human rights has informed neither affairs of state nor education. And this explains not just the political decline of the democrats, but their fragmentation. While debating the details of economic programmes or foreign and home policy, they have ignored the common humanitarian values they all share.

If civil rights organisations still function in Russia today, if a free press exists, it is thanks not to Yeltsin, but to democratically oriented politicians, social and human rights activists and ordinary, decent people.

Should Yeltsin win the June elections, the most important task facing democratic organisations will be to instil in the public mind an awareness of human rights as the foundation for state and society. The second, no less vital task will be the creation of a network of human rights organisations capable of defending citizens' rights and supporting democratic civil associations. To establish a broad spectrum of human rights work is the only way of creating a social basis for democratic political parties, assisting their consolidation and ultimately increasing their electoral success. In present circumstances, this sort of work has a distinct political significance. It is directed towards the establishment of an alternative political model for the country, opposed to the policy of the present authorities and, even more, to the Communist and nationalist models.

We have come to view work in the field of human rights and education in non-political terms. But in Russia today human rights is a legal and political issue. Any more moral or honest polity will depend on the priority given to them.

This kind of work is exceptionally difficult in any circumstances; under the Communists it may be dangerous. And it is here that the experience gained by dissidents in the 1960s, 70s and 80s may once again prove useful. Their struggle against Communism had a vital moral influence during the early stages of Russia's reforms, as the old system collapsed. Later, in the construction of a new state system, it was harder to make use of the negative experience of dissent, and the involvement of former rights activists in public life was severely circumscribed. Most chose not to return from emigration; of the dozens living in Russia, just a few went into politics. But I am sure that, if the threat of a totalitarian revival arises, whatever its rhetoric, many former dissidents will re-emerge.

That, I believe, is where my own future lies. I do not know whether we will have the strength or wherewithal to stir public opinion into resistance. But fight we must. Or we will not be worthy of our freedom.

Of Blood and Votes

Irena Maryniak

The reluctance of Russian politicians to recognise the rebel leader Dzhokhar Dudayev as a serious military and political opponent while he was alive has been matched only by their refusal publicly to acknowledge the real state of the Russian Federal Army. Now Dudayev is dead, reportedly killed in a rocket attack on the night of 21 April, and the blood feud which has long characterised relations between Russia and Chechnya can only be exacerbated.

Stories told by prominent Russian deputies, such as Yury Rybakov, who have visited the region and dodged army positions to talk to rebels, cannot easily be dismissed as 'negative reporting', in the way TV footage from Pervomayskoye was. The officially promoted distinction between Chechen fighters and the population at large is proving increasingly difficult to sustain. Following arbitrary massacres such as those in Sernovodsk or Samashki, civilians who have lost dozens of relatives are taking up arms. Children aged about 10 were seen shooting during the Chechen assault on Grozny on 6 March. Militiamen loyal to Moscow announced their refusal to fight Dudayev's men on local television. The March events in Grozny bore the hallmarks of a civilian insurrection. As Moscow's puppet president, Doku Zagayev, has confirmed, increasing numbers of Chechens are being drawn into the fighting.

The line that the war is being conducted by a few terrorist fighters has ceased to stand up. Today, an open trial for Dudayev's fellow commanders could prove more of an embarrassment for leading Russian politicians than their notion of public justice is worth. News of atrocities in an archipelago of Russian filtration camps has already seeped through to the West and the behaviour of the federal army has been denounced by independent human rights observers and the Organisation for Security and Co-operation in Europe (OSCE). At least 2000 Chechen civilians have disappeared. In some cases ransoms of thousands of pounds have been paid to Russian troops. The allegations of atrocities, corruption and arms trafficking rebel leaders could, and likely would, make are bound to make Russian politicians pause. But Dudayev's death may open the floodgates to all those blood vendettas in which Caucasian history abounds.

The Chechen struggle against Russia goes back to imperial incursions into the Muslim region in the eighteenth century. Sporadic warfare has erupted whenever Russian control has weakened, and the long-standing grievance nursed by the Chechen against its imperial neighbour remains the rebels' most powerful weapon. It has demonstrated Russia's capacity for genocide for the second time this century; it has encouraged the Chechen people to rally round; it has radicalised and militarised the population. It has played on the Chechen tradition that values freedom, the martial ethos and loyalty to a chosen leader more highly than anything else. As Dudayev remarked when interviewed by journalist Oleg Moroz in 1992, the principle of the blood feud holds fast in Chechnya; the weapon is a symbol of potent manhood; summary justice for violent crime is assured.

According to the tenets of this tradition, Boris Yeltsin has long been any Chechen commander's blood enemy, and Dudayev was cast as avenger for the thousands of Chechens who have died. If it is not practicable to dispatch Yeltsin physically, the new rebel high command may yet find its way to doing so politically. Shortly before his death, Dudayev made remarks which indicated that he would not be averse to peace talks with a Communist leadership. His close supporter Akhmed Zakayev said that the Communists are the most 'serious' contenders in the forthcoming presidential election. Dudayev, once a Soviet air-force general, indicated that he never gave up his Party card and that he was against the original dissolution of the USSR – a statement well in line withe the denunciation of the 1991 Bialowierza accords in the Communist-dominated Duma in march.

It is unlikely that the new rebel leadership can hope to secure full territorial independence from the Party that sanctioned the deportation of the Chechen people to Kazakhastan and Siberia in 1944. But any new presidency would doubtless seek to distance itself from the more disastrous mistakes of its predecessor. An agreement with the Communists, free of the burden of recent memories, could be a more serious proposition from the Chechen point of view than talks with Yeltsin.

Meanwhile, in the devastated towns and villages of Chechnya,

Russian troops are undernourished and unpaid. The use of drugs and alcohol is widespread: a soldier here is more likely than not to be drunk or high. Famished conscripts are fed by Chechen villagers in exchange for safe passage. They are willing to ignore orders for a meal or a telephone call home. On International Women's Day, Russian soldiers reportedly shared a few drinks with Dudayev's men and subsequently sold them a tank and an armoured vehicle for US$6,000. The role of an occupation army, persistently under threat, triggers untold brutality towards civilians and suspicion or fear of the media whose function it is to expose Russia's military shame.

Back home, amid sporadic bouts of misinformation and censorship, Russian television has been showing the funerals of conscripts killed in and around Grozny - some, most recently, bombed by their own troops. The upsurge in fighting, which preceded the announcement of President Yeltsin's peace initiative and the partial troop withdrawal on 31 March, may well have turned electors against Yeltsin. That was, perhaps, Dudayev's underlying intention and certainly the effect the president has since sought to counteract. Any further operations along the lines of the Grozny assault would bring the sight of more Russian losses to the television screens of countless families already resentful of Yeltsin's policies. This, together with the murder of hostages and prisoners of war or the threat of straightforward terrorism, remain strong cards in the hands of Chechen rebels if they fail to achieve the direct talks with Yeltsin which Dudayev demanded.

As the Russian president comes to grips with his new image as peacemaker, Chechnya is being offered autonomy within the Russian Federation (along the lines agreed with Tatarstan). There has been mention of an amnesty for Chechen fighters other than those who have committed common-law crimes (presumably the hostage takers of Budenovsk and Pervomayskoye) and promise of better humanitarian aid and government funds for reconstruction. This, of course, is a particularly tall order in a country where all economic aid has a tendency to vanish and where billions of roubles regularly disappear in the course of salary distribution.

On a more spectacular scale, there has been talk of a grand bargain to settle all conflicts in the Caucasus, including Abkhazia, South Ossetia and Nagorno Karabakh; there has been an economic integration agreement with Kazakhstan, Kirgizia and Belarus; and discussions are underway on the passage of an oil pipeline from Baku on the Caspian Sea, through Azerbaijan up to Novorossiisk on the Black Sea - via Chechnya. Lack of progress on the status of the Black Sea fleet based in Sevastopol, on Ukrainian territory, remains a thorn in the flesh, but it all adds up to a last ditch attempt to present Boris Yeltsin as the democratic leader who preserved the integrity of the state against all the odds, not just within Russia's borders, but equally in the independent republics of the former Soviet Union.

Without a withdrawal from Chechnya, as Yeltsin himself has admitted, his chances of winning the presidential election are minimal. He has remained ambivalently committed to a solution which combines hard military and judicial rhetoric with as much peace-making as pride will allow. 'It is above all a peace programme,' he has said. 'Second, it is a military programme. The criminals responsible for and implicated in terrorism must stand trial. Others must learn the lesson.'

Rebel leaders are unimpressed. General Vyacheslav Tikhomorov, the Russian commander in Chechnya, and General Alexander Lebed, another contender for the presidency, have said that a halt to military operations cannot be quickly implemented. It will take a great deal of determination to prevent the initiative from going the way of last summer's failed ceasefire. As some troops retire to the borders of Chechnya, reactions in Dagestan and Ingushetia to the prospect of an indefinite, battle-hardened military presence on their territory could be decisive.

Meanwhile, opinion polls continue to show that the Russian population is more deeply concerned about the Chechen débâcle than about poor living standards or organised crime. The 18-month-old conflict has cost an estimated 40,000 lives and created at least 250,000 refugees. It is a sorry tale of political paradox and misjudgement. And its legacy could cost still more, as Boris Yeltsin dons the mantle of peacemaker to salvage an election, and Chechen rebel leaders demand his moral capitulation and continue to woo the Russian people - by killing them.